From the Kitchens
of Pancho Villa

By

Karina Ann Betlem

Copyright   2012 by Karina Ann Betlem

ISBN 978-0-9907-254-0-4 Hardcover
ISBN 978-0-9907-254-1-1 eBook

Printed in the United States of America

Published November 2012
Updated August 2014

From the Kitchens of Pancho Villa
www.kitchensofpanchovilla.blogspot.com

FOR ROSIE

This book is dedicated to Rosalva (Rosie), without whom I could not have completed the project. Writing this dedication was perhaps the most difficult part of the entire project, as there is so much I would like to share with you about this most extraordinary lady, but time and space create restrictions that I cannot overcome. To my readers, please take the time to read this dedication and experience the inspiration that I have felt during the many years that Rosie ("Chava" to her closest friends) and I have been friends. We have enjoyed our relationship for so many years that, indeed, it feels as if I have known her my entire life.

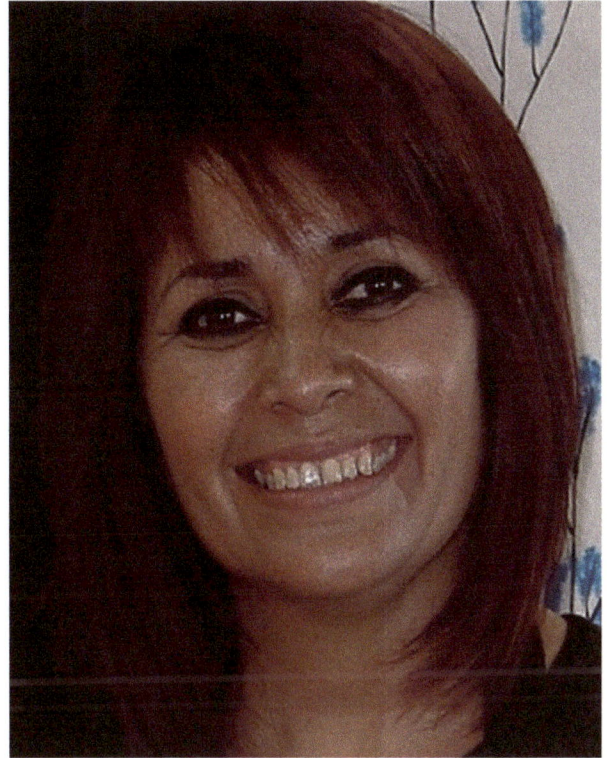

Like many of the contributors to this project, Rosie grew up in a poor family but has worked exceptionally hard all of her adult life to provide a good home for her own family and her parents. She met the man who would become her husband when they were both just thirteen years old. She was attending school; he was living on the street but working diligently every day to make a living for himself. Predictably, when they first met, her parents strongly objected to a relationship with a "street kid"—too poor, no future. But this was an early point in Rosie's life that demonstrated what was to become a lifetime trait. Rosie's ability to see the good in people and sense their hearts, without regard for their present circumstances, sets her apart from others. Rosie saw something good in this young, struggling teenager. At the young age of fifteen, Rosie convinced her parents to allow the marriage. Even her parents recognized that Rosie possessed wisdom beyond her years.

About twenty years ago, Rosie began driving around Mazatlán, giving haircuts to tourists in the local RV parks. Soon, she became a favorite among the tourists and would find people lined up when she arrived. After tending to her paying clients, she would return home to the *colonia* and give free haircuts to many poor neighbors. This practice continues to this day.

As her fortunes grew, Rosie was able to save enough money to attend beauty school and obtain her license. All the while, she was also honing her English skills—a valuable asset when your main clientele consists of English-speaking North Americans. Ten years later she had impressed some of her clients so much that they joined together to help Rosie set up a shop of her own. At the time, this made her extremely nervous, because she felt it was such a big step forward. It also created in her a strong sense of responsibility to succeed in the face of such generosity. The rest is history! Rosie has exceeded even the most enthusiastic expectations of her supporters. Not all of that success is counted in pesos, and this is where the real story begins.

Rosie's generous heart and willingness to help those who will help themselves shines through. At the latest count, there are seven young ladies working in her shop, because Rosie took them in, provided for their beauty school education, and taught them the secrets of her profession. Most recent was a young gal selling newspapers on a busy (dangerous) street corner. Sensing the young lady's desire to do more with her life, Rosie spoke with the girl's parents and, with their blessing, took this struggling twelve-year-old under her wing. Currently, Rosie is training her to be an assistant, and when she turns sixteen, Rosie will send her to beauty school. By many standards, Rosie has very little in the way of physical assets, but she finds it in her heart to give much of what she does have to others. "I have what I need, but many do not," Rosie has said.

Christmastime is especially joyous for Rosie and those around her. Annually, she hosts a *posada* and provides all of the food, hot chocolate, presents, and a piñata full of candy for approximately 150–200 neighborhood children. Having attended several of these events, I can attest to the tremendous amount of work that this requires, but most important, the love that shines through is an amazing thing to watch. Rosie also buys gifts for the children at a local orphanage and often brings them to her home in small groups for an overnight marathon of movies, pizza, and pop.

As I mentioned, this book would not have been possible without Rosie. Her constant efforts to set up cooking dates with our contributors, act as my translator, and encourage these ladies to complete their contributions to the book (no small task) was the part I could not do. I was accepted into many homes for cooking experiences solely because Rosie remained involved. Without exception, they look up to Rosie as a leader in the community and an inspiration.

And so, Chava, my friend, this is for you! You have been a loyal and loving friend. Without you, I could not and would not have been able to share the talents of your community with the rest of the world.

May God bless you.

Acknowledgments

Without the efforts of many people, this book could not have been written. The cooks that you will meet in these pages provided the enthusiasm, cooperation, and friendship that was essential to the success of this new approach to writing a cookbook. Because of the generous giving of their time and their willingness to share their knowledge with me, I have learned many new things about cooking and am pleased to share that knowledge with you. If you thought that good food required complicated recipes, you will learn, as I did, that even the simplest of recipes can result in a feast. The only things you need to complement these recipes are family and friends. These special friends have taught me more in the past three years about love, compassion, and generosity than I had learned in a lifetime. So to these wonderful people, I offer a heartfelt thank you for teaching me to be a better cook and a better person.

My husband and best friend, Pete (Pedro), you have supported me throughout this entire project. You never complained about the hours I spent at the computer or in the kitchen. You tasted each recipe several times while it was being perfected and never once complained or threw up! That is devotion, and I love you for it. You read each recipe for me to make sure it actually made sense and critiqued me lovingly. I will never forget the many laughs and giggles we had while you tried to figure out what I was trying to say. My favorite was trying to understand "beat with the eggs" ("How do you beat something with eggs?" he asked.) So Mr. Man, thank you!

Dianne Stillman, my buddy, we have been through 40 years of adventures together and they keep on coming. Thank you for all your help, and being by my side on this adventure.

I had many supporters who were always there with encouragement and a friendly ear to my whining and my excitement. So Alicia Gherke, Carolyn Bacon, Connie Gill, Debbie Wiggins, Jeanie Wix, and Judy Angell, thanks for being there for me. My niece Leslie Altamos, you kept prodding me on and providing valuable advice on the subtle nuances of writing recipes. Les, you will see your handiwork all over the pages of this book. My daughters Bethany Betlem and Saleia Mani (yes, Sal, I think you really are my daughter!), thank you both for spreading the word to all your friends about my blog and this book. I love you both! David Bodwell, you gave me a good lesson in publishing and answered all my questions without hesitation. As you will see in these pages, I have followed many of your suggestions. So to you and Richard Grabman, a big thank you! Tom Pixler, whom I have known since the seventh grade, thank you for turning that very ordinary photo of me into something acceptable for public viewing!

My first contact at Infinity Publishing was Laura Pici. After meeting Laura on the phone, I knew immediately that Infinity was the publisher for me. She took me by the hand and walked me through all I needed to know. Then, we had others join our little 'group', Michelle Shane and Brittany Lavin. Each one specializing in her field of expertise to help *me*. Then came the editing staff ... I cannot express my appreciation for the amount of time you spent making my manuscript the best it could be. Chris Masters of Infinity's art department created a beautiful cover for this book, and I know that some of the best talent in the business is at Infinity. A huge thank you to all of you at Infinity for making this book and the dreams of all the participating cooks of Colonia Pancho Villa a reality.

Contents

Karina Ann Betlem

Introduction

My husband and I lived our entire lives in the United States and for twenty years enjoyed visiting Mexico as tourists. It was during these times that we began to look increasingly at the possibility of retiring in Mexico. In 1997, we took a big step forward and purchased a home in Mazatlán. That home was our vacation destination for fifteen years as we completed final preparations to actually retire and move permanently. Mexico had become "the home of our hearts." Following a five-month remodel and updating of our Mexican home, we were ready to move in, and move we did! Everything we owned was loaded onto a moving van and shipped to Laredo, Texas. Here, Mexican customs inspected the shipment and gave the green light for a Mexican carrier to deliver it to our home. At 7:00 on a Sunday morning the truck arrived. It is now three years later, and we have never looked back.

Now, about this book … having lived most of our lives in California and Washington, we often dined out at typical "Mexican" restaurants. You know the ones—platters piled with enchiladas smothered with sauce and cheese, tacos that come in pre-shaped, overly crisp taco shells filled with lettuce, and a heaping side of rice and beans. That, my friends, is *not* authentic Mexican cuisine. The desire to share the real essence of Mexican home-style cooking prompted me to take the plunge and write this book.

With a great deal of assistance from Rosie (see the dedication page), I was able to record a large number of hand-me-down recipes from friends. These friends, accommodating to a fault, live in a poor area of Mazatlán known as Colonia Francisco Villa, commonly known as Pancho Villa. As a point of interest, residential areas in Mazatlán are generally divided into five classes, including upper-class homes (*residencias*), middle-class homes (*fraccionamientos*), low-income homes (*colonias*), homes with low-interest government-assisted mortgages (*infonavits*), and the poorest of all, *barrios*. You should know that while colonias are considered low income, it does not necessarily mean that they are dirty or rundown. Every home that I visited was clean, orderly, and comfortable. As you will see in the photographs, the kitchens are sparsely equipped, with only rudimentary utensils. Some kitchens are actually outdoors. Ovens are often treated as storage cabinets, because many cooks rarely, if ever, use an oven. Until recently, refrigerators in the homes were not common, so the cook would go to the store on a daily basis to purchase just enough food for the day. Most canned goods come with flip-top lids or are opened with a knife because can openers are still considered a luxury. In most kitchens, the clean dishes (washed by hand; no dishwashers here) are stacked neatly on the countertops because cabinets are expensive. However, despite these seemingly inadequate conditions, our friends create the most delicious dishes from recipes that have been passed down from generation to generation by word of mouth and parents teaching their children. Perhaps the most difficult part of this book was recording these recipes for the first time ever on paper.

Many of these recipes have changed very little over the years and then only with minor changes as ingredients evolve, but the basic traditions of the recipes remain the same. One example of the evolution of ingredients is with the old-fashioned Mexican crema, a thick, slightly sweet sour cream. Until just recently, this was a standard in most Mexican kitchens. A new product known as "Crema LaLa" (LaLa is the brand name) has taken its place. All of the cooks in this book now use Crema LaLa, which is also known as *crema acidificada,* a mild sour cream. Other recipes have been invented out of necessity to provide superior flavor while keeping costs to a minimum. Some meals cost less than fifty cents—for the entire meal!

The flavors of true Mexican cuisine are complex, building layers of flavor. Chiles (pronounced *chee-lays*), for example, are not added for heat but rather for an additional layer of flavor. Each type of chile has its own flavor and is not often interchangeable. Hot tip: mouth and tongue burning are not necessary! Onions and garlic are used sparingly, as are herbs—only to add another subtle layer of flavor. The use of cheese is minimal; sauces are light, not heavy; and the use of cream as an ingredient is to *enhance* the flavor, not drown it.

Many of the recipes take less than thirty minutes to prepare, with a combination of prepared and homemade ingredients. A basic underlying reason why so many meals take such a small amount of time to prepare is the weather. During the summer months, Mazatlán is extremely hot and humid. It becomes very uncomfortable for the cooks to spend a lot of time in the kitchen. If air conditioning is available, it is usually reserved for the bedroom. Another reason is time. Many of our cooks work outside of the home, raise the children, and do all the shopping, laundry, and house cleaning, so there just isn't enough time in the day for these hard-working people to spend hours preparing fancy meals. To get a more complete picture, visualize stepping back into 1940s and 1950s America. By the way, that is—for the most part—a good thing.

Sadly, for many of these families, the younger generations are showing less and less interest in learning the art of cooking. With the advent of cell phones, computers, and other modern technology, the youth of Mexico would much rather just eat out at one of the myriad taco stands to save time for other interests. This book may very well represent a final chapter in the art of Mexican home cooking, so it is with a great sense of satisfaction that so many recipes are now recorded for posterity.

You will note that the names of the recipes are in Spanish, with a translation to assist the reader in determining what he or she is actually making. Some of the titles may sound unappetizing, but a review of the ingredient list should help you realize that these really are tasty recipes and worth your time to experiment with them. Most of the recipes are simple, with only a few ingredients. All the recipes have been "field tested" with the cooks in their own kitchens and then re-created in my own kitchen, so you can be assured of the completeness and accuracy of these cultural dishes. I have tested acceptable substitute or equivalent ingredients when I felt that a certain ingredient might not be readily available outside of Mexico. However, one area of difficulty is cheese. If you have a good cheese department in your local grocery store, you may be able to find the exact cheeses specified. In other instances, you will need to do some substitutions. This is not a death knell to the recipe. Cheese is most often an "accent" ingredient.

Some of the processes and techniques, such as charring and peeling a chile, may seem a bit foreign, but I have described them step-by-step for you. Don't be intimidated; all techniques are foreign until we do them the first time. I once had a friend who called in a panic to tell me that she was having guests over for dinner, and the recipe required that she "blanch" an ingredient. She had no idea where to start! I told her that "blanch" only means to plunge the food into boiling water for a couple of minutes, drain and then plunge it into iced water to stop the cooking. To this day her nickname is Blanche.

The book is organized by the individual cooks who have contributed their recipes. You may find that certain cooks present recipes that are more to your liking than others. There occasionally are a number of recipes for the same dish, but you will find that each contributing cook offers a different twist on the same recipe, so take the time to browse the recipes, read the ingredients, and decide for yourself which one (or more) sounds the most appealing, and give it a try. I recommend that you follow the recipe exactly the first time you try it. The second time, do some experimenting. Cookbooks should be considered a guideline rather than a rule. If the cooks in this book can make these delicious foods in a simple kitchen with simple tools (one lady uses a rock!), then imagine what you can do.

Throughout this project, I have met many precious new friends. Although poor, they have a tremendous sense of community, of giving to their neighbors, and of helping others in need. I have been invited into their homes and lives and have met brothers, sisters, grandparents, and sometimes the entire extended family all at once! They treat me as a member of their own family, and I cherish that.

Good luck, have fun, and *¡buen provecho!*

Author's Notes

All the photos in this book are of the *real* food. We tried to plate the food so you could see exactly what it will look like when you prepare it in your own home. We did not use Photoshop, lacquer sprays, or other enhancements to make this food look more "artsy." Garnishes are at a minimum as well, as we didn't want to take away from the appeal of the food. If the recipe says to serve it with rice, for example, we did not include the rice. We all know what rice looks like but not necessarily the dish we are preparing. To see the color photos of each recipe, go to our blog at www.kitchensofpanchovilla.blogspot.com.

Being accustomed to US weights and measures, it became necessary to learn metric units of measurements when I moved to Mexico. Metric units give much more accurate measurements, and I urge you, if you are using ounces and pounds, to try metric. You will be amazed at how much more accurate and easier it is. Whenever possible, we have used cups, tablespoons, and teaspoons. It does not matter if you are using US, UK, or Canadian measurements; they are not different enough for the recipes in this book.

Since most of the cooks in this book have very small kitchens, some have no counter space at all. They organize their ingredients *mise en place* (everything in its place). All the ingredients are cleaned, chopped, and measured ahead of time and put in small bowls in the order they will be added to the recipe. This was a useful lesson that I learned from our contributors as they shared their time and talents with me.

Many cooks either don't have an oven or won't use it because of the heat it puts off. Desserts are made with ingredients that either can be cooked on the stove top, in a stove top bain-marie*, or cold using gelatins or canned milks. Very simple and very tasty!

The only special equipment that you will need is a blender. Most of the salsas require blending, and normally a food processor does not have the speed to puree thoroughly. There is another piece of equipment that is noteworthy: a pressure cooker. The frijoles refritos (refried beans) are always cooked in a pressure cooker, as are many meats. If you do not use a pressure cooker, you will need to cook some recipes the slow, old-fashioned way on the stove top or in the oven.

*Bain-marie or hot water bath: This method of cooking surrounds the food with very gentle heat from hot water and is used for cooking delicate dishes like custards. You will need a large baking dish or pan with high sides, 7.5–10 cm (3–4 inches). A roasting pan usually works great.

- Boil a large kettle of water.

- Put your pan of food inside the larger pan, and place that inside the oven or on the stove top. Very slowly add the boiling water to the larger pan so that the water surrounds the pan of food but does not splash into the food.

A Glimpse at Colonia Pancho Villa

A local business selling fresh mangoes from its own trees for one peso each (less than ten cents US)

One of the many "fruterias" located in the colonia—this one sells cocos helados

Not all homes belong to the poor. This corner has paved streets!

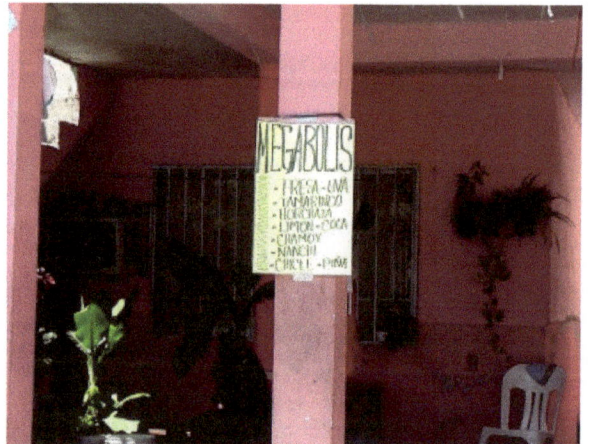

Selling "bolis" from a private home—cottage industries are encouraged and are a necessary part of their daily income

Inside one of the local churches—folding chairs will be set out before Mass or catechism

A typical side street, including chickens!

Karina Ann Betlem

Mazatlán's Humane Society located in Colonia Pancho Villa

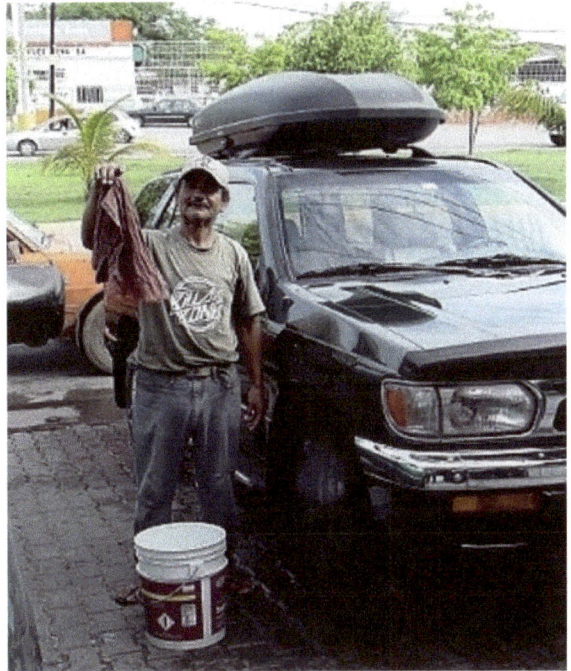

Sergio, a local car washer. Thirty pesos for a wash (about $2.30 US). I have a regular Friday morning appointment.

Almost 200 local kids patiently waiting their turn to smack the piñata after a Christmas posada.

Mexican version of the "Fuller Brush man." He travels the neighborhoods on his bike, selling brooms, brushes, and mops.

Saturday and Sunday you will always find pollos asados (barbecued chickens) for sale throughout the colonia—definitely a good time to drive through with the windows down.

Wash Those Veggies

(Something to ponder)

For at least the last twenty-five years I have been obsessed—yes, I think that is the word for it—with washing my fruits and vegetables with soap and water before I put them in the fridge.

Many years ago I was headed into the grocery store to do my usual weekly shopping. In the parking lot I passed a woman who was changing her baby's poopie diaper in her car before she went into the store. It was obviously a poopie diaper by the way the mother had to repeatedly wipe the offending bum to remove the residue.

I happened to meet a friend while I was close to the mother's car. We stopped to chat before I continued into the store. For some odd reason, I watched the mother finish her duty, pick up her baby, and start for the store. She didn't use baby wipes for her hands, so I assumed she would go to the restroom to wash her hands. Well, I was wrong.

Having finished chatting with my friend, I walked into the store behind the mother. She put her baby in the cart and headed for the produce section of the store. But wait—the restroom is on the other side of the store by the greeting cards. Not only did she not wash her hands or disinfect them, but she used those same diaper-changing hands to handle the fresh fruit! Holy poop! (Sorry about that.) From that day on, I have washed all of my fruits and veggies with soap and water—bananas, apples, pineapple, potatoes, broccoli.

I use a mixture of dish soap and water on a clean sponge or cloth. Scrub it all around and rinse it. The broccoli is a little different. I put some soap and water in a large plastic bowl with a bit of white vinegar and swish it around, rubbing the top of the florets, and then rinse it very well under running water. You are not using enough soap to taint the flavor, and because you are rinsing immediately, your family won't even know you used soap. The local cooks here use antibacterial drops in the wash pan when cleaning fruits and vegetables. They too understand the necessity for clean food.

Think about all the different people who have handled your produce—from farm workers to packers to retailers to customers. How many of those had a cold and coughed or sneezed on your food? Ever wonder what happens to produce that ends up on the floor? It goes right out into the bins, ready for you to buy it and take it home. Gross and disgusting, isn't it? You can protect your family by taking this one simple precaution.

I'm pretty sure after you use the bathroom that you wash your hands with soap and water, not just rinse them under running water prior to handling food. Unfortunately, not everybody does.

Is It Smoked Marlin or Smoked Tuna?

This has been a burning question through the ages and one that has sparked heated debates. To learn the truth, meet the one man who knows the answer: Señor Jaime (*Hi*-may) has had his *tuna*-smoking business for sixteen years. Despite Jaime's track record in business, there are still those who will disagree. Time and again, customers who place this delicious fish product on their plate will state conclusively that they are eating smoked marlin. If that is what they believe, who is Jaime to argue?

No one actually knows why people began to call it *smoked marlin* many years ago. Perhaps it was because restaurateurs thought it sounded more exotic. That moniker made its way into the *mercados* (markets) and today, the signs still read "Smoked Marlin."

Marlin is more of a trophy fish than an edible fish. The flavor is good, but the texture is tough and chewy. There is a layer of fiber between each flake of meat that resembles fiberglass strands. It is definitely not appealing to the palette. Tuna, on the other hand, is tender and juicy, with good flavor and texture. There are no smoke houses in Mazatlán that smoke marlin commercially.

Señor Jaime was kind enough to give us a tour of his smoking operation.

What a surprise—it *is* tuna!

They smoke between one and two tons of tuna per day, depending on the season. The tuna are brought to Mazatlán by boat and then trucked to the smokehouse, where they are cleaned, filleted, and cut into bricks weighing about one kilo each. From there, the bricks get injected with Jaime's private recipe brine before being moved to a very large, dual-purpose walk-in

---

refrigerator/freezer. Here, they are put into vats to marinate overnight.

The next morning, the bricks of tuna are placed on smoking racks and thoroughly dried with large floor fans. After two hours of drying, the racks are transferred to movable tracks, where they will be rolled into the smoker.

One long rack filled with tuna bricks is rolled into the smoker. After ten minutes, the bricks are checked to make sure there are no hot spots in the smoker. The rack is returned to the smoker, and a second rack is rolled in. After another ten minutes, the crew pulls the first rack back out. With gloved hands, two workers turn over each piece of fish and return the rack to the smoker. This procedure is repeated with the second rack. At the end of forty minutes, the first rack is done and rolled from the smoker. With thickly gloved hands, the men remove the hot racks and place them in a screened-in cooling shed. Here, huge fans are used to cool the bricks quickly. By this time, the second rack is ready, and the process is repeated.

When the bricks are cool, they are immediately transferred back to the refrigerator/freezer, where they are frozen. Once frozen, the bricks are vacuum-sealed and made ready for shipping.

Señor Jaime ships throughout Mexico and the United States. He sells strictly to businesses such as restaurants and small grocery stores.

No part of the fish is wasted. The leftover small bits and pieces of meat are formed into a brick of their own and smoked along with the underbelly bones that also have bits of meat attached. They are both sold to restaurants for "marlin" tacos. The fish carcasses are sold as by-products.

You need not be afraid to consume this delicious fish. When questioned about his outdoor operation, Jaime proudly points out that the health department visits several times a month, and he always passes with flying colors!

If you have a business and would like more information, you can call Señor Jaime at 044-669-148-2287 or his on-site manager Alejanadro at 044-669-147-0537. Both are cellular numbers in Mazatlán, Sinaloa, Mexico.

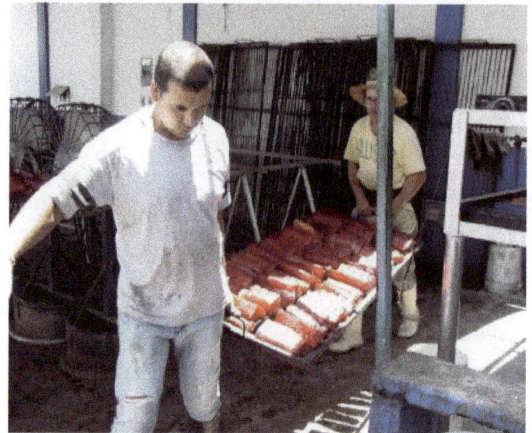

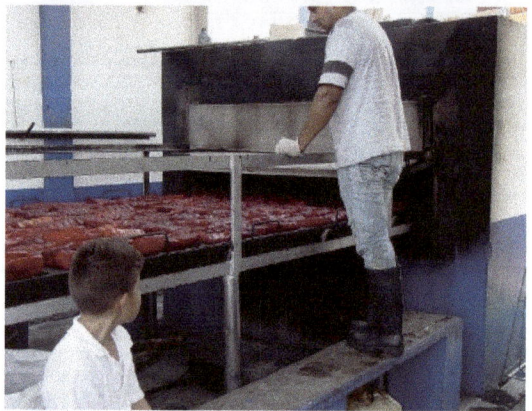

Ingredients

Almost all of the ingredients used in this book are available at regular grocery stores where you live. Most will have all the fresh ingredients you need in the produce section. Sometimes the names in other countries are not the names we use in Mexico. For instance, a store may call a poblano chile a pasilla chile; this can be very confusing because it is not correct. They are two totally different chiles with very distinctive flavors and heat scale. If you are not sure what it looks like, ask your produce manager. The other ingredients will be found in the Mexican, Hispanic, or ethnic food sections. If you live in an urban area, the section will most likely be called ethnic or Hispanic. If you live in an area where Mexicans live and work, the section will be called Mexican.

Fresh Ingredients:

Chayotes [chah-*yo*-tays] ~ Chayotes are actually a light green fruit with a pale green interior and can be eaten raw or cooked. When cooked, it is very similar in taste and texture to a summer squash. Raw chayote has a bland flavor, so in Mexico it is not normally eaten raw. The peel often gets tough when cooked, so peel it before cooking, and remove the seed. They are readily available in the United States.

Coconuts How-To
Coconuts are inexpensive here in Mexico or many times free for the taking. Because of the abundance, you learn early how to deal with them. A very popular treat here in Mazatlán is *cocos helados* or *cocos frios*—cold coconuts. Street vendors keep the green coconut on ice to chill the coconut water inside, so on a hot day their customers can have a ready-made cold beverage. They use machetes to hack off the top so that a straw can be inserted—you have the "glass" and the drink all in one. If you have never had this treat, I am sorry for you, my friend. Rush right down to that grocery store and do yourself a favor: buy a fresh coconut and try it! You will not be able to purchase one in the United States that still has the husk on it, but it still works the same. To savor this sweet beverage, poke a hole in two of the "eyes" of the coconut, and either insert a straw (that is what we do), or pour it into a glass. It actually is good at room temperature, but amazingly refreshing if it has been refrigerated or put on ice.

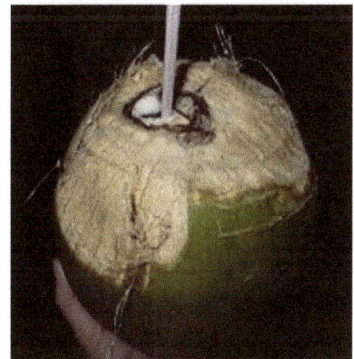

When you break open a coconut, the semi-clear liquid, coconut water, inside is a refreshing treat, but it is *not* coconut milk. Recipe for coconut milk follows.

To open a coconut, use the back of a heavy knife to break the outer shell. If you have already taken the coconut water out, then you shouldn't have a big mess. If you haven't taken it out, break the coconut over a large bowl. Hit it hard with the back of your knife (not the sharp blade) all around the center of the coconut until it breaks into halves.

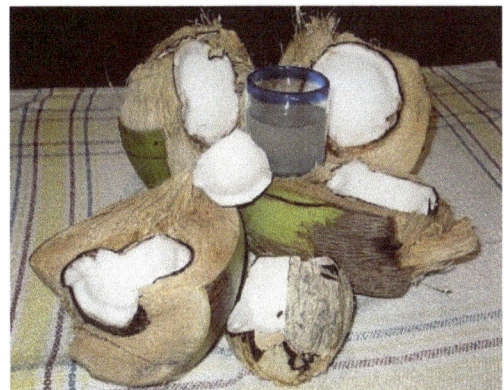

After you have it in large pieces, there are two ways to remove the coconut meat.

1. Heat the shell of the broken coconut directly on a gas burner for a few minutes to loosen the meat. Make sure you have the shell side on the burner, not the coconut meat. On a wooden board, using a clean screwdriver (I have one specifically for use in my kitchen), place the tip of the screwdriver between the meat and shell and pry to separate the two. *Note*: wrap the hand you use to hold the coconut in a thick towel so you do not cut yourself. The shell is very sharp and so is the screwdriver.

2. Do not bother to heat the shell; just use the screwdriver to pry the meat away. This is a bit more labor intensive because the coconut meat does not usually come out of the shell in one piece; it comes out in many smaller pieces that you need to pry loose individually.

Your coconut is ready to be used as you like. It can be shredded, toasted, or made into coconut milk.

Make Your Own Coconut Milk

You will need coconut (fresh or dried, unsweetened) and hot water.

For one coconut you will need four cups of hot water (not boiling). Place the coconut (without the shell) in your food processor or blender. Blitz until it is in tiny pieces or looks shredded. Add the hot water and continue to blitz until it is well pureed. Let it sit for five minutes. Place a piece of cheesecloth in a strainer over a bowl. Pour the pureed coconut into the cheesecloth. Wrap it up and squeeze as much of the liquid out as possible. This is the coconut milk. Use this instead of the expensive canned coconut milk (with all the junk in it) that you normally buy. Put it in a jar in the fridge, or use it immediately in curry, drinks, sauces, or a smoothie. The coconut can be used again in baking, ice cream, or anything you would normally use coconut for. The coconut also can be frozen for later use.

Epazote ~ is a dark-green herb which grows by the road in coastal Mexico. The strong fragrance, which can remind you of anything from petroleum to citrus, camphor, or mint, is difficult to describe, but once the scent has entered your nostrils, you will never forget it. I think of minty camphor as the closest match, although it does not taste like camphor. It is used sparingly in dishes like black beans, mole, tamales with cheese, and enchiladas. Most often you will see it in bean recipes, because it is believed to prevent flatulence. Who knows?

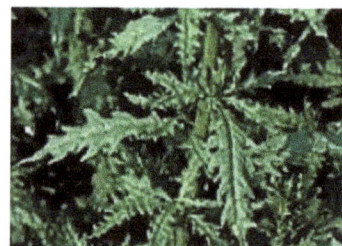

Mexican oregano ~ there is a big difference between the Italian, Greek, and Mexican oreganos. Italian and Greek oreganos are a different species, related to the mint family; the Mexican variety is an outsider. The flavor of Mexican oregano is somewhat more like savory than like the Italian or Greek oreganos. It looks like it has a bit of fuzz on the leaves, but there is no fuzzy taste. It should be available in the Mexican section of your market, and it will probably be packaged dried in a clear cellophane pack. This oregano is very easy to grow and has become popular outside Mexico, so you can probably either find seeds or starts to round out your herb garden. There is no satisfactory substitute for Mexican oregano.

Nopales ~ are a vegetable made from the young paddles of the prickly pear. Nopales are generally sold fresh in grocery stores and open markets. A stool and a knife are the only tools these vendors use to scrape off the spines before selling nopales. They have a slightly tart flavor, similar to fresh dill, and a smooth texture when cooked. They flower in springtime, as do many types of cactus. The nopales in the photo were "pilfered" from a neighbor's plant. The photo shows the four stages of nopale from off the plant to cooked. Throughout the book I will refer to these as *nopales*.

Onion ~ always refers to a white onion, not yellow. Occasionally, a purple onion or green onions will be called for in the recipe, but it always will be specified.

Plantains ("cooking bananas") ~ part of the same botanical family as a sweet banana, but they cannot be substituted for each other. The plantain must be cooked to bring out the smooth, creamy texture and sweetness of the fruit. On the exterior they look quite similar with one huge distinction: size. Plantains do not have the same flavor as a sweet banana, and the interior is a peach color rather than yellow.

Squash (Mexican) ~ calabaza – the texture is much more durable in the cooking process than its cousin the zucchini. This squash is the "neck" of a much larger squash and usually the only part sold in many stores. It is a very inexpensive vegetable, so it is used frequently. It can be peeled or left unpeeled, and it has no visible seeds to deal with. The flavor is similar to a strong-flavored zucchini.

Tomatillos ~ are small, round fruits resembling little green tomatoes, with a paper-like outer husk. Often called *tomates verdes* (green tomatoes), do not confuse these with unripe (green) tomatoes. Though they are usually green, they also can be yellow, purple, and red. The flavor is tart, and they are almost always used cooked. The photo shows three stages: in the husk, with husk removed, and cooked. Note the difference in color after they are cooked. Many recipes will call for them to be cooked in boiling water until the color changes. At this point, they will be very fragile and fall apart easily. A slotted spoon or a colander, rather than tongs, is the best method of retrieving them from the water.

Tomatoes ~ are always roma or plum tomatoes, unless otherwise noted.

Verdolagas ~ Purslane. This grows as a weed in Mexico and is also considered a weed in the States. Thus, it is very easy to grow. It can be eaten raw as a leaf vegetable, stir fried, cooked like spinach, or used in soups and stews. The stems, leaves, and flower buds are all edible. It has a slightly salty and sour taste, much like a mild pickle. You will probably have to go to a farmer's market or food co-op to find this if you do not grow your own. Try asking your produce manager to order it for you. There is no substitute for this vegetable.

Packaged Ingredients

First, a note about canned products called for in this book: most can sizes are the same, no matter where you live. For example, a can of evaporated milk in Mexico is the same size as you would find in the United States or Canada. Other canned products, such as mushrooms, vegetables, sweetened condensed milk, etc., are so close in size that the slight variance will not affect your recipe. If a specific can size is required, I have given that information in the recipe.

Achiote paste ~ is made from the slightly bitter, earthy flavored, red annatto seeds, mixed with other spices and ground into a paste. Annatto is a natural colorant and found in many foods all around the world, including the United States. The paste is dissolved in either lemon or lime juice, water, oil, or vinegar to create a marinade, or it can be rubbed directly on to the meat. Achiote paste is widely available in Mexican markets and on the Mexican food aisle of your grocery store. If you cannot find the pre-made achiote paste, look for annatto seeds and make your own. Many simple recipes on the Internet describe in detail how to make your own achiote paste.

Azafrán ~ Mexican saffron. Because Spanish saffron threads are very expensive, cooks all over Mexico use *azafrán de bolitas*, or saffron balls. The bolitas are brown to black in color and are about the size of peas. There is not much known about the plant these berries come from, other than they have no relation to Spanish saffron. I have asked many people what they know about these little balls, and no one seems to have much information. I did some research and found a botanical company from the state of Jalisco, Mexico, that had determined the plant is *Ditaxis heterantha* Zucc., of the Euphorbiaceae family, which honestly meant absolutely nothing to me. If you care to look into this further, that is your starting point. All we need to know here is that it is used for color and an extremely mild flavoring for food. I ate one of those little balls and only experienced a very mild flavor—but my teeth were yellow! Consider it is just for color.

Butter ~ Mexican butter comes either salted or unsalted. There is so little salt in the salted variety, however, that I can't tell the difference; they both taste unsalted to me. Be safe and always use unsalted butter. Margarine is *not* a substitute for butter in these recipes.

Chicken bouillon ~ and all other bouillons mentioned in this book. Knorr powdered or cube chicken bouillon is the choice of the cooks in the colonia. You can, of course, use the brand you like or make your own. I won't tell Leticia!

Cream cheese ~ Who would have expected to see Philadelphia cream cheese on the Mexican grocery store shelves? But that is exactly what we use; the only difference is the size. A regular package is 190g/6.7 ounces. When one package is called for in a recipe, you may have to reduce the size of the package you bought. The leftover cream cheese from your package can be used in a sauce or just popped into your mouth for a creamy treat! (Sh-h-h—hope no one is looking!)

Dried shrimp (*camarón seco*) ~ are packaged with heads, legs, and shells attached. They are very salty and probably have not been cleaned prior to drying and packaging. To clean them, soak in water for about ten minutes. Drain the water off and then remove the heads (remember, they have been dried, so the heads will come off easily), the shell, and legs. Rinse again with clear water to remove any additional salt or debris. Now they are ready for you to use. Look for them in either the Mexican food aisle or Asian food aisle. This ingredient is common in both cultures and is also popular in the southern part of the United States.

Lard ~ Good fresh lard tastes like lightly roasted pork. You only use a small amount in a few select recipes and the rich flavor it imparts to your food is better than butter. Normally a large grocery store will carry a good quality fresh lard in their meat department's cooler section. If you do not see it, ask. The non-refrigerated lard *(manteca)* is **not** ever an acceptable product.

Maggi ~ bottled seasoning sauce from Nestlé. Mexican cooks use this the way "Northerners" use Worcestershire sauce. Look for *Maggi Liquid Seasoning*. This should be available in the same area of your grocery store as the Worcestershire sauce. It is not used exclusively for Mexican cooking.

Media Crema ~ literally, "medium cream" or also called "table cream. It is very thick and has a mild flavor, similar to that of whipping cream. This is not to be mistaken for Mexican *crema*; they are two distinctly different products. Media crema can be substituted in most recipes that call for cream. Note, however, that there are two basic differences between the media crema and whipping cream. First, media crema does not need refrigeration until the package has been opened, so it is a wonderful pantry item. Second, it does not whip well. Media crema will only increase in volume slightly, so it is not a good substitute for actual whipping cream where you need volume and air. Two brands are popular; both have the same flavor. The first one is Nestlé and comes in a very short can

with 225 grams (7.6 ounces). The other is LaLa brand and is packaged in a box with 250 grams. (LaLa is my choice because it stacks well in my pantry.) I personally use this in all of my cooked dishes requiring cream, such as Shrimp Fettuccine, and I always pour some on my fresh strawberries.

Mexican crema ~ Usually, you will find this packaged in a jar located in the refrigerated section near the sour cream. It has a mildly sweet, acidic flavor but not quite as acidic as true sour cream. It is thick, like heavy cream, but tastes more like crème fraîche. There are no recipes in this book that require this ingredient, but many other Mexican cookbooks have this on their ingredient lists, so I felt this ingredient needed to be mentioned. Mexican cooking has evolved over the past few years to have a more "modern" flavor. Locally, almost all the cooks I know do not use the regular Mexican crema any longer but instead use LaLa Crema Acidificada, which is the mild sour cream called for in the recipes. They prefer the more acidic flavor instead of the sweeter flavor of the Mexican crema. If you cannot find LaLa brand sour cream, then use any other *mild* sour cream.

Mole in a jar (pronounced *mow-lay*) ~ Doña Maria mole is a favorite brand used in Mazatlán if the cooks are not making it themselves. This is a superb-quality jarred mole. It is readily available in the United States, so keep a few on the pantry shelf. You need not use the entire jar if you are making fewer than eight servings. Just scoop out what you need, cover the top with plastic wrap, and pop the lid back on. Refrigerate the jar after opening. It will keep almost indefinitely under refrigeration.

Peruano beans ~ are light-yellow beans and sometimes called Mexican yellow beans. Although the pinto is also used locally, in Colonia Pancho Villa, the peruano is the bean of choice used to make refried beans and bean soup—it cooks faster than a pinto bean and causes little or no gas. Your friends and family will love these!

Piloncillo (pee-loan-*see*-yoh) ~ is a type of sugar that gets its name from its cone-shaped "little pylon," and the color is either light or dark brown. In this book, we use the dark brown exclusively. In Mexico, the sizes vary from medium, about 4 ounces (122 g) to large, about 7.5–8 ounces (215–225 g). We will refer to one large cone or one small cone. Piloncillo is richer tasting and much harder than brown sugar. It is made from pure sugar cane juice, from cane that has been hand cut, crushed mechanically, and then heated to reduce its water content. The resulting thick syrup is poured into cone-shaped molds to cool. This sugar is extremely hard and must be either shaved with a serrated knife, broken with a hammer (my preference—great stress reliever), or melted in the liquid you will use in the recipe (this takes the longest time but also less mess). *Do not* try to break it up in your blender or food processor—it will damage your equipment.

Rice ~ is always long grain white rice.

Tomato purée ~ is actually thick tomato sauce, similar to what you can buy where you live. It is typically flavored with salt, onions, garlic, and a few herbs. You can use tomato sauce or tomato purée, they both work equally well. Tomato purée normally comes in a small box rather than a can. The size is 210 grams or 7.4 ounces.

Tuna ~ canned tuna comes in oil or water pack and is interchangeable in the recipes. The cans are the same size as they are in the United States and Canada.

Cheese

There are no real substitutes for Mexican cheese. In today's marketplace, with so many immigrants from Mexico, you may be able to readily find these wonderful cheeses in your grocer's deli case. Look for the real cheeses called for in this book *before* you settle for the alternatives. These real cheeses will make a world of difference in your finished dish.

Chihuahua cheese ~ is a pale yellow cheese, rather than a typical white usually found with Mexican cheese. It melts easily, has a creamy soft texture, and has a flavor ranging from very mild to an almost mild cheddar-like sharpness. Chihuahua cheese is often available outside Mexico and can be purchased online. If you cannot find this, you can use a combination of mild white cheddar and Monterey Jack. Although neither is a perfect substitute, a combination of the two comes close. A medium cheddar is not a good substitute.

Cotija cheese ~ is a hard white cheese from cow's milk. It has also been known as *añejo* (aged) cheese. With a high salt content, cotija is not eaten as a table or dessert cheese. Instead, it is used crumbled or grated as a topping to add flavor to refried beans, tostadas, tacos, salads, and soups. When it is cooked, it softens slightly but does not melt. It is normally used the same way you would use Parmesan and is commonly sold already grated.

Manchego cheese ~ Apart from the name, this cheese has nothing in common with the true Spanish variety of manchego, which is made from sheep's milk in a specific region of Spain. In Mexico and Spanish-speaking areas of the United States, *manchego* or *queso tipo manchego* (manchego-type cheese) is the name given to a cow's milk cheese similar in taste to a Monterey Jack cheese. It melts very well but does not grate well unless it is very cold. It is considered a medium soft cheese.

Queso (kay-so) fresco ~ fresh cheese, also known as queso ranchero and panela. Panela cheese has less salt than a typical ranchero type. Queso fresco is one of life's little delicacies. It is a creamy, soft, and mild unaged white cheese. The flavor is so mild that it picks up the flavors of other ingredients in your recipe. It can be eaten plain (my favorite) or mixed with other ingredients to make toppings, spreads, or dips. A word of warning: *it does not melt*. Make sure to always buy the very freshest queso fresco you can find.

Meat

Chicken ~ There is no difference between a chicken in Mexico and where you live. A chicken is a chicken the world over.

Beef ~ Most beef sold in Mexico is grass-fed and not grown in feed lots. Corn is a main food staple of the country, so corn is for the people to eat, not the animals. The beef is very lean and not aged. What has been butchered yesterday, you can have on the barbecue tomorrow. Since it is not aged, Mexican beef must be cooked longer, in most instances, than beef that is available in other parts of the world. Keep this in mind when a recipe calls for longer cooking times; you may need to decrease the cooking time for your type of beef. The cuts of meat are normally not as thick as US cuts. A steak, for instance, can be 6 mm–13 mm / ¼–½ inch thick. This also impacts the cooking time. Beef is usually purchased in Mexico without the bone, except for a few types of steaks, like porterhouse or T-bone. People here cannot afford to pay for a bone that will be thrown away.

Pork ~ There are many recipes in this book for pork. If you have a problem eating commercially grown pork due to the chemicals that are routinely fed to kill parasites, then try to buy either organic pork or have your butcher order some from a local farmer who raises pork without chemicals. By the way, whole milk fed to piglets will kill those parasites, but chemicals are much cheaper for commercial lots. Pigs in Mexico are not fed those chemicals. Other than ribs and occasionally pork chops, pork is generally purchased without the bone.

A Day without Chile …
Is Like a Day without Sun
(as the saying goes in Mexico)

Mexicans eat chiles with almost every meal. The chiles are not necessarily eaten for the heat they impart but for the flavor. Every chile has its own distinct flavor, as well as its own heat index (see the Scoville chart). You cannot substitute one chile for another and expect perfect results. *Not all chiles are created equal.* For instance, if a recipe calls for an ancho chile, you should use an ancho chile. Using a Colorado chile, even though it looks much the same as an ancho, will give you a totally different flavor. A dried chile is not the same as a green or fresh chile. Almost every variety of chile, both dried and fresh are available either in the produce section or Mexican food aisle in your grocery store. There is no good reason for substitution. After you have tried these recipes, feel free to experiment on your own. By that time, you will know the distinct characteristics of each chile and how you can alter the recipe for your palette.

There are some basic ground rules in handling these little beasts. There is, of course, the old myth (maybe not a myth) that you should eat ice cream *before* you eat any spicy chiles to keep *tender areas* from burning the next morning. Alas, I have not tried this to see if it really works.

The precautions (*rules*) below are not myths, and I urge you to follow them for your own protection. You will be glad you did!

1. **Always (and I mean it!)** wear gloves when handling any type of chile.
   - If you forget this rule, and your hands feel like they are on fire, you can tame the heat with some fresh lime juice. This will *tame* the heat, not make it disappear. So follow rule #2.
2. Do not touch your eyes, nose, or any other vital parts of your anatomy with hands that have handled chiles. You will be very sorry you did (use your imagination here).
3. If you have eaten a chile dish that is too spicy for you, *do not drink* water or beer! This is the worst thing you can do, as it only spreads the fire; it does not extinguish it. A piece of bread, tortilla, or cracker will help. If you have butter handy, put some on the bread; it will work better. A glass of milk (*not* non-fat) will help also. Almost any food with some fat in it will save you.

Many years ago, my husband wanted to learn to make salsa cruda (fresh salsa). I gave him instructions on the ingredients and how to cut and chop and also how to protect his hands against the chiles. Being the manly man he is, he didn't need no stinkin' gloves! An hour later, he was walking around with hands aflame, not just burning but actually beet red. He was soaking his hands in a bowl of iced water on the front patio when a dear neighbor Victoria (Toya) came over and starting laughing hysterically. She asked him why he hadn't used gloves. He looked at me and hung his head but had no answer. She told us about using lime juice on his hands. That was a good lesson, so now he always uses those stinkin' gloves, and he has become the best little salsa maker around.

In Mexico, summer gives more heat to the chiles than in winter. If you live in the United States, this does not apply. Commercially grown varieties in the States have gotten very mild over the past few years, to the point that jalapeños and poblanos have almost no heat at all, due to hybridization. When you purchase chiles at your local grocery store, the commercially grown chiles will be much milder than the organic varieties, no matter what time of year. They have good flavor but not much heat. So, if heat is what you are looking for, always opt for the organic varieties. Now on to the chiles …

Varieties of **Fresh Chiles**

Jalapeño—the most famous chile of all. It is usually about 5–7.6 cm/2–3 in. long and plump at one end. The membrane (veins) and seeds are the hot parts. If you want flavor but not much heat, remove the seeds and membrane (using your gloves) before chopping or slicing. These typically are used raw (by non-Mexicans) for salsas, added to a bean pot, or stuffed with cheese. They can be roasted and chopped in a blender with roasted tomatoes for a lovely salsa. The skin is a bit thick, and the taste is rather a "biting" grassy flavor, not a smooth flavor, as with a serrano. Perhaps that is why Mexicans most often use jalapeños cooked or pickled. Smoked, they are called chipotle chiles.

Serrano—looks like a smaller version of the jalapeño but with two major differences: it is much hotter (four to five times hotter) and tastes nothing like a jalapeño, as discussed above. Serranos have a thin skin and a smooth, slightly fruity flavor. Mexicans use them in salsa cruda (pico de gallo) for those very reasons, the same reasons you would use jalapeños. Many cooks in Mexico also roast this chile and use it as a condiment alongside meats, such as carne asada (grilled meat). Roasting this pepper does *not* make it milder.

Poblanos—are the "stuffing" chile. When you order chiles rellenos, a stuffed poblano is what you get. They are large, very mild (low on the Scoville chart), and have a fresh grassy-type flavor. They are almost always cooked and can be eaten hot or cold. The skin is removed by charring and rubbing it lightly under slowly running water. The seeds and membrane are then removed, and the chile is either sliced, chopped, stuffed, or pureed in the blender.

To prepare the poblano chiles: In a dry, heavy skillet or grill pan over high heat, place the poblanos and allow them to char. You will see wisps of smoke as they char. Now is the time to turn on that stove fan! Turn and char on all sides. Immediately after charring, place them in a large bowl with a lid (I use a dinner plate to cover the bowl). Repeat with all the chiles. Set them aside to steam in the bowl

Poblanos - raw, charred, peeled

for ten minutes. If you are not stuffing them, you can leave them in the bowl longer.

Under slowly running water, slip off the charred skin (remember those gloves). Remove the stem, seeds, and veins (membranes).

- *If you are making rajas (slices) or chopping them, you can slit them up the side to reveal the inside and remove the seeds and veins.*
- *If you will be stuffing them, be careful not to split them up the side. Remove the stem neatly with a knife and remove the seeds through the opening created by removing the stem. (If you do accidentally split them, don't worry; just slit all the others up the side and stuff them "open face," pretending that you planned it that way.)*

NOTE: you can also char them over a direct flame, but you need to watch them closely so they do not burn beyond the char stage.

If you are already charring and preparing poblanos, why not do a few more to freeze? I normally freeze them in packages of three poblanos each, so that I can use them in almost any recipe I have. After rinsing, let them drain. Place them flat in freezer bags so you can make a recipe that calls for poblanos without any fuss.

Karina Ann Betlem

Árbol—also known as *bird's beak chile* and *rat's tail chile (chile ratón)*. It is small and *very* spicy. These chiles are about 5–7.6 cm/2–3 inches long, and about 6 mm / ¼ inch wide. The peppers are a bright red color when mature and can be found fresh, dried, or powdered. Generally, they are sold dried in clear cellophane packages on the Mexican food aisle. I personally don't get much flavor from these little chiles, only heat.

Varieties of **Dried** *Chiles*:

Ancho—Probably the most widely used dried chile in Mexico. Very mild with a rustic smoky flavor, reminiscent of an old English tobacco, and lovely red/rust color. Many cooks in Mazatlán use this chile strictly for its color. It is a mature, dried poblano chile. You can make your own chile powder using an ancho.

To prepare these for chile powder, rip off the stem end (this is therapeutic), open up the chile, and remove the seeds and veins. Before you start ripping stems off chiles, remember rule #1. Put the opened chile in a dry cast-iron pan until a few wisps of smoke appear, just a few seconds per side. Let them cool for a few minutes. Grind them in your coffee grinder and put in an airtight jar. That's it! You can find these on the Mexican food aisle in your grocery store in clear cellophane packages.

Chipotles—Dried jalapeños smoked whole with seeds and membranes. They have much more heat than canned jalapeños because they are left intact. Although you can purchase them dried, they are most often sold in cans, packed in adobo, a red tomato-type sauce. You will find them in the canned chile row. By the way, the adobo from the chipotles is spicy hot also. Removing the seeds after they have been canned does not make them milder.

Morita—purple in color, smoked, dried jalapeños or chipotles (not in adobo sauce) but used dried. Do not be confused by their appearance. Although they look a bit like an ancho chile, that is where the resemblance ends. They are much smaller and have a strong smoky flavor. This type of chipotle is grown in the northern Mexico state of Chihuahua. Most dried chipotle chiles found in the United States are of the *morita* variety.

Guajillo—has a shiny, thin, deep-red flesh with a green tea flavor and slight berry overtones. (Gosh, sounds like a wine or chocolate!) It is mild in flavor, with only a small amount of heat. Preparation for use is the same as for ancho chiles. This also makes a wonderful chile powder. It is the dried marisol chile.

Cascabel—These little chiles are also called bell chiles because the seeds rattle around inside. Very mild, ranking below the jalapeño on the Scoville chart. They are used for their nutty, smoky flavor without adding heat.

Pasilla ~ (*pah-SEE-yah*) have a wrinkled, dark, blackish-brown skin and is sometimes known as the chile negro or black chile. If you have ever had Oaxacan black mole, then you have had pasilla chiles. It is mild to medium-hot (Scoville rating 2,500) and has a rich distinctive grape flavor. It is a long, slender looking chile and can be ground into powder, pureed for sauces or used whole for stuffing.

These are not dried poblano chiles (anchos) as some would have you believe, but rather, the dried form of the long and narrow chilaca pepper.

Scoville Chart

The higher the number, the hotter the chile. This is only a guideline and is not the complete scale, but it may help you to decide which chiles you want to try. I have highlighted those chiles you will find within these pages.

15,000,000–16,000,000	Pure capsaicin
5,000,000–5,300,000	Law-enforcement-grade pepper spray
100,000–350,000	Habanero chile, Scotch bonnet pepper, Peruvian white habanero, Jamaican hot pepper
30,000–50,000	Cayenne pepper, ají pepper, Tabasco pepper, **chipotle, árbol chile**
10,000–23,000	**Serrano pepper**
3,500–8,000	**Jalapeño pepper, guajillo pepper**, new Mexican varieties of Anaheim pepper, Tabasco sauce
1,000–2,500	Anaheim pepper, **poblano pepper, ancho, cascabel**
100–500	Pepperoncini pepper
0	Bell peppers

Beans and Salsa

**Beans, beans, the magical fruit,
the more you eat the more you toot …**

(oops … sorry about that! It just came right out.)

Authentic Mexican refried beans is one of those recipes that seems to vary just a wee bit from household to household. This is a basic recipe that was given to me by several of these cooks and is probably the best one to pass on to you. Instead of choosing just one cook's chapter in which to include it, I chose to separate it so it would be easier for you to find when you need it.

Before we start, I think we should talk beans. In my part of Mexico, the bean of choice for *frijoles refritos*— refried beans—is the peruano bean, also known as the Mexican yellow bean.

If your Mexican grocery does not have peruano beans, then use pinto beans. This is also a very common bean used in Mexico, although it does cause a bit more gas. (Definitely not the choice for a romantic evening meal. Choose wisely!)

The first thing I do with dried beans of any kind is sort them on a white plate, so that I can easily see the tiny stones or shriveled beans at a glance. Discard anything that looks foreign or discolored.

To soak or not to soak—in Mexico, it is not necessary to soak beans because they are not *old* beans. In other parts of the world, the turnover in dried bean supplies may not be as active, so if the beans are old, soaking is the way to go. If you choose to soak, then you will need to plan ahead, as they will need to soak overnight. Rinse the beans in a colander and then put them in a large pot. Cover them with cold water to about 7.62 cm/3 inches above the beans. Let sit until tomorrow. In the morning, drain and rinse again. They are now ready to be cooked.

Or …

Rinse the beans in a colander and then put them in a large pot with a well-fitting lid. Cover them with cold water to about 7.62 cm/3 inches above the beans. Heat the beans over medium heat until they have come to a rolling boil. Keep the lid on—no peeking. Turn the heat off, and let them sit undisturbed for one hour. After one hour, drain the beans and rinse again. They are now ready to be cooked.

Now, what you have been waiting for … (drum roll) …

Refried Beans … THE RECIPE

Frijoles Refritos

2½ cups dried beans
1 clove garlic, roughly chopped
½ onion, roughly chopped
2 teaspoons salt
1 Tablespoon dried epazote (optional)
3 Tablespoons real pork lard (fresh, if possible; not that white canned stuff) or oil
(both are commonly used)

After you have either soaked the beans overnight or hydrated them by cooking for an hour, you are now ready to really cook them.

In your pot, put the newly rinsed beans, the onion, and garlic and add enough water to cover by 5 cm/2 inches. You will salt them a bit later.

Over medium heat, cook the beans 1 hour. Add the salt and epazote. Cook for another hour. Test for doneness at this point. Taste one to see if it is totally soft. If it is, they are done. If it still has a bit of chew to it, keep cooking. Check them at 30 minute intervals.

NOTE: The times may differ, depending on the age of the dried beans. The older the bean, the longer the cooking time.

When the beans are done, drain them, reserving about 1 cup of the cooking broth. Now is the time to mash the beans, onion, and garlic. The way to mash them offers another choice: you can mash them with a potato masher and have some lovely little chunks of beans mixed with the bean purée, or you can use the back of a large wooden spoon to mash them for a smoother texture. I like them really smooth, so I use an immersion blender. If your beans are too stiff, add some of the broth you kept—not all of it, just a little at a time to thin them out.

When you have the consistency you like, heat the lard or oil in a large frying pan. When it is *hot*, add the beans and let them fry, stirring occasionally until they are heated thoroughly and all the lard/oil has been absorbed. Adjust your salt, if necessary. Serve.

Salsa Mexicana
Salsa Cruda (Raw Salsa)

Fresh (raw) salsa is another of those recipes that is almost the same in every household in Colonia Pancho Villa. I have therefore placed the recipe in this general section, rather than bury it in an individual chapter. You will (or should) make this often.

The recipe is made with either serrano chiles or jalapeños, depending on whose kitchen you are in. Serrano chiles are more prevalent in some kitchens, while jalapeños are more prevalent in others. Both are wonderfully fresh tasting. The ratio of chiles and tomatoes are a personal preference, even in Mexican kitchens.

I find jalapeños very mild but also very flavorful, so I do like to use them in my salsa. My ratio of 1 chile to 1 tomato may be too hot and spicy for you. Feel free to adjust the quantity. I do, however, remove some of the seeds because I just don't like chomping down on so many seeds in my salsa. I am going for good flavor and texture. If you do use serranos, it is not necessary to remove all the seeds, as they are quite tender.

Although you will find this salsa on tables throughout most of the year, it is important to always have it for Mexican Independence Day. The colors of the salsa are the colors of the Mexican flag—red, white, and green. It is considered very patriotic!

Ingredients

6 ripe roma tomatoes, seeds removed
6 jalapeños or serranos (use your own discretion on the quantity)
½ white onion
½ cup cilantro
2 limes

Chop the tomatoes into a medium-sized dice. Remove the seeds as you go; they add no flavor, just moisture.

Okay, go get your gloves on! Remove the stem end from the jalapeños, stand the chile on the flat end, and carefully slice down the chile between the flesh and the seeds. This is actually the easiest method to remove those pesky seeds. When you have finished this step, dice them into very tiny squares. If you are using serranos, you can de-seed them the same way or just dice them up with the seeds.

Chop the onion into a small dice. Chop the cilantro leaves roughly.

Combine all the tomatoes, onion, cilantro, and as much of the chiles as you want. Then squeeze the juice from the 2 limes over the salsa and gently stir to combine.

Under *no* circumstances should you add salt! Salt draws out the water, and you will end up with your salsa swimming in a pool of watery tomato juice.

Karina Ann Betlem

ADELAIDA

Meet Adelaida Chávez López

(This was a difficult photo to take of Adelaida because she kept laughing hysterically at everything. Of course, she made me laugh, and I could not hold the camera still!)

Adelaida (Ah-day-*lye*-da), a true Mazatleca (a native of Mazatlán), has never lived anywhere else and has never traveled outside the state of Sinaloa. She comes from a family of seven children. When she was a little girl, she says she was nosy and wanted to learn about everything, so her mother began teaching her about house chores and cooking. Although Adelaida was going to school full time, she still enjoyed the time spent learning from her mother.

By the time she was eleven years old, Adelaida could prepare the *nixtamal*—the corn used to make tortillas. The process of preparing the corn is laborious, consisting of boiling it in a slaked lime solution, rinsing, removing the husks, and then grinding (by hand). This process is difficult even for some adults! She would mix the *masa* (dough), form the tortillas, and then briefly cook them on a hot comal—a round cast iron plate for cooking tortillas. Adelaida became a valuable helper for her mother.

When she was fifteen, Adelaida fell in love. She wanted to get married, but her parents would not allow it. Regrettably, she did what many other teenagers have done through the years—she ran off and got married. Today, Adelaida works hard to discourage other teenagers from making the same mistake. Her marriage lasted only two years, but by then she had two children In spite of her unfortunate circumstances, she rarely asked her family for help but knew they were always there for her, if needed. Adelaida accepted responsibility for her youthful indiscretions and was determined to make her own way in life. Eventually, she found work, cleaning and cooking in the homes of more affluent Mexican families.

Most of the kitchen is in the backyard, and off to the right is the bathroom.

By this time, Adelaida was already a good cook, and the things she had learned from her mom about cleaning paid off. At last she was able to make her own way, with only minimal assistance from her family.

A few years later she remarried, saying she was much wiser. For eight years now, she has worked, cleaning and cooking for one family. She loves her job; they pay her well and treat her with respect. Adelaida's employers joke that she can never leave their employ, as they would not be able to survive without her! She is a trusted and much-loved part of their family and in return, she brings good work and laughter to their home every day.

Corn Tortillas
Tortillas de Maiz

Makes 16 tortillas

Adelaida grew up making tortillas, so it is only fitting that she share her recipe with us. We will not go into soaking the corn in slaked lime or grinding it.

We will use the purchased Maseca*—corn flour "nixtamalizado" or nixtamal corn flour. This is *not* to be confused with cornmeal, plain corn flour, or cornstarch. Corn flour for tortillas is a cross, of sorts, between corn meal and corn flour—not as coarse as corn meal and not as fine as corn flour. Make sure the package you purchase says "For Tortillas." You will find this product on the Mexican food aisle or near the flour and corn meal. *Maseca is a brand that is widely available outside Mexico, but any brand will work, as long as it is the specified type of flour.

You may be wondering why anyone would bother making homemade corn tortillas when they are so readily available at the grocery store. I offer you a challenge: make a batch of these homemade tortillas and compare them, side by side, with ones you've bought. I already know which you will prefer. (Don't despair; you can cut the purchased ones into triangles and fry them up for chips!)

If you do not have a tortilla press, use a rolling pin. (You may want to purchase a press after you taste the difference in homemade tortillas.) A press makes this entire process so much easier. You can purchase one in metal or wood, available at most kitchen specialty stores.

Ingredients

2 cups nixtamal corn flour
1¼ to 1½ cups warm water
¼ teaspoon salt

Mix the flour, water, and salt. Knead with your hands for 2 minutes to completely mix. If the dough seems dry and falls apart, add 1 or 2 tablespoons more water and knead again. If the dough is too wet and sticky, add a bit more flour.

Divide the dough into 16 equal pieces and roll each piece into a ball. Cover the balls with a damp towel while you work so they do not dry out.

Take two pieces of plastic wrap or wax paper, and cover both sides of the press (or cover the dough, if you are rolling with a rolling pin). Place the dough ball slightly off center to the rear of the press (by the hinge). Gently close the press and press down firmly until the dough has spread to a diameter of about 15 cm/ 6 inches.

Heat a griddle or a large skillet on medium-high heat. Working one at a time, carefully remove the top piece of plastic wrap from the tortilla. Gently remove the tortilla from the bottom plastic and place the dough in the hot pan. Cook the tortilla for 30 seconds, and then carefully flip and cook 30 seconds on the other side.

Remove the cooked tortillas to either a tortilla warmer lined with a clean cloth, or wrap them in a clean cloth to keep them warm and soft. Serve immediately.

Chiles Rellenos

7 servings

If you thought you were in love with traditional chiles rellenos, you will fall head over heels for this one! Super easy to make (and eat). There is no breading, and the sauce is a light orange-cream sauce—no cheese on top. After you char and peel the poblanos, the entire recipe takes less than 10 minutes.

Ingredients

7 poblano chiles
250 grams (8.8 ounces) Chihuahua cheese, divided into 7 pieces
½ cup oil
3 onions, sliced
¼ cup mild sour cream
1½ Tablespoons chicken bouillon powder
1 cup orange juice

Char and peel the poblano chiles as directed in the "A Day without Chile …" section. Carefully remove the stem and seeds without splitting the chile down the side. (You will only have an opening at the very top where the stem was.) If you split the chile accidentally, get another chile, and try again.

After the chiles have been cleaned, place them in a pan of simmering water for 5 minutes. Drain and thoroughly pat them dry. Fill each chile with a piece of cheese, and then close with a toothpick.

Heat the oil in a large pan. Sauté the onions until they are translucent and have separated into rings. Remove them from the pan and arrange them in a layer on a large platter. In that same oil, fry the chiles on both sides until they are "toasted." Be careful when turning them so they do not break. Gently place them on top of the sautéed onion.

Mix the sour cream, bouillon powder, and orange juice together, and heat in a covered pan for 5 minutes. Pour over the rellenos. *Listo!* (Ready!)

Tortilla Soup
Sopa de Tortilla

3 servings

A very different kind of tortilla soup—one with no chiles or lime. The broth is a light tomato with garlic and a hint—just a hint—of onion. The tortillas give the soup its body, and the garnishes add yet another layer of flavor. A great recipe to add to your list of everyday soups.

Ingredients

6 corn tortillas, a day or two old
oil to 6 mm / ¼ in. deep in small frying pan
3 tomatoes
3 cloves garlic
1 slice onion
½ teaspoon salt
3 cups chicken stock or broth
6 teaspoons Chihuahua cheese, shredded

6 teaspoons mild sour cream

Let the tortillas air dry a day or two (you want them dry and stale). Cut them into small squares and then brown them in hot oil. They need to be well browned and crisp. Drain on paper towels.

In a blender, purée the tomatoes with the garlic, onion, and salt. Pour this into a pot and cook on low heat to blend the flavors, about 5 minutes. Add the broth to the tomato mixture. When it comes to a boil, add the fried tortillas and cook another 20 minutes.

Ladle the soup into bowls. Serve with 2 teaspoons each of cheese and sour cream on top. Do not stir; cheese and sour cream should sit on the top.

Beef Meatballs
Albondigas de Res

9 servings

Did you know that Mexicans ate meatballs? This is a traditional version and fairly easy to prepare. The aroma of the meat and mint poaching in a poblano/cilantro broth is irresistible. You get only a hint of flavor from the broth ingredients. If you close your eyes and taste it, you might not be able to pinpoint any individual ingredient. This meal will warm the cockles of your heart.

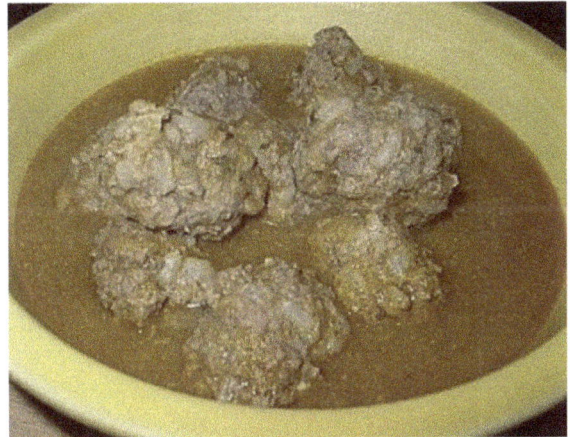

Ingredients

For the broth:
3 Tablespoons oil
1 onion, chopped
1 clove garlic, chopped
1 poblano chile, chopped, seeds, veins and stem removed
2 tomatoes
2¼ cups water
¼ cup cilantro, chopped
1 teaspoon salt

For the meatballs:
500 grams (1 pound) ground beef
¼ teaspoon salt, or to taste
1 pinch ground black pepper, or to taste
1 Tablespoon mint, finely minced
¼ cup rice, pre-cooked
1 egg
¼ cup dry breadcrumbs

It is not necessary to char and remove the skin from the poblano chile for this recipe (unless, of course, you have nothing else to do with your time).

Heat the oil in a small frying pan; then sauté the onion, garlic, and chopped poblano chile.

Put the tomatoes in a small pot of boiling water until the skins split, 5 minutes. Drain and discard the water. Place them in a blender jar with the 2¼ cups water, cilantro, salt, sautéed onion, garlic, and poblano. Purée. Then pour into a large pan and heat to a slow boil.

Knead all the meatball ingredients until they are thoroughly mixed. Form the meat into walnut-sized balls. Carefully drop each meatball into the boiling broth. Cook them for 20 minutes.

Serve with white rice, mashed potatoes, or pasta.

Slow-Braised Beef
Birria de Res

8 servings

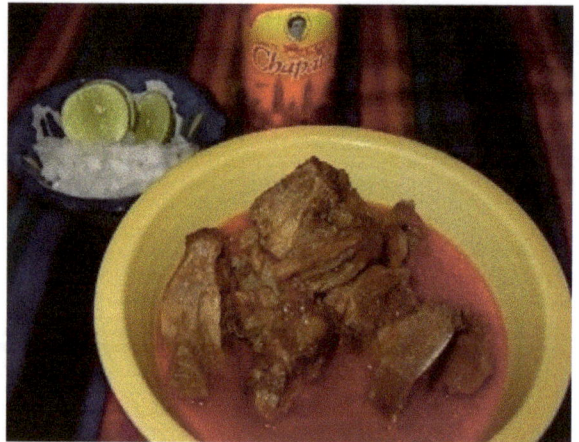

Birria comes in many forms including *birria de chivo* (goat), chicken, lamb, turkey, pork, and beef. This recipe uses beef ribs. First, you brown them; then you slow cook them. It almost cooks by itself. When finished, you can eat the meat in a taco or by itself with rice and beans. The sauce (broth) is fragrant and flavorful. Although crock pots are not prevalent here in Mazatlán, this would be a perfect recipe in which to use one.

Ingredients

3 Tablespoons oil
1 kilo (2.2 pounds) beef ribs
10 bay leaves
½ teaspoon salt
1 large ancho chile, stem and seeds removed
2 cloves garlic
1 cube chicken bouillon
100 ml (3.5 ounces) white vinegar
2 whole cloves
10 whole black peppercorns
1 onion
sliced limes

Heat the oil in a deep pan. Brown the ribs on all sides. Add the bay leaves, salt, and enough water to cover the ribs. Bring to a slow boil and simmer for about 2 hours, until the meat is fork tender.

Put the chile to rehydrate in a small pan of boiling water. Let it boil for about 3 minutes; drain and discard the water. Put the softened chile in a blender with the garlic, bouillon, and vinegar. Purée, and add to the cooked meat.

Grind the cloves and peppercorns in a mortar and pestle or spice grinder. Add to the meat. Allow to slowly boil for 10 minutes, and serve with chopped onion, lime, and bottled hot sauce.

Shredded Beef
Carne de Res Deshebrada

7 servings

Looks like beef stew, right? It is—Mexican style! Unlike other cuts of beef, brisket has a unique texture that allows it to be easily shredded. There is only a wee bit of spice, even though you have a few árbol chiles in the sauce. Boiling them before you add them to the blender removes some of the heat but retains the flavor. Remember that chiles are not interchangeable, so do not try to substitute one for another.

Ingredients

500 grams (1 pound) beef brisket
1 teaspoon salt
1 onion
1 whole black peppercorn
2 potatoes, peeled and cubed
1 carrot, peeled and cubed
1 bay leaf
3 árbol chiles, dried
2 tomatoes
1 clove garlic
1 poblano chile, minced (not charred or peeled)

Cook the meat in a little water with salt, onion, and peppercorn until it can be shredded. You can cook the meat using any method you wish. Brisket takes about 2 hours to cook in a pot on the stove top. Adelaida uses a pressure cooker, which reduces the cooking time to about 45 minutes. You also could use a crock pot and cook it overnight. No matter which way you cook it, make sure it is tender and shreds easily.

Shred the meat and return it to the pan. Add the potatoes, carrot, and bay leaf.

Cook the árbol chiles with the tomatoes in boiling water until the tomato skins split. Remove the tomatoes with a slotted spoon and place in a blender jar. Continue to cook the chiles for 3 more minutes; then remove them and put in the blender with the tomatoes. Discard the cooking water. Add in the garlic and liquify.

Add the minced poblano chile to the meat, and pour in the tomato mixture. Cook until all the vegetables are tender, about 15–20 minutes.

Serve in bowls or on plates with a rim to capture all the broth.

Enchiladas in Beans (Sauce)
Enchiladas Enfrijoladas

4 servings

Normally, the tortillas for making enchiladas are dipped in either warm oil or warm sauce, but in this unique version, the tortillas are dipped in warm liquefied beans (frijoles). The queso fresco is fresh and salty; the tomatillo/serrano sauce is tart. These enchiladas are prepared with meat and tortillas that have been heated, so there is no need to heat them in the oven. If, however, you are an inexperienced and/or a slow enchilada maker and the ingredients cool down, you can reheat them in the oven or microwave.

Ingredients

1 cup beans, cooked (peruano or pinto)
2 Tablespoons oil, plus ¼ cup for the tortillas
½ onion
1 clove garlic
4 serrano chiles (remove the seeds if you like)
3 stems cilantro
¼ teaspoon salt
2 cups tomatillo sauce, bottled or canned (salsa verde)
12 tortillas
250 grams (¼ pound) beef brisket, cooked, shredded, and kept warm
500 grams (1 pound) queso fresco (fresh cheese), grated

If you have made your own beans, they should remain very watery after you mash them.*

Heat 2 Tablespoons oil in a small frying pan. Lightly sauté the onion, garlic, and chiles—the object is to remove the "raw" taste. After about 5 minutes, pour the contents into a blender and liquefy with the cilantro, salt, and canned tomatillo sauce.

Heat ¼ cup oil in a small frying pan, just large enough to fry one tortilla. Pour the watery beans into a flat container, large enough to submerge a tortilla. Dip the tortillas, one at a time, in the watery beans, and allow the excess to drip back into the container. Immediately place the tortilla in the hot oil for 3 seconds, flip it over, and fry on the other side for 3 seconds. Carefully remove it to a plate. Do *not* allow the tortillas to brown or get crisp.

Put a large spoonful of meat in a line on half of the tortilla. Place a spoonful of the queso fresco on top of the meat. Roll the tortilla into a tube and place seam side down on a plate. Repeat with all the tortillas and filling. Serving size is 2 or 3 enchiladas per plate. Pour the tomatillo sauce over the enchiladas and then cover with the remainder of the cheese.

Serve immediately while they are very hot.

*If you use canned beans, make sure to add ample water to them so they are watery.

Chicken Mole
Mole de Pollo

6 servings

This particular mole (*mo*-lay) packs a mild punch from the use of these little red chiles. If you feel challenged by the spicy heat, no problem—before you pop them in the blender with the other ingredients, just remove two of them, blend the other ingredients, give it a taste, and add more chiles if you like. The boiling of the chiles takes out some of the heat but not all. The heat of these chiles blends nicely with the warm scents and flavors of the cinnamon and cloves.

Ingredients

1½ chickens, cut in pieces, skin removed but with bones
1 teaspoon salt
1 pinch ground black pepper
1 onion, quartered
1 clove garlic, cut in half
3 chiles de árbol
3 Tablespoons oil
15 Maria's cookies—vanilla-flavored cookies
2 sticks cinnamon
2 whole cloves
90 grams (1 disk) Abuelita brand Mexican chocolate

Cook the chicken in some water with the salt, pepper, onion, and garlic for about 20 minutes or until it is cooked through.

Boil the chiles in a little water for 5 minutes, until they are soft. Drain and discard the water.

In a medium-sized frying pan, heat the oil, and sauté the drained chiles, cookies, cinnamon, and cloves until the cinnamon and cloves release their scent, about 3–4 minutes. Put them all in a blender jar, and add the chocolate disk. Blend until it is perfectly smooth. If necessary, add some of the chicken water to thin it out.

Add this all to a large pot, heat thoroughly, and then add the cooked chicken. Heat together for 5 minutes.

Serve with red rice.

Chicken with Mushrooms
Pollo con Champiñones

10 servings

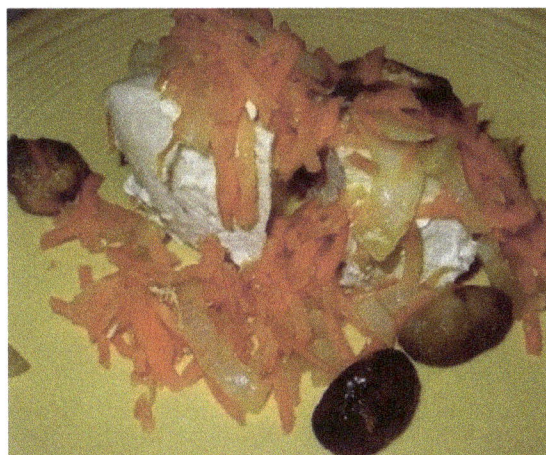

Chicken and mushrooms just seem to be a natural duo, so the combination is used often and embellished differently with each recipe. Today, Adelaida uses carrots and celery for a fresh flavor and bit of crunch. Serving a meal that is pretty to look at as well as delicious is important. Make sure to use chicken with the bones so that you get an extra shot of flavor in the sauce.

Ingredients

90 grams (6½ Tablespoons) butter
1 onion, cut into rings
1 chicken, cut into pieces, skin removed
salt and pepper, to taste
200 grams (7 ounces) fresh mushrooms, sliced
4 carrots, grated
2 stalks celery, finely diced

Melt the butter in a large pan with a lid. Add the onion, and cook for 3 minutes. Add the raw chicken, salt, and pepper. Cover and cook over medium to medium-low heat for 20 minutes.

After 20 minutes, add all the other ingredients and continue cooking until tender, about 7 minutes more.

Serve with white rice.

Chicken Tacos
Tacos de Pollo

6 servings

I know she says this serves six, but that only gives three tacos to each person! When you bite into these crisp, moist chicken tacos with the fresh taste of salsa, I'll bet you can't eat just three!

Ingredients

1 chicken breast, skinless, with bone or without
18 corn tortillas
lard or oil for frying

3 tomatoes
1 or 2 serrano chiles
1 onion
salt and pepper to taste

Poach the breast in salted water until it is completely cooked, about 10 minutes. Remove from the poaching liquid and when it can be handled, shred the meat.

Lay the tortillas out on a board or counter. Divide the meat equally among the 18 tortillas. Place the meat in a thin line down the tortilla, about 2.54 cm/1 inch in from the side. Roll each tortilla tightly into a small tube.

Heat the lard or oil in a medium-sized frying pan so that the liquid is about 13 mm / ½ inch deep. (Adelaida's pan is not very wide, so she doesn't have to use too much lard or oil to get the correct depth.) Fry each roll, seam side down, in the oil until it is crisp. Then turn over and fry the other side. You will know when the tortillas are crisp by their golden color. Drain on paper towels.

For the salsa: Drop the tomatoes and serrano chiles into a small pot of boiling water. Leave the tomatoes in the water until their skins split; then remove with a slotted spoon to a blender jar. Leave the chiles in the boiling water until the color changes from bright green to dull green, 3–4 minutes longer. Remove the chiles, cut the stem off, and add the chiles to the blender jar. Discard the water. Roughly blend with the onion, salt, and pepper (there should be a few small chunks remaining). Heat the salsa for 2–3 minutes until it is hot. Then serve drizzled over the fried tacos.

Cowboy Beans
Frijoles Charros

10 servings

There are so many flavor layers in this soup, it is difficult to describe the taste. The first flavor is cilantro, then bacon and ham, tomatoes—a complete flavor array in one spoonful. The broth is light; the jalapeños give a little crunch without much heat; the cilantro is fresh. The beans Adelaida uses are peruano. They cook up more white and yellow, not speckled or brown like a pinto bean, and have a smoother texture when you bite into one. Pinto beans work well in this soup but will take longer to cook and will not be quite as smooth textured. (Note also: pinto beans cause more gas than peruano beans, so if you have a hot date, stick with the peruanos!)

Feel free to diminish the quantity of the cilantro if you're not sure you want the amount the recipe lists, but please do not leave it out altogether. The dish just would not be the same!

Ingredients

1 kilo (2.2 pounds) dried beans, peruano or pinto
250 grams (8 ounces) bacon, chopped
3 sausages, sliced
4 slices ham (not turkey ham)
250 grams (8 ounces) chorizo
1 onion, diced
2 tomatoes, diced
½ cup cilantro, leaves only, chopped
1 or more jalapeño chiles, to taste
¼ bottle beer, Pacifico or Corona

Cook the beans in water until they are tender, about 30 minutes. When they are tender, continue to simmer them in their own broth while you prepare the other ingredients. Pinto beans take longer to cook, so adjust your bean cooking time accordingly.

In a separate pan, fry the bacon until it is crisp; then add it to the beans. In the same bacon pan, fry the sausage, ham, chorizo, and onion. When the sausage is almost cooked through, stir in the tomatoes and cook for 3 minutes. Incorporate the sausage mixture into the beans. Bring it to a boil, add the beer, jalapeño, and cilantro. Cook for 1 minute; then remove the pan from the heat.

This is usually eaten as a first course but can be eaten as a side dish or as a main course. Don't forget the tortillas!

DULCE

Meet Dulce Ibarra Camacho

When Dulce was growing up in Veracruz, Mexico, her family was able to afford a nanny to watch the children and teach them the basics of living. Her nanny was very strict and believed in the old-fashioned notion that all children should grow up knowing how to cook and clean. Dulce and her siblings all learned those lessons well.

At eight years old, Dulce would stand on a chair (she is still very short) to help with basic kitchen tasks, such as chopping and stirring. She was taught to be clean and safe in the kitchen, and today you can see those traits in her everyday living habits.

It is very difficult to find Dulce at home. She works, cooking and cleaning, six days a week from 9 AM to 4:30 PM. Saturdays, she volunteers at the local church to help teach catechism to the neighborhood children, and following that, she stays to clean the church itself.

Dulce labored successfully to see her three children complete their public school education. Two of them have earned their degrees at the university. She still pays half of the college costs for her youngest daughter. At the same time, she is saving to get the part of the street in front of her house paved. The government will pay half, but the homeowner pays the other half. For Dulce, that is 5,000 pesos (approximately $390 USD, as of June 2012). (Consider that the average wage for a job like Dulce's is about 1,250 pesos a week, or $96 USD.) In addition to helping with her daughter's college expenses, she still has to pay for food, propane, electricity, and all the other normal costs of living. If there is any money remaining, she saves it for the paving.

Education in Mexico is not free. For example, high school alone has a tuition of 950 pesos a year, plus the cost of uniforms and books. Dulce has worked many years for her family and still finds time to volunteer, helping others. She is an inspiration!

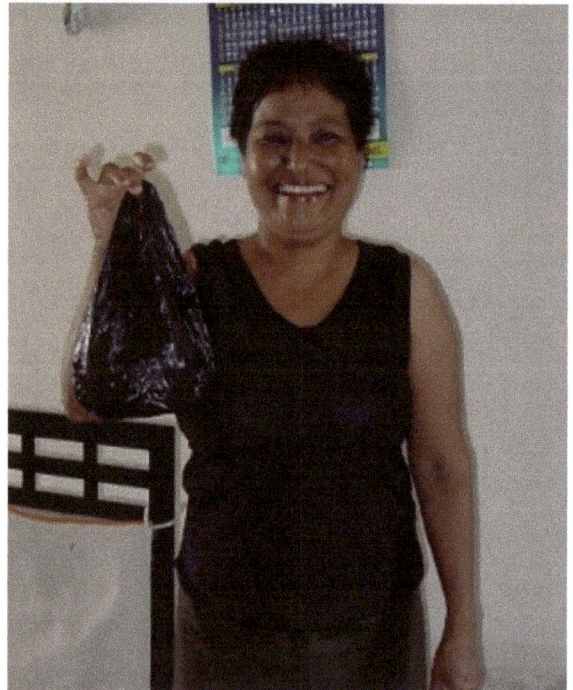

I always go home with a doggie bag.

Squash with Corn
Calabaza con Elote

4 servings

A rich-tasting side dish of shredded squash, sautéed with onions, garlic, and corn. Use a Mexican squash if you can find it. If not, use a zucchini with no seeds.

Ingredients

1 Tablespoon butter
1 Tablespoon olive oil
2 Tablespoons onion, minced
1 small garlic clove, finely minced
175 grams (6 ounces) shredded squash
½ teaspoon salt
¼ cup corn kernels, canned or frozen

Melt the butter with the olive oil in a pan over medium-low heat. Sauté the onion until it is soft; then add the garlic, squash, and salt. Stir to combine. Continue cooking until the squash is tender, about 5 minutes. Add the corn kernels and heat thoroughly. Serve as a side vegetable.

Mushrooms with Slices of Chicken
Champiñones con Rajas de Pollo

6 servings

Here's chicken with that homestyle flavor of celery, onions, and mushrooms, without taking all day to cook! In less than 15 minutes total cooking time, you have a meal that is perfect for your family or guests. Using bouillon to season the chicken instead of salt adds even more flavor. After eating this for the first time, my husband's eyes widened as he said, "Oh, my gosh! This is great! We need to have it more often."

Ingredients

600 grams (1⅓ pounds) chicken breasts
1 teaspoon ground black pepper
1 or 2 teaspoons powdered chicken bouillon
300 grams (10.5 ounces) fresh mushrooms
3 Tablespoons olive oil
2–3 cloves garlic, smooshed but kept whole
1 medium onion, chopped
2 stalks celery, sliced

Cut the chicken breasts into thin slices. Sprinkle with the pepper and a little chicken bouillon. This will be in place of salt.

Slice the mushrooms into rounds.

Heat the olive oil in a large pan and add the garlic. Cook until the garlic is golden; then remove it and discard.

To the hot garlic-flavored oil, add the chicken, onion, and celery. Cook for 5 minutes. Stir in the mushrooms. Cook for an additional 5–7 minutes. That's it—it's done!

Serve with rice.

Grilled Peppers with Herbs
Pimientos Asados con Hiervas

6 servings

The pretty colors of this dish are just the beginning. Wait until you taste the tender, crisp slices of green and red bell peppers, and the poblano with a bite of grilled onion, fresh herbs, and a light olive oil and lime vinaigrette! The poblanos add no heat, only a fresh, grassy flavor that complements the sweetness of the red bell pepper. Serve this as a side dish to just about any main course for lunch or dinner.

Ingredients

3 medium red bell peppers
2 medium green bell peppers
4 medium poblano chiles
2 medium onions, cut into quarters
2 Tablespoons fresh marjoram or basil leaves
2 Tablespoons fresh thyme leaves
¼ cup olive oil
¼ cup fresh lime juice
freshly ground black pepper and salt, to taste

Place the peppers and the chiles on a very hot griddle or grill pan. (When you char bell peppers, this is the best method.) Turn them over as their skin blisters on each side. Do this for all the peppers. When they have been blistered, put them in a large bowl with a lid, and allow them to rest for 10 minutes.

Remove the peppers one at a time from the bowl. Carefully remove the outer skin, being careful not to tear the pepper. Cut around the top of the pepper to remove the stem, seeds, and membrane. Slice each whole pepper across into 1-inch slices. These slices will be whole rounds.

Place the onions on the griddle, and cook 5 minutes, turning so each side gets golden.

On a plate, arrange the peppers, chiles, onions, marjoram, and thyme. Drizzle with lime juice, olive oil, black pepper, and salt.

Honeyed Sweet Potatoes
Camote Enmielado

4 servings

This is an absolutely perfect dessert any time of the year. (*See the note below.) The flavor is unique, and the preparation is a snap, because you use unpeeled sweet potatoes. You wash them, cut them in half lengthwise into large pieces, and cook. Anyone can do that, right?

The title is a bit deceiving because there is no honey in the recipe. The sugar thickens into a honey-like syrup because of the long cooking time. Do not substitute regular brown sugar for the piloncillo; there is *no* similarity. Piloncillo is readily available in almost every grocery store on the Mexican food aisle. You can read more about this sugar in the "Ingredients" section of this book.

Ingredients

2 kilos (4.4 pounds) sweet potatoes or yams
3 large cones piloncillo, 7–8 ounces each (see note below)
1 cup granulated sugar
1 teaspoon salt
½ cup water

Scrub the sweet potatoes. Cut in half crosswise; then in half lengthwise. Place potatoes with the **skin side up** in a pan. Add the whole piloncillo (no need to break it up), granulated sugar, salt, and water. Cover the pan with a lid, and cook on a very slow simmer for 45–60 minutes. The "honey" will get thick and dark. As it cools, it will get much thicker.

Put the sweet potatoes on a plate with the skin still attached. Scrape the cooked sweet potato meat from the skin as you eat.

Piloncillo is a very dark, unrefined brown sugar, formed into cones. If you cannot find piloncillo, buy the darkest brown sugar you can find (you will need 3 cups) and add 1 tablespoon dark molasses for each cup. This is not *an optimal substitution, but it will work if that is your only option.*

When using piloncillo, **do not** *try to break it up with your blender or food processor (unless you need a new one!), as it will severely damage the blades.*

Dulce also has a variation she wants to include: **Honeyed Pumpkin**

In the fall, when there is an abundance of pumpkins and other squash varieties ripening in the fields, Dulce makes this dessert a bit differently. She uses different types of squash, depending on what is available at the time. You can use hubbard, butternut, acorn, pumpkin—any hard-shell squash. Wash it, cut or break it into large pieces, remove the seeds and stringy fibers from the inside, and cook.

The remainder of the preparation is the same, with the exception of the cooking time. Cook it for 2–3 hours instead of 45 minutes. Check it periodically for doneness. Put on a plate with the outer shell of the squash still attached. Scrape the cooked squash from the shell as you eat.

Meatballs
Albondigas

4–6 servings

Another version (there are four meatball recipes in this book) of this most popular dish. The mint is cooked in the broth, rather than mixed with the meat, but it does not give it a minty flavor. The addition of azafrán* helps give the broth a rich color.

Ingredients

For the Broth:
6 cups water
6 tomatoes, roasted
2 cloves garlic
¼ onion
¼ teaspoon azafrán*
3 Tablespoons mint, leaves only, chopped

For the Meatballs:
500 grams (1 pound) ground sirloin
2 eggs
½ cup rice, precooked
½ teaspoon salt
pinch ground black pepper

Prepare the broth: Put the water in a pan to boil. Roast the tomatoes in a dry pan until small char marks appear on the tomatoes. Purée them in a blender with the garlic, onion, and azafrán. Pour this into the boiling water, and add the chopped mint leaves to the water. (Do not add the mint to the blender.)

Prepare the meatballs: With your hands, knead all the meatball ingredients until they are well mixed. Form the meat into walnut-size balls. Carefully drop each one into the boiling broth. Cook until they are fully cooked, about 30 minutes.

Serve with red rice and lots of tortillas!

* Azafrán is a type of Mexican saffron, although not a true saffron. Unlike the saffron threads from Spain, Mexican azafrán is made up of little pellets about the size of peas and is very inexpensive. You can substitute Spanish saffron if these are unavailable. See complete description in the "Ingredients" section.

Pork Ribs with Purslane
Costilla de Puerco con Verdolagas

6 servings

Both of these main ingredients—ribs and *verdolagas*—are favorites in the colonia. Cooking ribs does take an investment in time to pre-cook them, but you can just set the timer and walk away for a couple hours while they cook.

You will probably have a more difficult task finding the verdolagas (purslane). If you have a local food co-op or farmer's market, they probably will have it or can get it for you. A bunch is quite small, about 10–12 stems, so you don't need an armful. Cooked, it has a delicate flavor a bit like fresh dill, only much milder. You can easily grow it yourself. It grows like a weed and is considered one of the healthiest greens you can eat.

Ingredients

750 grams (1.5 pounds) pork ribs, cut into pieces, with 2 to 3 ribs per section
2–3 cloves garlic
1 medium onion
2 teaspoons salt
2 Tablespoons olive oil
1 bunch fresh verdolagas (purslane), rinsed and tough stems cut off
2 ancho chiles (stems, seeds, and veins removed)
4 tomatoes, charred
20 grams (7 teaspoons) corn flour (not the same as cornstarch)
1 teaspoon chicken bouillon powder

In a large pot, place the pork ribs, garlic, onion, and salt. Add water to cover the ribs. Cook the meat at a slow boil for 2 hours. It will be tender at the end of the boiling time.

Drizzle the olive oil into a large, hot frying pan. Remove the ribs from the broth, and carefully add them to the hot oil. Remember, water and oil do not like each other, so stand back! Brown ribs on both sides. After they are well browned, turn down the heat to just a bit more than simmer.

Cut the verdolagas (purslane) into 5.1 cm/ 2 inch pieces. Place pieces in the pan with the ribs. Sauté them slowly—you want to cook them, not brown them. Purslane cooks quickly, so 5–7 minutes should do it.

Cook the chiles in boiling water to soften them, about 5 minutes. With tongs, remove the chiles from the water and place in a blender, discard the water. Add the roasted tomatoes, corn flour, and bouillon to the blender. Dig the garlic and onion from the pork cooking water, and put in the blender also. You will need a ladleful (or two) of the cooking water to allow the ingredients to blend properly. Purée until very smooth.

Pour this over the ribs and verdolagas. Heat (do not cook) for 10 minutes to flavor the meat.

Serve in a bowl with rice. Refried beans on the side is traditional.

Pork with Purslane
Carne de Cerdo con Verdolagas

6 servings

Morita chiles have the most wonderful smoky scent and flavor of any chile I have ever tasted. They have a bit of spicy heat, but the media crema tames it somewhat. You may have to look long and hard to find morita chiles, but there is no substitution for the amazing smokiness in this sauce. If your Mexican grocery aisle does not have morita chiles, you can purchase them online from several sources. Do not substitute regular chipotle chiles for them. Remember: not all chiles are created equal.

Ingredients

500 grams (1 pound) boneless pork roast
500 grams (1 pound) purslane
4 morita chiles
6 tomatoes

3 cloves garlic
¼ onion
3 Tablespoons oil
1 Tablespoon chicken bouillon
1 can media crema

Dulce cuts the pork roast into bite-sized pieces and then boils it until it is tender, about 30 minutes. Feel free to cook the roast as you like, but make sure it is quite tender.

Cook the purslane in salted boiling water for 5 minutes; then drain and set aside.

Put the tomatoes in a small pot of boiling water until the skins split, 3 minutes. Drain and discard the water.

Remove the stems, seeds, and veins of the chiles. Put the chiles in a small pot of boiling water for 3 minutes. Drain and discard the water. Put chiles in a blender.

Cook the tomatoes by dropping them into boiling water until the skins split, remove them with a slotted spoon, and place in the blender jar with the chiles. Add the garlic and onion and blend until smooth.

Heat the oil in a large pan. Pour the blender ingredients into the hot oil and fry for several minutes. You want to evaporate some of the tomato liquid. Add the bouillon, pork, and the purslane. Let it boil for 2 minutes; then add the cream.

Serve immediately over rice. Have some fresh warm tortillas or crusty bread for the sauce.

Shrimp Au Gratin
Camarónes Gratinados

6–8 servings

Shrimp is one of Mazatlán's major industries, so it is usually inexpensive and is always easy to prepare. This shrimp recipe has a cream sauce infused with two liquid seasonings, plus onion and garlic. The flavor is unique—and not one I would have considered, had Dulce not introduced it to me. As we were preparing this one afternoon, I kept asking her, "Are you sure?" She was, of course, and the meal was delightful!

Ingredients

1 kilo (2.2 pounds) shrimp
garlic salt to taste
ground black pepper to taste
90 grams (6⅓ Tablespoons) butter
1 small onion, chopped; reserve 2 thin slices for completing the dish
2 cloves garlic, finely minced
1 large can sliced mushrooms, drained
2 cans media crema
2 Tablespoons soy sauce
2 Tablespoons Salsa de Jugo Maggi
250 grams (8 ounces) Chihuahua cheese, shredded

Preheat the oven to 175°C/350°F.

Peel and devein the shrimp. Sprinkle them with the garlic salt and pepper. Set aside.

Melt the butter in a frying pan over medium-low heat. Add the chopped onion and garlic; sauté until the onion is translucent.

Add the shrimp and sliced mushrooms. Remove any juice that is released and discard it.

Mix the cream with the soy sauce and salsa Maggi; incorporate into the shrimp mixture.

Place the shrimp mixture in a greased casserole. Cover with the reserved 2 slices of onion, separated into rings and distributed over the top, then the grated cheese. Bake for 15 minutes.

Shrimp Chop Suey
Chop Suey de Camarónes

6 servings

I know this looks Asian, not Mexican, but Asian food is popular in Mazatlán. Bean sprouts are sold fresh, in bulk, in the grocery stores. If you can purchase fresh bean sprouts, it will make a huge difference over the canned variety. The crunch of the carrots, celery, and sprouts adds another dimension to the textures in this colorful dish. Surprise your friends by having them over for Mexican food and serve this … and then watch their faces!

Ingredients

750 grams (1½ pounds) fresh shrimp, cleaned and deveined
¼ cup soy sauce
1/8 teaspoon ground black pepper
500 grams (1 pound) fresh bean sprouts
3 Tablespoons olive oil
2 cloves garlic, smooshed but kept whole
1 small onion, chopped
2 stalks celery, sliced
3 medium carrots, sliced
½ small head of broccoli, cut into small florets

Clean the shrimp by removing the shell and then making a slit up the back and removing the vein. Rinse in cold water. Place the cleaned shrimp in a bowl of cold water while you clean the remainder of the shrimp. When all the shrimp are cleaned, drain and place them in a bowl with the soy sauce and pepper. Stir well to make sure the marinade has covered all the shrimp.

Wash the bean sprouts and disinfect, if necessary. (Here in Mazatlán, it is common practice to use a food disinfectant, such as white vinegar, for lettuce and bean sprouts—things that cannot easily be washed.)

In a large pan, slowly heat the oil with the garlic. Remove the garlic when it is semi-golden in color. The object is to flavor the oil with the garlic. Discard the garlic.

Raise the temperature to medium-high heat. Add the onion, celery, carrots, and broccoli. Stir-fry for 5 minutes. Add the marinated shrimp (including the marinade). Cook for 3 minutes. Add the bean sprouts; stir and cook for about another 5 minutes.

Serve with white rice.

Shrimp Packets
Tortas de Camarón

6 servings

Tortas have many definitions—some are sandwiches, pies, or a filled roll or "packet." This torta is a filled packet bursting with shrimp. It might sound strange to batter and fry shrimp and then boil it in broth, but when you make this dish, you will fully understand. This is one of the most wonderfully fragrant and flavorful broths I have ever eaten. Dulce and I sat around the table after making these, and I had bowl after bowl of the broth, long after my portion of shrimp was devoured. If you like shrimp, this recipe will become one of your favorites—I guarantee it!

Ingredients
1 kilo (2.2 pounds) fresh shrimp
1½ liters (6⅓ cups) water
3 large tomatoes, roasted (or charred)
1 serrano chile, roasted
1 clove garlic
¼ onion
9 pellets Mexican azafrán
3 Tablespoons powdered chicken bouillon
5 eggs, separated
olive oil for frying, 13 mm / ½ in. deep

Clean and devein the shrimp; reserve the heads and shells. Place the cleaned shrimp into a bowl of cold water while you prepare the other ingredients.

Place the shells and heads in a large saucepan. Add the 1½ liters of water and bring to a slow boil. Cook the shells and heads slowly for about 15 minutes while you prepare the other ingredients. This will be the broth for your *caldo* (soup).

Strain the shrimp broth into a larger pan. Discard the shells and heads. You will put the cooked shrimp packets into this pan also, so make sure you have enough space. Turn the heat to medium low, and bring to a slow boil.

In a dry heavy skillet, char the tomatoes and chile until they have black char marks. Place them in a blender with the garlic, onion, azafrán, and bouillon. Purée until smooth.

Pour this mixture into the boiling broth. Cook for 10 minutes.

Shrimp packets: Beat the egg whites until stiff. One by one, add each egg yolk, and beat well after each addition. Add all the shrimp to the egg mixture, and stir slightly to make sure all the shrimp are covered with egg.

Heat the olive oil to *very* hot. Using a large cooking spoon (the type you use to stir food in a pan), scoop up a few shrimp (3–4) with some batter, and drop it in the hot oil. When they are browned on one side, flip and brown the other side. It only takes about a minute or so to brown the batter. Drain on paper towels. Repeat until all the shrimp packets have been browned.

Add the cooked shrimp packets to the hot broth and simmer for 5 minutes. Serve in bowls with plenty of the broth!

* Azafrán is a type of Mexican saffron, although not a true saffron. Unlike the saffron threads from Spain, Mexican azafrán is made up of little pellets about the size of peas and is very inexpensive. You can substitute Spanish saffron if these are unavailable. See complete description in the "Ingredients" section.

EDUARDA

Meet Eduarda Hernandez Cruz

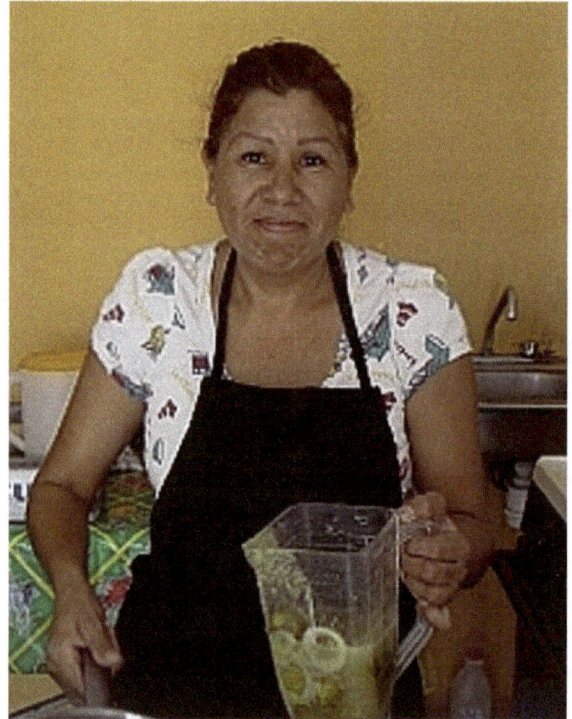

Señora Eduarda originally is from the town of Puebla in the Mexican state of Puebla. Puebla is located in the center of the country, east of Mexico City. Señora Eduarda began cooking when she was fifteen years old, learning recipes from her grandmother and father. When she married Vacilio, they moved to Mazatlán, and the rest is history (or *her* story)!

Señora Eduarda launched her cooking career at a small, local *loncheria* (luncheonette), making pies and cakes.
She worked there for six years, until she gave birth to twins (currently sixteen years old). With the birth of the twins, Señora Eduarda had four children, so a change in her career was required. Because baking pies and cakes was not her real passion anyway, she decided to start her own loncheria from her home. Utilizing her formidable skills as a cook, Señora Eduarda developed several new recipes of her own and began selling lunches to the local workers, taxi and bus drivers, and others who wanted a reasonably priced, good homestyle meal. Right from the start, her food was prepared in an exceptionally clean environment. Thefood was healthy and always was served with a smile and a stack of fresh tortillas!

After fifteen years of building her reputation from her home location, she made the decision to rent a storefront and move the entire operation. In January 2011, she started in her new location.

Now, she has a basic kitchen, including a stove, sink, refrigerator, and microwave. The counters are actually tables covered with clean plastic tablecloths. Her pans and other utensils are stored neatly on a wooden shelf at the far end of the room. Her patrons sit at two long picnic-style tables, where they can enjoy her varied lunch menus. Her tables are always full of satisfied customers.

Señora Eduarda works seven days a week. Cooking starts about 8:30 AM, with customers stopping by on their way to work for takeout tortas. (A torta is a thick, grilled sandwich that usually includes at least two different meats, cheese, lettuce, tomatoes, onions, chiles, and mayo. Want one?) The lunch menu (two different dishes each day) is always ready about 11:30, and that is exactly when her hungry patrons start to arrive. She continues working until her food is sold out in early afternoon. Regardless of which menu selections she chooses to make that day, you are guaranteed to receive an ample serving of fresh, wholesome, and delicious food.

Señora Eduarda's husband pitches in to make the daily supply of *limonada* (limeade), entirely from scratch. He squeezes the limes, adds just the right amount of sugar and water, and supplies their customers with the most refreshing of drinks on a hot summer day. Appropriately, the drink is called a *refresco*. He is also the "gopher" man.

Need ice? No problem—he is on his bicycle and back in a flash. Need lunches delivered? He is again on his bicycle, speeding to his next destination.

Señora Eduarda's older daughters, Gaby and Claudia, are always standing by to do whatever is needed to assist their mom.

Gaby, Eduarda, and husband Vacilio

Claudia, peeling garlic for Sunday "menudo"

It should be noted that Señora Eduarda's recipes are designed to feed a crowd, but all of them can be reduced for smaller groups. No measurement is exact, so let your taste buds be your guide.

One final note: Señora Eduarda hasn't baked a pie or a cake in sixteen years! I have personally observed her daily routine, from start to finish, many times—a most remarkable lady!

White Rice
Arroz Blanco

12–15 servings

White rice in Mexico is not just plain white rice, unless it is a base for another "saucy" type dish that is served over the top. It has a variety of other ingredients. Each cook (*cocinera* or *cocinero*) has her or his own recipe for rice, and they are all a bit different. When it is not the base for a saucy dish, it is always served on the side, without gravy or other sauces.

Please note that this recipe makes 12–15 servings of rice. Feel free to reduce the ingredient quantities by a half or a third for a smaller serving amount.

Ingredients

45 grams (3 Tablespoons) butter
500 grams (2¾ cups) rice, white, uncooked
1 large carrot, 6 mm / ¼ in., diced
3 Tablespoons onion, finely diced
7 cups chicken broth (*ratio is 2.5 liquid to 1 cup rice)
1½ Tablespoons powdered chicken bouillon
130 grams (¾ cup) corn kernels, canned (drained) or frozen corn

In a large frying pan, melt the butter. Add the rice, carrots, and onions; stir until the rice changes to a chalky-white color. Slowly stir in the broth and powdered bouillon. Cook until the rice has absorbed almost all the broth; then add the drained corn and continue to cook until the corn is hot.

*The ratio of broth to rice is higher than normal because you do not cover the pot, and some of the liquid will evaporate.

Red Rice
Arroz Rojo

15 servings

You know the rice you love at Mexican restaurants? Well, this is it! Remember that taco party you were thinking about having? This is the side dish you need. Add a pot of refried beans, chill the *cerveza*, and pour the margaritas!

Keep in mind that this recipe makes a lot of rice! If your party includes 6–8 people, you may want to reduce the recipe by half. When it comes to the tomatoes, just use one. Even if you divide the recipe in half or quarter, still use just one tomato; you don't need to cut one in half.

Ingredients

2 tomatoes
1 large chicken bouillon cube
¼ cup oil
1¼ kilo (6½ cups) rice, uncooked
2.37 liters (2½ quarts) water
½ teaspoon salt

Cook the tomatoes in boiling water for 3 minutes, until the skins split. Drain, discarding the water. Put the tomatoes in a blender with the bouillon. Purée until it is very smooth, no chunks.

Heat the oil over medium heat in a large pan. Sauté the rice until it turns white. Add the tomato purée, water, and salt. Bring to a slow boil; then reduce the heat and cover with a lid. Allow this to slow-simmer for about 10 minutes. Check to make sure there is still water in the pan. If it is dry, add 1 more cup of water and continue to cook. Check again in 5 more minutes for doneness. If needed, cook an additional few minutes. When done, remove from the heat, and let sit until you are ready to eat.

Mashed Potatoes
Puré de Papas

6 servings

You might be thinking that you know how to make mashed potatoes, but this is a new twist on the old standby. It has a more complicated flavor than normal mashed potatoes. Your friends and family will bow down to your mashed potato skills!

Ingredients

6 large potatoes, peeled, quartered
200 grams (7 ounces) butter, melted
1 cup (+/-) evaporated milk, heated
1 teaspoon salt
1 teaspoon ground black pepper

1 cup Chihuahua cheese, grated

Cook the potatoes in boiling salted water until they are tender but not mushy.

Drain the cooked potatoes. Once they are well drained, pour them back into the hot pan you cooked them in. Mash with a potato masher. Using the masher will leave some small potato lumps—this is a good thing.

Add the butter, hot milk, salt, and pepper. Mix well with a large spoon. (You may need to adjust how much milk you use, depending on the type and size of your potatoes.) Keep stirring to fully incorporate the milk into the potatoes. Add the cheese and continue stirring until it has melted. Serve hot.

Spicy (Hot) Salsa
Salsa Enchiloso

10 servings or 100 servings
(depending on how brave you are)

The heat overpowers the flavor of these little red chiles, so if you don't like the heat, keep them out of your kitchen. *Enchiloso* means hot and spicy.

These little beasts, called *chile de bola*, are so hot and spicy that most non-Mexicans simply cannot eat them. Mexicans laugh like crazy when a *gringo* accidentally eats some of this potent salsa. (I have never actually

Matchstick is 2 inches long

seen anyone breathe fire after eating this, but I think I saw smoke once!) When mixed with the four tomatoes, the heat is tamed, but for the real old-timers, Eduarda blends the chiles with only a little water and salt. Using your imagination, test a spoonful of the Salsa Enchiloso, and then picture yourself diving head first into a watering trough!

Ingredients

4 tomatoes
3 chiles de bola (*pequeñas*—small ones)
¼ cup water
1 Tablespoon cilantro, chopped
¼ cup onion, finely minced

Put the tomatoes into boiling water for 3 minutes until the skins split. With a slotted spoon, remove them to a blender. Discard the tomato boiling water. Add the chiles to the blender, and purée until smooth.

Pour that mixture into a bowl. Rinse the blender jar with ¼ cup water, and pour that into the bowl with the tomatoes. Add the cilantro and onion to the bowl of tomato/chile, mix, and enjoy!

Remember the tip I gave in the "A Day without Chile …" section: if you eat something too spicy, *do not drink water or beer*! Water or beer will only spread the fire, *not* extinguish it. A piece of bread, tortilla, or cracker will help. If you have butter handy, put some on the bread; it will work better. A glass of milk (not non-fat) will help also. Almost any food with some fat on or in it will save you. Good luck!

Limeade
Limonada

Nothing is more refreshing in the summer than fresh limeade (it seems like summer here all year long). It is not often that lemons are available here, but limes are always in abundance. They cost an average of about 20 cents a pound, so they are used on or in almost everything. The limes we use are key limes, the same ones you find in Florida. Do not even try to make *limonada* with bottled lime juice—this drink is all about freshness!

Here, it is usually made by the pitcherful and seems to always be available if you stop by a friend's house for a chat.

Ingredients

¾ cup fresh lime juice (about 10–15 limes, depending on the size)
1 cup granulated sugar (use ¾ cup sugar if you like it less sweet)
1 cup water plus more water and ice to fill a 2 liter/2 quart pitcher

Heat the 1 cup water until it is very warm but not hot. Make a simple syrup by adding the sugar and stirring to allow it to dissolve so you don't have grainy limeade. This simple syrup will cool while you squeeze your limes.

Roll the limes on the counter using pressure from the heel of your hand to release more of the juice, especially if the limes are a bit hard. Cut the limes in half. Over a small strainer, squeeze the juice from the limes until you have at least ¾ cup. You can use a squeezer, a reamer, or your hands to squeeze them; it doesn't matter. The hand-held squeezer is the most common utensil for this task. Nearly every household in Mexico owns one.

Pour the lime juice and simple syrup into your pitcher. Stir to mix well. Add about 1½ liters/1½ quarts of cold water. Give it a taste. It should not make you pucker; it should just have a lovely refreshing flavor. If it tastes just perfect, add ice, and go sit out under the tree. If it needs a bit of adjusting, do so now. If it needs more sugar, make sure to melt it in some warm water before adding it to the limeade to avoid that gritty sensation. Too strong? Just add a bit more water. Not enough lime? Squeeze another.

Everyone has his or her own tastes when it comes to limeade, lemonade, or any other citrus drink. You will quickly find how to adjust yours to your taste buds. If you adjust the recipe, make sure to write it down so that the next time you make it, you will look like a pro.

A quick tip about limes: outside Mexico, limes tend to be a bit more expensive, so when limes go on sale in your area, buy as many as you can. Juice them into ice cube trays. When they are frozen, remove from the tray and place them in a freezer bag. Then, when you want a tall glass of limeade, pop 1 cube into a glass, add some simple syrup, cold water, and ice.

Beef Stew
Cocido de Res

9 servings

Not quite like Momma used to make but very close! The broth is rich and flavorful; the meat, fork tender. Eduarda serves this by first putting one of each vegetable in the bowl, then meat, and then some broth. No one has dibs on all of the corn or all of the potatoes!

It is extremely important to have warm tortillas to sop up the broth, as the broth is so flavorful and there is lots of it. Serve with a bowl of Salsa Enchiloso for those brave souls who would like to add it to their stew for heat.

Ingredients

4 liters (4 quarts) water
3 kilos (6½ pounds) beef shanks, cut into 2.5 cm/1 in. slices, with bone
3 large ears of corn, cut into 3 pieces each
1 onion, diced
1 poblano chile (stem, seeds, and veins removed), cut in 2 pieces
2 large chayotes*, seeded, cut into 6 pieces each

6 tomatoes
2 cloves garlic
½ teaspoon ground black pepper
2 Tablespoons salt

3 large white potatoes, with skins, cut into large pieces
1 Mexican squash (about 20–23 cm/8–9 in. long), cut into 2.5 cm/1 in. lengths
3 large carrots, unpeeled, cut into 4 cm/1½ in. long rounds
1 large head cauliflower, parted into large, palm-sized pieces
½ cup cilantro, roughly chopped

In a large soup pot, put the water, beef, corn, onion, poblano chile, and chayotes. Bring to almost boiling, skimming off, and discarding any scum that forms on the surface. Scum forms naturally when you boil meat, but it doesn't taste very good and looks terrible in your finished dish. Turn down the heat and simmer for 2 hours or until the beef is tender.

Cook the tomatoes in boiling water for about 3 minutes until the skins split. Remove with a slotted spoon to a blender. Discard the tomato cooking water. Add the garlic, pepper, and salt to the tomatoes in the blender; purée until smooth. Set aside.

After the meat is tender, remove the chayote to a bowl and continue simmering the beef. Add the potatoes, squash, and carrots to the pot of beef. After 15 minutes, add the cauliflower, and remove any of the other vegetables that are tender. If they are not tender yet, leave them in the pot to continue cooking, checking them often to prevent overcooking. Pour in the tomato mixture and gently stir. Cook for an additional 15 minutes, continually removing any vegetables that have become tender during this extra cooking time. Add the chopped cilantro and turn off the heat.

*Chayotes—see "Ingredients" section.

Chicken in Mushroom Cream Sauce
Pollo en Crema de Champiñones

12 servings

Mere words cannot describe the aroma that comes from this chicken! You will savor the aroma of rich, creamy mushroom-scented chicken by just standing over the boiling ingredients. Breathe deep and enjoy! Please—if you only try a few of the recipes in this book, make this one of them. You cannot imagine the flavor in that first forkful of chicken and sauce.

Ingredients

1½ chickens, cut in pieces, with bone, skin removed
salt
2 cloves garlic
¼ onion
½ cup butter
1 large can sliced mushrooms, drained but reserving ¼ cup liquid
(380 grams w/liquid/228 grams drained)—(13.5 ounces/8 ounces)
8 Tablespoons cornstarch
250 grams (1 cup) mild sour cream
1 Tablespoon powdered chicken bouillon

Put salt, garlic, and onion in a large pot of water (about 3 liters). Bring it to a boil; then add the chicken pieces. Boil these until they are cooked through but still tender, about 15 minutes after it starts to boil again.

Remove the garlic from the chicken broth and place it in a blender with the mushrooms and the reserved ¼ cup of their liquid. Blend but do not purée—you want some small chunks remaining.

Melt the butter in a large frying pan. Add the blended mushroom mixture and 2 liters/2 quarts of the chicken broth (your chicken cooking liquid). Continue cooking.

Mix the cornstarch with 1 cup *cold* water, and add this to the pan of blended mushrooms, stirring constantly to prevent lumps. When it has thickened, add the sour cream, chicken pieces, and chicken bouillon. Heat through, but do not boil again. Remove from the heat and serve.

You can serve this with *arroz blanco* (white rice) or pasta. The mushroom sauce should not be wasted—it is really tasty, so make sure to serve warm, crusty bread to sop it up!

Baby Back Ribs in Green Sauce
Costillitas con Salsa Verde

12–15 servings

These tempting little bites of tender, saucy ribs are a favorite of ours. In fact, we like them so much that I called on Señora Eduarda to make a large batch for a dinner party that we were attending.

The tomatillos add a light tart flavor to the sauce—a nice complement to the rich, meaty ribs. You will be glad you tried this unique variation.

Ingredients

3 kilos (6½ pounds) baby back ribs, cut into 2-rib pieces
2 poblano chiles
1 teaspoon ground black pepper
6–7 tomatillos (depending on size)
3 slices white onion (6 mm / ¼ in. thick slices)
3 teaspoons oil
½ Tablespoon salt
6 Tablespoons flour mixed with ½ cup cold water, for thickener

Boil the ribs in water for 1½ to 2 hours, until the meat is very tender.

In the meantime, char the poblanos on all sides, and place in a covered bowl to steam for a few minutes. Remove the charred skin under slowly running water and remove the stem, seeds, and veins. (For more information on charring poblanos, see the "A Day without Chile …" section.) Put them in a blender jar.

Remove and discard the papery skin from the tomatillos. Keeping them whole (do not chop), place them in a small pot of boiling water. Let them boil until they change from bright green to a dull green color. Drain them and discard the water. Put the drained tomatillos in the blender jar with the poblanos.

Heat the oil in a large, deep pan. Add the onion slices and cook for 1 minute. Empty all the onions into the blender jar with the poblanos, cooked tomatillos, and black pepper. Make sure there are no pieces of onion remaining in the pan. Purée until no chunks remain; this needs to be a *very smooth purée*.

Pour the puréed mixture back into the hot pan (where you just finished sautéing the onion), and cook this liquid on medium-high heat for 2 minutes, stirring occasionally. Sra. Eduarda uses about ¼ cup of water to rinse the remainder of the purée from the blender and adds it to the pan. Add the salt.

Remove the ribs from their cooking broth using a slotted spoon, and place them into the sauce. Pour enough of the ribs cooking broth back onto the ribs until it reaches the top of the ribs without actually covering them.

Cover with a lid and bring to a full boil. As soon as it boils, add the thinned flour mixture to the hot sauce while stirring. Stir well, as this will start to thicken the sauce, and it could stick to the bottom of the pan. You don't want lumps, so keep stirring. After it has cooked for a minute or two and has thickened, turn off the heat.

Serve with arroz blanco and refried beans, if you like.

Fried Fish Fillet
Filete Pescado Frito

10 servings

You know the fried fish you get at the really good fish-and-chips place? This fish is better! There is no thick batter coating, just a light dredging with flour. It will probably take you less time to make this from scratch than it would to drive to the restaurant.

I don't usually like fried food, but this fish just wouldn't be the same if it were cooked any other way. I fry this fish on the patio, using the side burner of the gas grill to keep the frying odors outside.

Here it is served with refried beans and red rice. Feel free to serve it with the traditional French fries if you like. Blend up some salsa to serve on the side. I have several recipes for different salsas in this book, so pick one you like—you can't go wrong.

Ingredients

1 kilo (2.2 pounds) fish fillets (mahi mahi, halibut, cod—any firm white fish)
salt and pepper to taste
salsa Maggi*— a couple of drops per fillet
½ lime
½ cup flour
½ cup oil or enough to reach 6 mm / ¼ inch in the pan

Rinse the fish and pat dry with paper towels. Sprinkle salt and pepper, and squirt a couple of drops of Maggi on both sides of each fillet. Place the fillets in a large bowl and squeeze the lime juice over top of the fish. Rub the seasonings and lime juice all over the fish. Cover and let sit for about 10–15 minutes. No need to refrigerate.

Heat the oil in a large frying pan until it is very hot but not smoking.

Lightly dredge each fillet in flour and place it in the hot oil. Fry on each side until it is golden brown, about 5 minutes per side.

Serve with red rice and refried beans. Cut more limes to serve with the fish if desired.

*Salsa Maggi is made by Nestlé. It does contain wheat gluten and MSG, so if you don't want these ingredients, use a few drops of Worcestershire. Find it in the Mexican food section or with the Worcestershire sauce in your grocery store.

ELVA LETICIA

Meet Elva Leticia Tostado Garcia

As you can see, Señora Elva is a happy woman who loves to laugh and loves to cook! Her utensils, silverware, and dry goods storage are on the countertop and on a small table in the corner. She also has cabinets underneath the countertop to store her dishes. She is proud of her clean kitchen *and* her new stove! There is a small chest freezer in the corner of the living room to store the *bolis* (frozen tubes of sweet milk or milk mixed with fruit or cookies) that she makes and sells for extra income. Yes, her recipe for bolis is in here too!

We had a good laugh about her kitchen being so clean. She said she has to wash the walls at least once every two weeks because she makes bolis. The base is milk and unfortunately, Señora Elva has a tendency to multitask while the milk is cooking on the stove. When milk boils, it sends off *bombitas*, or "little bombs." I guess that even after so many years, her ability to multitask does not include tending to that boiling milk and the resulting bombitas.

Señora Elva was born and raised in Huajote (Wa-*ho*-tay), a small *puebla* (village) about twenty minutes outside Mazatlán. She laughs about the huge family gatherings at the *rancho*, because there are so many family members. She is the third oldest of eight children. Her parents have twenty-nine grandchildren and four great-grandchildren.

When she was fifteen years old, Señora Elva went to work to help support the family. She was hired by a family in Mazatlán with three children to clean their house and be a nanny to the children. During the week, she lived with her employer, but on weekends she would take the bus back to the rancho to spend time with her own family. At sixteen years old, her employer began teaching her to cook. This education continued for a year while she learned the basics of cooking and her employer's favorite recipes. By the time she was seventeen, she was still doing the cleaning, being the children's nanny, and cooking all the meals. She continued to work for this family until she was twenty, when she got married. Señora Elva is still thankful to her employer for teaching her to cook and, in typical Mexican fashion, she has tried to pass this knowledge on to her daughter, Leticia. But that is another story …

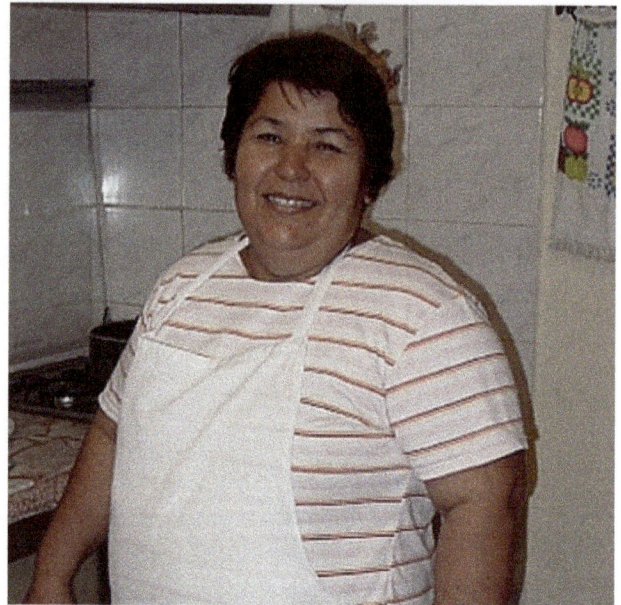

Creamy Bean Soup
Crema de Frijoles

4 servings

This is bean soup like you have never tasted before. It is totally blended, with no chunks whatsoever—that was a big difference for me between this soup and others I'd tried. The tomato purée is a perfect match with the beans. It makes a lovely presentation and is easy to prepare. Make it for guests, and see how many ask for the recipe!

Karina Ann Betlem

Ingredients

90 grams (6⅓ Tablespoons) butter
2 cans tomato purée, 210 grams each (7.4 ounces each)
½ teaspoon salt
2 cups cooked dried beans, unsalted (Elva uses peruano or pinto beans)
2 cups evaporated milk
1 Tablespoon powdered chicken bouillon
fresh cheese (queso fresco), crumbled, as a topping

Melt the butter in a large saucepan, and add the tomato purée and salt. Bring to a slow simmer.

In a blender, liquefy the beans with the milk and bouillon, so there are no chunks remaining. Pour this into the tomato mixture. Bring it to a boil; then immediately remove the pan from the heat.

Ladle into soup bowls and serve with the fresh cheese on top.

Cream of Carrot Soup
Crema de Zanahoria

4 servings

This soup will warm your heart! Other than the bouillon, there is no added salt, so if you are watching your salt intake, get the low-salt version of the bouillon. For a decadent soup you don't need to change a thing.

Ingredients

6 large carrots
1½ cups water
¼ onion, finely minced
3 Tablespoons butter
2 cups milk (2% or whole; please do not use skim)
2 cubes chicken bouillon
2 slices toasted or grilled bread cut in cubes for garnish

Peel and cut the carrots in cubes. Place in a saucepan with the water. Cook until they are tender and *do not* drain.

Sauté the minced onion in butter over low heat.

Liquefy (Elva uses a blender; I use an immersion blender) the cooked carrots adding only enough of the cooking water to allow the carrots to blend well. Add the carrot purée to the saucepan with the onion. Let it cook for 3 minutes. Incorporate the milk and bouillon cubes. Stir until it comes to a slow boil; then remove from the heat.

Ladle into bowls and serve, garnished with the bread cubes.

Elbow Macaroni Soup
Sopa de Codito

6 servings

Elva cooks this pasta with bay leaves in the cooking water. What a great idea! Elva laughed at me when I said I had never tried this. You will love the subtle flavor in the pasta.

By using fresh tomatoes instead of purchased tomato purée, the sauce has a fresh, light tomato flavor. There is nothing heavy about this pasta dish, unless, of course, you load on more cheese.

Ingredients

200 grams (7 ounces) small elbow macaroni
3 bay leaves
1 Tablespoon powdered chicken bouillon
3 tomatoes
1 clove garlic
45 grams (3 Tablespoons) butter
2 cups chicken or beef broth
50 grams (¼ cup) Chihuahua cheese
salt to taste

Cook the pasta in boiling water with the bay leaves and the bouillon. When *almost* cooked, drain and discard the liquid. (You will boil it for 5 more minutes later on, and you do not want to overcook the pasta.)

Cook the tomatoes for 3 minutes in boiling water. Remove with a slotted spoon and liquefy in a blender with the garlic.

Sauté the tomato mixture with the butter; then add the pasta and the broth. Bring it to a boil and let it cook for 5 minutes. Add more salt, if necessary. Remove from the heat, and serve with grated Chihuahua cheese on top.

The usual accompaniment is *frijoles puercos* (pork beans). See the recipe for this tasty dish in the section featuring Elva Sanchez, page 77.

Asparagus Pasta
Sopa de Esparrago

10 servings

Literally, *sopa de esparrago* is "asparagus soup" … *but* this is not a soup; it's a pasta cooked in a soup mixture. Elva usually makes this for a crowd at the rancho, where her family often gets together. The recipe can be increased for huge crowds of fifty or sixty people or reduced for five servings. The flavor of the asparagus really comes forth in this pasta sauce. She never cooks pasta in salted water but flavors the pasta with onions, garlic, and chicken bouillon. It really does add a whole new dimension to the pasta.

Ingredients

For the pasta:

400 grams (14 ounces) elbow macaroni
¼ onion
1 clove garlic
½ teaspoon powdered chicken bouillon

For the sauce:
2 cans Campbell's cream of asparagus soup
375 grams (13 ounces) mild sour cream
250 grams (8 ounces) Chihuahua cheese, shredded
90 grams (6 Tablespoons) butter
½ cup milk
½ teaspoon powdered chicken bouillon

Cook the elbow macaroni in boiling water with the onion, garlic, and bouillon. When it is tender, drain and discard the liquid, onion, and garlic. Set the macaroni aside.

Melt the butter in a large saucepan over medium heat. Add the cream of asparagus soup, sour cream, chicken bouillon, and milk. Stir well to blend.

When it begins to make "little bombs" (Elva's term for splattering), add the pasta and stir. Continue cooking until it again begins to make little bombs (hopefully, you'll be wearing an apron).

Add the cheese and continue cooking until the cheese has melted. Serve.

Tomato Salad
Ensalada de Tomate

4 servings

A very simple tomato salad to serve any time with just about any main dish. The olive oil and vinegar bring out the sweetness of the tomatoes. That flavor is accented by sliced green onions and a touch of garlic.

Ingredients

4 large tomatoes
salt and pepper to taste
2 large green onions
1 clove garlic
4 Tablespoons olive oil
2 Tablespoons apple cider vinegar
2 Tablespoons chives

Cut the tomatoes into slices and remove and discard the seeds. Season with salt and pepper.

Finely chop the onion and garlic. Sprinkle over the tomatoes.

Mix the oil with the vinegar. Pour over the salad, and toss to mix.

Serve with chopped fresh chives.

Señora Elva serves this fresh salad alongside a fried fish.

Homemade Custard
Flan Casero

8 servings

Flan is a dessert that is made often and does not require a special occasion. The ingredients are few, and it is usually made in a bain-marie* on the stove top, not in an oven. The sweet custard has a caramelized topping that adds a rich, sweet, caramel flavor to the simple custard.

There are basically two types of flan made in the colonia: Flan Casero and Flan Napolitano. The only difference between the two is the amount of evaporated and sweetened condensed milks. Flan Casero has 1 evaporated and 2 sweetened condensed. Flan Napolitano has 2 evaporated and 1 sweetened condensed. Flan Casero is therefore sweeter than Flan Napolitano. A recipe for Flan Napolitano is included in the section featuring Rocio, page 154.

Ingredients

75 grams (6 Tablespoons) granulated sugar
7 eggs
1 can evaporated milk
2 cans sweetened condensed milk
1 Tablespoon vanilla extract

Place the sugar in a heat-proof mold or pan, and place on the stove over a very low flame to slowly allow the sugar to caramelize. The sugar slowly will start to liquefy and change color. Gently stir around the edges to mix the liquefied sugar with the undissolved sugar so it does not burn. (Elva uses a Pyrex dish, so she can caramelize the sugar over the burner and then cook the custard in a bain-marie using the same dish.) Set the dish aside to cool slightly, allowing the caramelized sugar to set.

Blend the eggs, milks, and vanilla extract in a blender to thoroughly mix. Pour over the caramel.

Cover the mold with foil and cook in a bain-marie* for 60 minutes on medium-low heat.

Remove the mold to a cooling rack. When it has cooled, refrigerate until it is cold.

To serve, turn the mold upside down on a serving plate and remove the mold. The caramel will cover the top and run down the sides, making a beautiful presentation.

*See "Author's Notes."

Milk Bolis
Bolis de Leche

Makes about 24

Bolis (bow-lees) are very popular here, especially in the summer. They are sold by individuals who make them in their homes and sell them either to neighbors or on the street corners. They are frozen tubes of sweet milk or milk mixed with fruit or cookies. Bite off the end of the plastic bag and squeeze it up, sucking out the sweet goodness—this is similar to the old-fashioned Push-Ups ice cream you would buy from the Good Humor man.

The cups that you see in the freezer in the photo are treats Señora Elva made for her grandson. One is strawberry pulp and cream; the other is mango pulp. No sugar was added to either one. Just put the pulp in a plastic cup, pop in a stick, and freeze.

Ingredients

2 cans evaporated milk
1 liter (4.25 cups) whole milk
½ cup sugar, more or less (taste as you go)
2 liters (8.5 cups) water
2 Tablespoons cornstarch, mixed with some of the cold milk
1 Tablespoon vanilla extract
#7 food-safe plastic bags

Boil the water in a large pot. Add the milks, sugar, and cornstarch. Bring to a slow simmer, stirring occasionally so the cornstarch doesn't stick to the bottom. When it is cool, strain the milk, and add the vanilla. Ladle into the bags and tie the end into a knot. Place in the freezer until frozen solid.

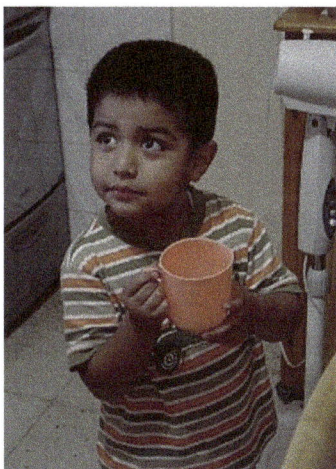

"Si, Abuelita, it's ready."
Quality Control

Oops, we forgot to write the recipe

Straining the milk

Filling the bolis bag

Oreo bolis: Prepare the basic recipe omitting the vanilla. Place 2 Oreos in the bottom of each bag and crumble them, using your fingers. Add the bolis mix, tie the end, and freeze.

Strawberry bolis: Put 10 strawberries in the blender. Add 200 grams/7 ounces media crema; then fill the blender ¾ full with the basic bolis mixture. Blend, leaving a few small chunks of strawberries. Fill the bags, tie the end, and freeze.

Coconut bolis: Put 1 cup shredded coconut (not sweetened) in the blender. Add enough basic bolis mixture (with *no* vanilla added) to the blender to reach ¾ full. Blend, leaving a few small bits of coconut. Fill the bags, tie the end, and freeze.

As you can see, the flavors are limitless. If you cannot find skinny bolis bags at your restaurant supply store, use any other food-safe bag that you can tie closed.

Sweet Coconut Cookies
Cocada

4 servings

Yes, it *is* worth it to grate your own coconut. See the "Ingredients" section for instructions on how to deal with a whole coconut. Fresh coconut is moist and chewy, without any additives or funny sugary taste. If you decide to use dried coconut (gosh, why would you do that?), you will need to rehydrate it for 20 minutes before making this cookie. These remind me of the old-fashioned "haystacks" my mom used to make. These cookies are never drizzled with chocolate, but … just thinking out loud.

Ingredients

2 Tablespoons water
2 cups granulated sugar
2 fresh coconuts, grated (about 3–4 cups)
vegetable dye, any color you like—we used yellow
butter, for greasing mold or pan

Preheat oven to 200°C (375–400°F).

Grease muffin tins or a cookie sheet with the butter. Set aside. (The muffin tins act as a mold).

Place the sugar and water (you can use the water from inside the coconut too) in a saucepan. Over medium heat, melt the sugar and constantly whisk until you see the bottom of the pan. Add the vegetable coloring to your liking and whisk so the melted sugar is a uniform color. Add the grated coconut. Mix until all the coconut has a uniform color.

Using spoons, form the coconut into balls and place on a greased cookie sheet.

Bake until they are golden, about 15 minutes. By the way, stay in the kitchen as they bake, because the aroma from the oven is pure heaven!

Spring Bananas (Plantains)
Plátanos Primavera
4 servings

This recipe calls for plantains (cooking bananas). In Spanish, they are called *plátano macho*. Do not confuse this with a sweet banana. They may look similar, but they are nothing alike. Sweet bananas fall apart when cooked, but plantains must be cooked to tenderize them and allow their sugars to come out. Look in the "Ingredients" section of this book for more information on how to deal with one and how to choose a ripe one. Once you have eaten one, you will be hooked! And besides, this recipe has rum, so that's an added bonus.

Ingredients

3 Tablespoons butter
3 Tablespoons granulated sugar
3 ripe plantains, peeled and cut in half lengthwise, then cut into chunks
¼ cup rum, light or dark (not flavored rum)

Melt the butter in a frying pan and mix in the sugar until it dissolves. Add the plantain chunks and cook until they are tender.* When they are cooked through, add the rum. Serve hot!

You also can add a bit of vanilla ice cream or whipped cream!

Note: The amount of time the plantains need to cook depends on their level of ripeness. Use a fork to test for tenderness. If they are not tender, the texture will be like eating an unripe banana—not very pleasant to the palate.

Peasant Steak
Filete de Res Campirano

4 servings

This is a great recipe to stretch your meat dollars. By cutting the steak into bite-sized pieces, you don't need individual steaks for your meal. A little goes a long way. Serve with several side dishes, such as rice, salads, and vegetables.

The serrano chiles add only a bit of spicy heat to the pan of oil and meat. For more heat, eat a fried serrano piece with a bite of meat—whew! Soy sauce adds only a slight flavor, as you do not use much—but do not omit it; you will definitely know the difference.

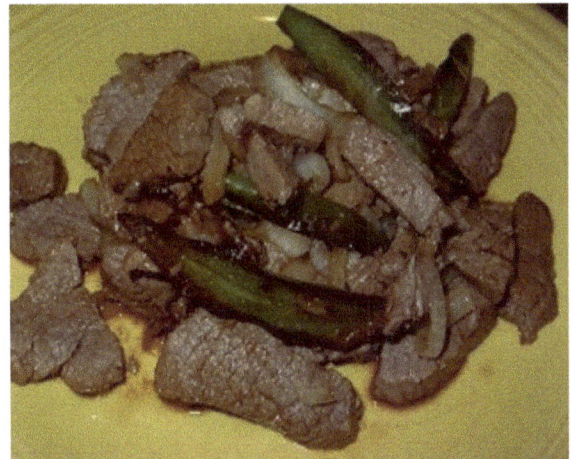

Ingredients

600 grams (1⅓ pounds) beef steak—your choice of any tender steak
salt and pepper to taste
6 serrano chiles
3 Tablespoons oil
1½ onions, cut in half, then cut into slices (half moons)
2 Tablespoons soy sauce

Cut the steak into small bite-sized pieces. Season them with salt and pepper.

Cut the serrano chiles in half, and remove the stem and seeds (remember to use those rubber gloves).

In a frying pan, heat the oil to medium. Sauté the onions and chiles until they have a little color but not well browned. Add the steak pieces and sauté for 1–2 minutes on each side. Drizzle on the soy sauce.

Continue to cook until the meat is done the way you like it.

Chicken in Cheese Sauce
Pollo en Salsa de Queso

4 servings

The pimentos in this recipe give the sauce a bit of tartness. Not too much, but your mouth will say, "Oohhh, that's not what I expected. I love it!" Between the cheese and the bread, the sauce is very thick and clings beautifully to the chicken breasts. One of the easiest sauces to make—another one you will want to make often.

Ingredients

4 chicken breasts, boneless and skinless
salt and pepper to taste
3 Tablespoons butter
4 slices American cheese
½ cup sour cream
1 small can pimentos (185 grams/6½ ounces)
1 Tablespoon onion
1 Tablespoon powdered chicken bouillon
2 slices bread, white or wheat
½ cup water

Season the chicken breasts with salt and pepper. Sauté them in butter until cooked thoroughly (about 10 minutes).

In a blender, liquefy the remaining ingredients and add to the cooked breasts. Slowly bring to a low boil. Remove from heat and serve with white rice or mashed potatoes and vegetables.

Baby Back Ribs in Green Sauce
Costillitas en Salsa Verde

4 servings

After you have cooked the ribs, the sauce is a snap to make. Tomatillos have a slightly piquant flavor that blends perfectly with pork. The serrano chile adds more flavor than spicy bite, so be sure to include it. If you have leftovers, you will enjoy them the next day even more than you did the first day. (Make extras, if you like, so that you do have leftovers! Gosh, I like that idea.)

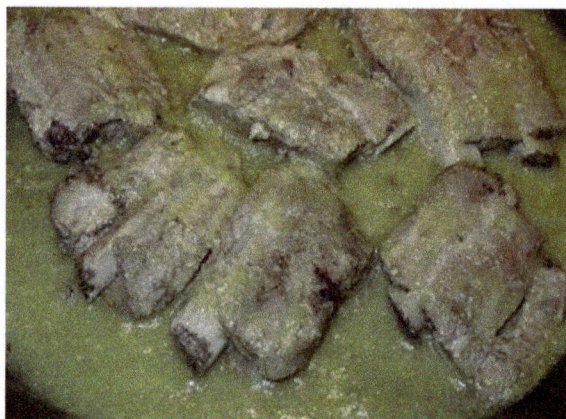

Ingredients

1 kilo (2.2 pounds) pork ribs, baby back
2 cups water
1 bay leaf
½ onion
1 teaspoon salt
ground black pepper to taste
500 grams (1 pound) tomatillos
1 serrano chile
1 clove garlic
1 Tablespoon cilantro
1 teaspoon oil
1 pinch baking soda

Cook the ribs in the water with the bay leaf, onion, salt, and pepper for 2 hours. Check periodically to make sure there is enough water to cook the ribs; add 1 cup at a time if needed.

In a separate pan of boiling water, cook the tomatillos and serrano until they are soft. Drain and discard the water. Cut the stem off the serrano and remove the seeds, if you like it milder. In a blender, purée the tomatillos and serrano with the garlic and cilantro.

Into a large pan (you will be putting the ribs in it), pour the oil and add a pinch of baking soda; mix. Add the tomatillo/chile liquid to the pan. Remove the ribs from their cooking water and place into the tomatillo/chile mixture. Adjust salt and pepper to your taste.

Heat over medium heat for 10 minutes. Serve.

Bits of Pork in Chile Colorado
Trocitos de Carne de Puerco en Chile Colorado

4 servings

The "in Chile Colorado" in the name of this recipe does not refer to the type of chile but to the preparation of the ancho chile. Señora Elva and I went round and round on this, but that is her story, and she's sticking to it! Ancho chiles are one of the most flavorful chiles and are used more often in cooking than any other dried chile. Put your nose in a bag of these chiles, and you will know why. (Okay, no one has to see you do that.)

Once the pork is cooked, the remainder of the recipe is a breeze. All of it can be done ahead of time while the pork cooks. This is not really a soup, but Señora Elva loves to serve lots of sauce with the pork because it has so much flavor.

Ingredients

500 grams (1 pound) lean pork meat, cut into bite-sized pieces
3 cloves garlic (divided usage)
2 dried ancho chiles, stems and seeds removed
1 Tablespoon oil or pork lard
1 Tablespoon flour
salt to taste
finely minced onion to garnish

Cook the pork pieces in a pot of slowly boiling water, with salt and 2 cloves of the garlic, for about 1½ hours. In a small saucepan, heat a bit of water, and cook the ancho chiles until they are limp, 3 minutes. Drain and discard the water. Liquefy the chiles in a blender with the remaining clove of garlic. If necessary, add about ¼ cup water to blender.

Heat the oil (or lard) in a large skillet. Add the flour and cook until it is slightly golden in color. Mix in the blender ingredients. Slowly add some of the pork broth to the flour mixture, stirring constantly so it does not get lumps. This should be the consistency of a thin gravy, and the meat should "swim" in the bowl. Add the meat. Cover the pan, and cook 5 minutes.

Serve in bowls and sprinkle finely minced onion over the top. Of course, it is almost a law to serve fresh tortillas alongside!

Fish in a Raincoat
Pescado a la Gabardina

4 servings

I have no idea where the "raincoat" part of the title came from—perhaps because the fish is coated with the sauce. The fish will swim (wade, actually) in the sauce on your plate and will have a texture more like a gravy than a sautéing sauce. With every bite, you get a little sauce as well.

Ingredients
4 fish fillets, such as snapper or mahi mahi (nothing delicate)
2 eggs, slightly beaten with a whisk
1 bottle beer (Corona or Pacifico type, not dark beer)
¼ cup flour
½ teaspoon total: mixture of white pepper, garlic salt, onion salt, and celery salt
½ teaspoon Worcestershire sauce
2 Tablespoons oil

Season the fillets with ¼ teaspoonof the salts and pepper mixture.

Mix all the rest of the ingredients in a shallow pan with the remainder of the salts. Add the raw fish, and sauté the fillets in the mixture. Stir the sauce periodically so it does not stick to the pan. Turn the fish over to cook the other side in the sauce. Serve the fish with the sauce poured over and around it, along with white rice and steamed vegetables.

Steamed Fish
Pescado al Vapor

4 servings

This recipe is actually *en papillote*-style fish—fish steamed in a packet. Very moist and flavorful, and one throw-away packet contains all the veggies and fish. Elva makes this in one packet for the family, but for a fiesta, she makes individual packets so that she can keep them hot, and each person can open his or her own.

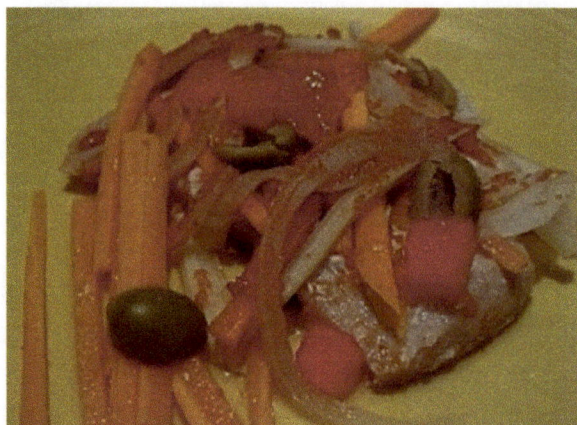

Karina Ann Betlem

Ingredients

1 kilo 2.2 pounds small fillets (mahi mahi, red snapper, halibut, etc.)
salt and pepper to taste
3 carrots, peeled, cut in julienne-style (matchsticks)
3 stalks celery, cut in julienne-style (matchsticks)
½ onion, thinly sliced
2 tomatoes
½ teaspoon whole oregano, not ground
¼ teaspoon salt
50 grams (1.75 ounces) green olives, pitted, cut in half
chopped tomato, for garnish

Preheat oven to 175°C/350°F.

Season the fish with salt and pepper. Place the fish fillets on a long sheet of heavy-duty aluminum foil with a cookie sheet underneath for support.

Arrange the carrots and celery around the fish. Add the onion slices around and on top of the fish.

Liquefy the tomatoes with oregano and ¼ teaspoon salt. Pour over the fish and vegetables. Add the olives on top of the sauce. Wrap tightly, making a sealed pouch. Remember the object is to *steam* the fish and vegetables, so do not allow the steam to escape. Bake for 20 minutes.

Remove the cookie sheet from the oven, carefully open the packet of fish. The steam will come billowing out, so make sure to have some potholders—steam burns skin very quickly. Serve from the aluminum with chopped fresh tomato as garnish.

Serve with white rice and fresh tortillas.

ELVA SANCHEZ

Meet Elva Sanchez Cruz

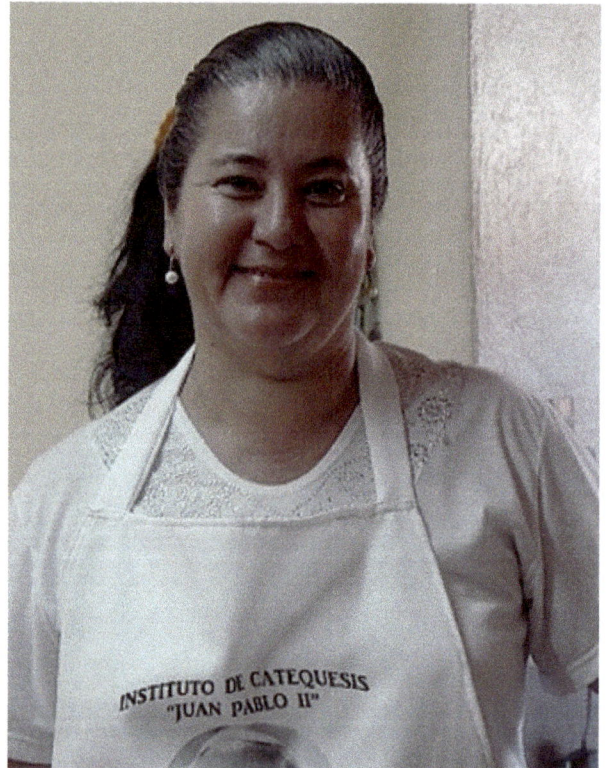

Señora Elva is from Santa Catarina, a little *puebla* (village) about 1½ hours from Mazatlán. Unlike many homes in the pueblos, being the only girl in her family definitely had its benefits. She confesses that she was pampered and "spoiled," never having to do laundry, clean up her room, or cook. She was allowed to go to school and concentrate solely on her studies. Her face gets a bit of blush when she tells me that she would have her fingernails done because she had no housework to do.

At eighteen years old, she married, and her new husband had quite a surprise coming. His new wife could not even boil water!

Out of necessity, while Elva's husband looked for work, they moved in with his parents in La Noria, which is closer to Mazatlán. Her dear mother-in-law, Señora Zeferina, took pity on Elva and decided to teach her to cook. They started with the basics, one of which was *frijoles* (beans), a main staple in the Mexican diet.

Elva readily admits that cooking did not come naturally to her. She could not remember recipes, which were never written down, and would forget something was on the stove and walk away. Many meals were ruined at her hand. As an example, she talks about a day she was very tired. Señora Zeferina was going to be gone most of the day, so she asked Elva to make the daily pot of beans. Sounds simple enough. She put the ingredients in the pressure cooker (*olla express*), thought she had enough time to take a tiny nap, and fell dead asleep. She was

awakened by an explosion that sounded very near. She soon found the pressure cooker had run dry and exploded. Burned blackened beans were everywhere, and the lid had embedded itself in the ceiling—a *concrete* ceiling! Obviously, there was no meal that day.

Since that day, she has turned her cooking life around. She made a promise to Señora Zeferina to pay attention to her and never walk away while cooking again. Elva and her husband lived with Señora Zeferina and her husband for nine years, and she kept her promise. Elva has turned into an exceptional cook, and as her son Brian says, "She is a perfectionist with the food she prepares."

When she moved to Mazatlán, Elva felt a bit lost—it was a big city, and she had never worked. She tried to find things to do in her neighborhood to help others. Then, eight years ago, she found her calling. She started to cook at the local church for the forty to sixty missionaries that passed through once a month and has become the leader of the other cooks who also volunteer at the church. She smiles and says she is happy now!

Soy Ceviche
Ceviche Soya

8 servings

I had to hunt for textured soy before Elva made soy ceviche (pronounced: say-*vee*-chay) for me Textured soy is a ground-meat substitute that actually looks a bit like dry dog food as it comes out of the package. You will need to rehydrate it before using; I have given instructions below. After the soy is rehydrated, it looks like tasty pieces of meat—and it makes great ceviche! It does not have much flavor of its own, so it picks up the fresh taste of the vegetables and the limes.

Ingredients

200 grams textured soy (one bag is 330 grams)
2 cucumbers, peeled, seeds removed, and diced
2 carrots, shredded
½ cup cilantro, leaves chopped
¼ cup red onion, finely chopped
12 limes, juiced
1 pinch ground black pepper
salt to taste
1 teaspoon ground black pepper
small packaged tostadas *(horneadas)*

Cook the soy in boiling water for 5 minutes. Take the pan off the heat, and let the soy rehydrate for 15 minutes. Drain through a colander with large holes, and squeeze out as much water as you can. Put the soy in a clean bowl. It's now ready to use.

Add to this the cucumber, carrots, cilantro, onion, lime juice, salt, and pepper. Stir well, and let sit for 30 minutes to absorb the flavors.

Serve on small, crisp tostadas.

Cold Macaroni Salad
Codito en Frio

5 servings

An interesting version of macaroni salad. It includes ham and sausage as well as the usual celery, mayonnaise, and sour cream. The sour cream actually tames down and thins out the mayonnaise, so you don't have a heavy sauce. It is light and tasty and a perfect complement to grilled or fried chicken.

Ingredients

250 grams (8–9 ounces) small elbow macaroni
1 cup sour cream
¾ cup mayonnaise
200 grams (7 ounces) ham, diced
200 grams (7 ounces) mild sausage, cooked
1 stalk celery, diced
1 pinch ground black pepper

1 teaspoon chicken bouillon powder

Cook the elbow macaroni until tender but not overcooked, approximately 7 minutes. Strain and rinse with cold water. Drain thoroughly. Pour into a bowl and add all the remaining ingredients. Stir, and refrigerate until you are ready to eat.

Enchiladas Durango Style
Enchiladas Estilo Durango

5 servings

Each of the thirty-one states in Mexico has a unique culture and cuisine. This recipe is from the state of Durango, just east of the state of Sinaloa, where Mazatlán is located. These are genuine Mexican enchiladas, made without an oven. Many of the traditional Mexican foods are prepared without the use of an oven. Most of the cooks in this book do not own ovens, but as this recipe demonstrates, the lack of an oven is no handicap to producing great flavor. Please notice that these enchiladas are *not* drowned in melted cheese!

Ingredients
½ chicken, skin removed
oil
500 grams (1 pound) fresh corn tortillas
250 grams (8 ounces) ancho chiles
1 clove garlic
4 Tablespoons sugar
1 pinch salt
125 grams (4 ounces) dry Mexican cheese (*cotija* cheese), shredded

Poach the chicken in boiling water until cooked thoroughly. Shred the chicken and set aside, keeping it hot.

In a frying pan, heat about 6 mm / ¼ in. of oil to medium hot. Fry the tortillas on each side until they are "wilted" but not crisp, 3 seconds each side. Use tongs and a spatula to turn them carefully, because they will be very fragile at this point. Drain on paper towels, but keep them hot.

To make the chile salsa: Pour a bit more oil into the frying pan. This time you will heat it until it is very hot but not smoking. When the oil is hot, add one ancho chile and fry on both sides (about 5 seconds on each side). Remove from oil and put into a blender (no need to chop). Repeat with the remaining ancho chiles. Also to the blender add the sugar, garlic, and salt. Add some of the poaching water to the blender, so that it will actually blend; start with 1 cup. Purée until totally smooth. You may have to add a bit more liquid, but do not add too much. The sauce should be thick enough to adhere to the tortillas. Pour the blended sauce into a pan, and heat until it is hot.

Dip a wilted tortilla into the sauce, lay it on a plate, and then fill with some shredded chicken, placed in a line on the tortilla, and roll it up. Repeat with the other tortillas. Place 4 of these on a warmed plate, seam side down. Bathe the enchiladas with more of the sauce, and top with about 1 teaspoon of cheese.

Enchiladas are usually served with a scoop of refried beans on the side.

Chicken in Mole
Mole en Pollo

10 servings

There are as many recipes for mole as there are people in the entire country of Mexico, and each has its own unique flavor. Try as many of these mole recipes as you can. The difference will be quite clear to the palate. Some moles are spicy, and others, such as this one, are not. The moles in this book are very simple to prepare, unlike the variety you would find in Oaxaca, which might require grinding together thirty or more spices. If you are not an experienced mole maker, then these will work great for you.

Ingredients

1.2 kilos (2½ pounds) whole chicken, with bones, skin removed, cut into pieces
3 Tablespoons oil, plus more, if needed
1 guajillo chile
1 piece whole cinnamon
1 whole clove
50 grams (⅓ cup) sesame seeds
100 grams (3.5 ounces) animal crackers (yep, the sweet animals from your childhood)
1 slice onion
90 grams (1 disk) Abuelita brand Mexican chocolate
½ tomato

Place the chicken pieces in a pot, and cover the chicken with water. Simmer the chicken until it is cooked through, about 20 minutes.

Heat the oil in a medium frying pan to very hot but not smoking. (You will use this same pan and oil to fry or toast everything, from the chile to the onion.) Clean the chile by removing the stem, seeds, and veins; wipe the outer surface with a towel to remove any dust. Fry the chile in the hot oil for 10 seconds each side, and remove from oil and place in a blender jar.

Fry the cinnamon and clove for 1 minute, until they release their aroma; then place them in the blender.

Toast the sesame seeds with the animal crackers until they are golden brown; add to the blender. Sauté the onion until it is soft. Remove to the blender.

Add the tomato and chocolate to the blender as well. Now you have all the ingredients in the blender except the chicken. Using a ladle, put some of the cooking water from the chicken in the blender to help smooth it out. Keep adding in small amounts until it flows freely in the blender and can be poured out into a pan. Don't worry if you add too much; you can reduce it if needed. Keep blending until the mixture is completely smooth—no lumps at all. Empty the contents into a pan. Add the cooked chicken pieces, and allow them to heat in the sauce, about 5 minutes.

Serve with red rice.

Breaded Chicken Breasts
Pechugas Empanizadas

5 servings

A recipe for crispy, tender chicken breast that cooks in 4 minutes should be in everyone's repertoire. Elva used dried corn flake crumbs but says she uses whatever she has on hand. The flavor is always excellent. The crust is crunchy, and the chicken moist. Picture serving this chicken on rolls as a hot chicken sandwich with your favorite salsa or guacamole on top. (Is your mouth watering yet?) Make this for a quick (yes, I said quick) meal—start to finish in less than 10 minutes!

Ingredients

oil, enough to cover the bottom of your frying pan
500 grams (1 pound) chicken breasts, boneless and skinless, pounded thin
salt and pepper to taste
½ clove garlic, very finely minced or pressed
1 egg
150 grams (1⅓ cups) dried bread crumbs or corn flake crumbs

Heat the oil in a large frying pan until it is hot. If it is not hot enough, the coating on the chicken will absorb the oil, rather than fry it. (To test your oil to make sure it is hot enough, place a cube of bread in the oil. When it sizzles, it's hot enough.)

Salt and pepper both sides of the chicken breasts. Beat together the minced garlic and the egg in a flat, shallow bowl. Dip the chicken breasts into the egg; then dredge each piece with the bread crumbs. Set the coated pieces on a plate. Repeat this process for all the chicken pieces. Quickly fry the chicken breasts in the oil until they are golden brown, 2 minutes on each side. Drain on paper towels. Serve.

Chinese Chicken
Pollo China
(poy-yo Cheena)

5 servings

Soy sauce with just a hint of oregano brings an explosion of flavor to this chicken. Very simple flavors with an elegant presentation. Using the low-sodium form of soy sauce allows the chicken to absorb the wonderful soy sauce flavors without all the saltiness of traditional soy sauce. A great base for a home-cooked Chinese menu.

Ingredients

1.2 kilos (2½ pounds) chicken, cut into parts, with skin and bones
1 Tablespoon butter
¼ teaspoon oregano
355 grams (12½ ounces) low-sodium soy sauce

Wash the chicken and blot it dry with paper towels. Melt the butter in a large frying pan. Add the oregano and chicken pieces. When the chicken is browned on all sides, pour the soy sauce over top. Cook slowly, uncovered, for 30 minutes, turning the chicken occasionally, until the sauce is dry and the chicken is the color of the sauce. Serve with white rice.

Karina Ann Betlem

Cowboy Beans
Frijoles Charros

5 servings

This is a very popular soup here. It's often served at traditional (non-tourist) restaurants. It is always served as a side dish, rather than a main dish, in small bowls or cups. This is a hearty soup with a light broth. Adjust the amount of jalapeños to suit your own taste buds.

Pork lard is a natural fat and will be in the meat cooler, while processed manteca is on the shelf with all the other solid shortenings. If you'd prefer not to use real lard, you can substitute with extra virgin olive oil. (No, you may not use Crisco or other oil. You need good flavor in those beans. You will thank me.)

The chorizo you need looks like ground sausage with red chile powder mixed in. It is not encased as a solid meat like link sausage; it cooks up as a loose sausage. The type called for here is *not* spicy.

Ingredients

500 grams (1 pound) dried beans, such as peruano or pinto
125 grams (4½ ounces) chorizo
125 grams (4½ ounces) bacon
125 grams (4½ ounces) sausage, sliced into thin disks
100 grams (½ cup) lard, pork
1 or 2 jalapeños, finely minced

Sort the beans, discarding any dirt, stones, or beans that are damaged, wrinkled, or shriveled. Rinse at least two times, very well. (Remember, you will be eating this broth.)Our cooks do not soak their beans overnight. Beans bought here are dried but are not old. The beans are not stored for any length of time; they are used at the time of purchase. You can choose to soak your beans or use the tip below.**. Cook in ample water until they are tender but not mushy. Set aside.

Heat the lard in a large pot. Add the chorizo and fry until it is fully cooked. To this, add the bacon and sausage disks. Continue cooking until the bacon is crisp.

Add the cooked beans with their liquid and then the minced jalapeños. Let it simmer for 15 minutes.

Ladle into small bowls for a classic Mexican side dish to accompany *carne asada* (grilled beef).

** *To bypass having to soak beans overnight*: after rinsing the beans, put them in a large saucepan and cover them with water to about 1 inch above the beans. Cover with a lid. Bring to a boil, and turn off the heat. Do not open the lid. Let them sit on the stove for 1 hour. At this point, you can just turn on the heat and continue cooking them or, to rid yourself of some of the gas your beans may cause, drain and add new water. Cook until tender. Your cooking time will be reduced dramatically.

Pork and Beans
Frijoles Puercos

20 servings

Yes, this is enough for a crowd, but if you don't eat it all, freeze the leftovers for next time. If you can find peruano beans, you may never go back to pinto beans. They cook very fast and produce little or no gas—you have to love that!

You will find instructions for the preparation of the beans and discussion about the chorizo and pork lard in the recipe for *Cowboy Beans* in this chapter, page 77.

Ingredients

500 grams (1 pound) dried beans, cooked (peruano or pinto beans)
125 grams (4½ounces) chorizo
125 grams (½ cup) pork lard
1 can tuna, water pack
125 grams (½ cup) Chihuahua cheese, shredded
1 teaspoon salt
1 Tablespoon hot sauce
2 slices jalapeño chiles, chopped

Sort the beans, discarding any dirt, stones, or beans that are damaged, wrinkled, or shriveled. Rinse at least two times very well. (Remember, this is food.) Cook the beans in ample water until they are very soft. Drain. Mash the beans with a potato masher. It is best to have some small chunks and not be puréed.

In a large frying pan, fry the chorizo in the lard until it is totally cooked. Add the beans and all the other ingredients to the chorizo. Continue cooking all of this mixture over **very low heat** until no fat is visible, about 15 minutes. Do not stir.

Serve with *carne asada* (grilled meat).

Giant Squid Ceviche
Ceviche de Calamar Gigante

6 servings

This ceviche is unusual because it actually is cooked on the stove with heat, not chemically "cooked" with limes. The large squid found in the waters off Mazatlán really *are* big! Many are 123 cm/4 feet in length or larger. These are not to be confused with the giant squid that recently have been found in the Gulf of Mexico. The giant squid that we are talking about here are caught commercially. They call these large slabs of squid meat "calamar steaks." If you cannot find the giant variety, get the largest you can find. If you purchase the squid with tentacles instead of as steaks, remove the tentacles and fry them up separately for snacks.

Ingredients

1 kilo (2.2 pounds) giant squid steaks
500 grams (1 pound) carrots, peeled and cut into small dice
500 grams (1 pound) tomatoes, seeds removed
4 cucumbers, peeled, seeds removed
1 white onion, chopped into small dice
1 kilo (2.2 pounds) limes, juiced
1 pinch ground black pepper
salt to taste

1 bunch cilantro, leaves finely chopped, stems discarded

Cook the squid in a pot of salted boiling water for about 40 minutes or until it is tender. Remove from the water, and when it is cool enough to handle, cut into small dice. Refrigerate.

While the squid is cooking, dice the carrots and cook them in boiling water until tender, about 5 minutes. Drain and refrigerate.

Dice the tomatoes and cucumbers into small dice.

Add all the ingredients together in a large bowl. Stir well to combine. Allow this mixture to chill in the refrigerator for 1 hour for the flavors to blend.

Serve with crackers, tortilla chips, or on tostadas.

Sierra Ceviche
Ceviche Sierra

10 servings

Sierra is a fish caught in Mexican waters, also known as the Mexican mackerel. It is mild tasting and very inexpensive, so it is a favorite for ceviche and is sold freshly ground by the fish vendors. The recipe is similar to Rogelio's only in that it uses sierra. Give them both a try—it will make a ceviche lover out of you!

You may think that because you marinate the fish in so much lime juice that lime would be all you taste, but such is not the case. After squeezing out as much of the lime juice as possible and adding the vegetables, what you taste are the individual vegetables and a very mild fish, enhanced with just a background flavor of the lime—quite pleasant to the palate.

Remember: when making any type of ceviche, the fish or shellfish must be fresh. By that I mean it must smell fresh and not have been left out unrefrigerated for any length of time. Let your nose be your guide. Fresh fish does not have a "fishy" scent. If it does, do not use it for ceviche. (Frozen fish is fine, but it must be raw.)

Ingredients
1 kilo (2.2 pounds) sierra, ground
fresh limes, juiced (reserve 2 tablespoons juice for finishing the dish)
(20 limes for each ½ kilo/1.1 pound of fish)

3 large carrots, shredded
3 Tablespoons red onion, finely chopped
1 pinch ground black pepper
salt to taste
1 serrano chile, finely chopped
(remove the seeds before chopping if you don't want too much heat)
½ bunch cilantro, chopped
small crisp tortillas or tortilla chips

Put the ground fish (sierra) into a bowl, and cover with the lime juice and stir it in. Place the bowl in the refrigerator for 30 minutes.

Meanwhile, prepare all the vegetables and set aside.

After 30 minutes of marinating, slowly squeeze the lime juice from the fish using a strainer. Make sure to remove as much as the lime juice as possible; the fish should almost feel dry. Place the strained fish into a large clean dish.

Add the carrots, onion, salt, pepper, and cilantro to the fish. Stir well to incorporate. Drizzle over the reserved lime juice.

Serve at once on small crisp tostadas (*horneadas*) or with crisp tortilla chips as dippers.

Note: When serving this ceviche on an hors d'oeuvres table, keep the bowl cold by placing it inside a larger bowl filled with ice. Make sure to place a decorative towel under the bowl of ice to absorb the condensation.

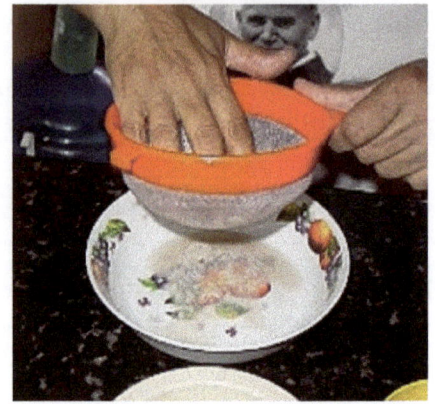

GABRIELA

Meet Ana Gabriela Cruz Hernandez

Although Gabriela is a beautiful name, she prefers to be called Ricky. She is actually one of the few people I know who was born and raised in Mazatlán, not "transplanted." Ricky and I met about five years ago when she was just finishing high school and training after school at a local *estetica* (beauty shop). Ricky assisted with pedicures and manicures until she could save enough money to attend beauty school. She learned her trade quickly and over a short period of time had acquired her own clientele. This particular beauty shop caters to tourists, most of whom speak English. It is imperative that the beauticians and manicurists/pedicurists speak English. When Ricky began work at the beauty shop, she knew only a few basic words in English, such as "good morning," "thank you," and "how are you?" Never a shy violet, she quickly began chatting with the customers the best she could. She learned English quickly and today still practices and tries to learn as much as she can from chatting with her customers.

When Ricky was about thirteen years old, her mother, a small restaurant owner, needed some help. Ricky is the oldest of six children, so it was only natural for her mom to bring Ricky into the business and teach her to cook. Ricky's grandmother stepped in to teach her to cook some of Ricky's own favorite foods, making it much more fun to learn! Ricky says she likes to cook tostadas, gorditas, and mole, but she likes to eat them even more than she likes cooking them. Who doesn't?

Ricky was married in January 2011. She and her husband set up housekeeping in one of the outlying colonias. They both worked very hard to save money for furniture, a new bed, a decent car, and kitchen appliances—all the things you need to equip your home. They were very proud of their accomplishments and the fact that they were able to furnish their new home by themselves. In August 2011, there were three separate rainstorms, dropping over 18 cm/7 inches of rain *each*. The resulting floods came through their colonia and their home. They lost almost all of their furniture, clothing, and appliances. Their car was floating but was submerged *under* the water. Some people died in that flood. Ricky and her husband salvaged what they could and moved back to Colonia Pancho Villa. The government of the state of Sinaloa gave some assistance to everyone affected by the floods. Ricky and her husband received 5,000 pesos (about 400 US dollars) to help replace some essentials. This amount does not go far when you need to replace everything.

Ricky and her husband are quick to tell you they are very thankful that their lives were spared. They don't even mind not having a stove or refrigerator, because they are able to work, and together they can save for those "luxuries" again.

,

Cauliflower with Cheese in the Oven
Coliflor con Queso al Horno

6 servings

I used to hate—yes, hate—cauliflower! I wouldn't even look at it out of the corners of my eyes for fear it would jump into my shopping cart, and I would have to deal with it. Then, Ricky made this recipe and oh my goodness—I am hooked on this stuff! Somehow the milk takes away that strong "cauliflowery" taste that I never liked. I have tried this with broccoli as well, and it is delicious too. I hope this will become a family favorite for you.

Ingredients

1 head cauliflower, florets separated, steamed to partially cook
1 teaspoon butter
1 cup sweet cream
¼ cup milk
1 teaspoon salt
½ teaspoon ground black pepper
2 eggs
1 Tablespoon fresh parsley, finely chopped
¼ cup grated Parmesan cheese

Preheat the oven to 170°C (325°–350°F).

Grease an oven-proof dish with the butter. Put the partially cooked cauliflower in the dish. Mix all the other ingredients, except the cheese, and pour this mixture on top of the cauliflower. Sprinkle the cheese over top. Bake in the preheated oven for 20 minutes or until it is golden.

Serve immediately.

Penne in Green Sauce
Plumilla en Salsa Verde

6 servings

The green poblano and tomatillo sauce cling to the grooves of the penne, making it look quite festive. Tomatillos give a somewhat tart flavor to the sauce, while poblanos give an earthy, grassy flavor. Combine these with cream, garlic, and onion, and you'll have a complex pasta sauce that is a snap to make. No spicy heat in this sauce, just flavor.

Ingredients

300 grams (10.5 ounces) tomatillos, papery skin removed
6 poblano chiles (not necessary to char)
3 Tablespoons oil
¼ onion
1 clove garlic, rough chopped
1 cup water

1 Tablespoon powdered chicken bouillon
200 grams (7 ounces) penne pasta, cooked and drained (keep hot)
1 can media crema

Cook the tomatillos and chiles in a small pot of boiling water until the tomatillos turn from bright green to a dull green color. Drain them (discard the water), and put the tomatillos in a blender jar. Carefully remove the stems, seeds, and veins from the poblanos, and place them in the blender with the tomatillos.

Heat the oil in a small skillet. Sauté the onion and garlic for 5 minutes; do not brown. Place them, including the oil, in the blender with the tomatillos and chiles. Blend until very smooth. Pour the blender ingredients into a cold pan. Add the 1 cup water and the bouillon. Bring to a boil and cook for 2 minutes; then add the cooked pasta and the crema. Mix well and serve immediately.

Bimbo Rapid Roll
Rollo Rapido Bimbo

6 servings

Okay, I hear you laughing at the name, but **Bimbo** is a brand of bread and is the largest bakery company in the United States. The name means *baby* in Italian but does not mean anything in Spanish. The pronunciation is given on the packaging as "Beembo" to distinguish it from the American slang term "bimbo." A standard loaf size is twenty slices.

This dish is similar to a rolled-up ham sandwich. The bread is compressed so it stays rolled up. Great for lunch, a snack, or hors d'oeuvre.

Ingredients

9 slices of sliced white bread
3 Tablespoons butter
1 Tablespoon mustard
1 cup ham, finely chopped
¼ onion, finely chopped
3 Tablespoons mayonnaise
1 Tablespoon cilantro leaves, finely chopped

Remove the crusts from the bread. Lay the slices evenly, 3 rows of 3 slices each, on a clean and damp cloth, overlapping the edges slightly. Level the bread with a rolling pin.

Melt the butter together with the mustard, and mix well. Spread this mixture on all the slices of bread. Mix the ham, onion, mayonnaise, and cilantro together. Spread evenly on top of the mustard mixture.

Using the cloth as an aid, roll up the bread, jellyroll fashion, using slight pressure to compress the roll. Then wrap the roll in the cloth and refrigerate for at least one hour. Before serving, slice the roll into 6 equal parts. For an hors d'oeuvre, slice into thin bite-sized pieces.

Mexican Bread Pudding
Capirotada de Leche

6 servings

Although *capirotada* is a classic Mexican bread pudding usually eaten during Lent, this version is different. Ricky makes it several times during the year. The classic capirotada is not made with sweet bread but with *bolillos*—a hard white bread-type roll. There is a recipe for the more traditional version in the section featuring Maria de Los Angeles. This version, however, has its own character and delicious flavor. For a bread pudding to serve with tea or coffee, this is it!

Picones are sweet, dense Mexican bread rolls. If this is not available in your bakery, use any other sweet dense bread, such as raisin bread.

Ingredients

750 ml (3-1/8 cups) milk
1 stick cinnamon
250 grams (8.8 ounces) sugar
4 eggs, separated
6 Mexican sweet bread rolls (*picones*), ½ sliced and ½ dried (sliced into small rectangles and dried overnight)
250 grams (8.8 ounces) shredded Chihuahua cheese
200 grams (7 ounces) butter
50 grams (1.75 ounces) raisins
50 grams (1.75 ounces) each dried fruits: figs, prunes, apricots, mango, peanuts or almonds, diced

Preheat the oven to 200°C/400°F.

Simmer the milk with the cinnamon stick and half of the sugar for 5 minutes; remove from heat and chill.

Beat the egg yolks until thick and add to the chilled milk mixture. Set aside.

Mix the dried bread with the shredded cheese and the remainder of the sugar.

In a 13 x 9 oven-proof dish greased with butter, place a layer of the dried bread mixture; dot with butter. Add pieces of the fruit and then a little of the reserved milk mixture. Top with some of the dried bread mixture. Continue to make layers, finishing with a thick layer of the dried bread/cheese mixture.

Put in the oven until it has absorbed all the liquid and looks dry, about 15 minutes.

Beat the egg whites until a stiff meringue forms. Spread over the capirotada, and put back in the oven until it is beautifully browned, 10 minutes.

You can eat this warm or cold, but I have never seen this last long enough to get cold.

Pineapple Gelatin with Milk
Gelatina de Piña con Leche

10 servings

I think Mexicans must have written the book on ways to use gelatins. This dish is almost like a creamy chiffon dessert—light and fruity but not stiff. By using only a small amount of sugar, the flavor of the pineapple bursts forth. Make sure that you do *not* use fresh pineapple because the gelatin will not set up.

Ingredients

1 large can sliced pineapple, chopped into small pieces (800 g/28 ounces)
½ cup sugar
1 pinch baking soda
70 grams (2½ packets) gelatin, unflavored
1 cup cold water
1 can evaporated milk
2 cans media crema

Drain the juice from the can of pineapple into a pan. Add the sugar and baking soda. Heat over very low heat until the sugar melts.

Dissolve the gelatin in the cup of cold water. Let it sit for approximately 3 minutes. Add the gelatin and water to the pineapple juice. Continue to heat. Pour in the evaporated milk, stirring occasionally. Just before it comes to a boil, remove the pan from the heat. Pour this mixture into a bowl, and allow it to cool completely in the refrigerator.

Beat the media crema until it has doubled in volume. *Please note that it will not get as stiff as a whipping cream does, but it will increase in volume.* Fold the beaten cream and the chopped pineapple into the cold gelatin mixture. Pour into a mold and refrigerate for at least 1 hour. The dessert will be thick but not set up as a stiff gelatin normally does.

Lime Ice Cream
Helado de Limón

6 servings

A light ice cream that is full of lime flavor but not enough to make you pucker. It reminds me of the old-fashioned cheesecake my mom used to make that had the same lime flavor. She used limes instead of lemons, and it was so refreshing. I can still taste it, even after many years. (Exactly how many years is not for publication!) The ice cream is on the light side, as it does not use heavy cream but rather media crema.

Ingredients

2 eggs
1 can media crema
1 can sweetened condensed milk
1 zested lime
scant ½ cup fresh lime juice

Break the eggs into a heat-proof bowl. Whisk well, and add in the can of media crema. Place the bowl over a pan of simmering water and continue whisking until the egg/milk mixture is thickened. The eggs will be cooked at this point.

Whisk in the remaining ingredients; then empty this mixture into a wide container and freeze for 6 hours or until frozen.

Custard (not Flan)
Jericalla Violila

6 servings

Custards and flans are traditional Mexican desserts, so there are as many versions as there are households. *Jericalla*, originating in the state of Jalisco, is a creamy, very sweet egg custard, similar in texture to both flan (without the caramel) and crème brûlée. The flavor of the jericalla differs from these two custards, because it is infused with the warm scent of cinnamon instead of vanilla.

This is an extremely easy dessert to prepare. Only takes about 5 minutes preparation time, and then it goes into the oven. Done!

Ingredients

1 liter (4¼ cups) milk
1 stick cinnamon
200 grams (1 cup) sugar, granulated
3 egg yolks
2 eggs
1 Tablespoon butter, for greasing dish(es)

Preheat the oven to 200°C/400°F.

Slowly simmer the milk with the cinnamon and sugar for 10 minutes. Remove the pan from the heat, and set aside to cool.

Whisk the egg yolks and eggs together. While continuing to whisk, slowly add the warm (not hot) milk mixture. Strain the custard into a buttered oven-proof custard dish or dishes.

Place the custard dish(es) into a hot water bath (bain-marie*) in the oven for 35–40 minutes or until a knife inserted into the middle comes out clean.

* See "Author's Notes."

Vanilla Snow
Nieve de Vainilla

8 servings

This is a sweet, vanilla iced milk that is definitely a refreshing treat on a hot afternoon. Mexico is known for its vanilla, and this recipe is a good example. Using 5 tablespoons of vanilla extract gives you a real burst of vanilla flavor. By freezing, thawing, and freezing again, this iced milk has fewer ice crystals than you would normally get by not using an ice cream freezer.

Ingredients

2 cans sweetened condensed milk
2 cans evaporated milk
2 cups milk, whole or 2%
5 Tablespoons vanilla extract

Blend all the ingredients in a blender. Pour into a bowl and freeze for 2 hours. Remove from the freezer and allow the iced milk to thaw and liquefy. Return it to the freezer and allow it to freeze again for 3 hours.

Banana Cake
Pastel de Plátano

12 servings

A dense, not-too-sweet banana cake that is perfect for sharing. Use bananas that are "just" ripe, not overly ripe, so that you do not have a strong banana flavor, just a light fresh taste. This cake is about subtlety, not intense flavor. Take it with you on your next outing or pot luck. It needs no adornment such as frosting, but use your imagination if you want something more elegant-looking.

Ingredients

170 grams (6 ounces) butter
1 can sweetened condensed milk
3 eggs
1 cup milk
3 cups flour
2 teaspoons baking powder
½ cup mild sour crema
1½ teaspoons baking soda
1 lime, juice of
3 bananas, smooshed
1 Tablespoon vanilla extract

Preheat oven to 200°C/400°F. Grease and flour an oven-proof bundt pan.

Cream the butter with a mixer until it is light and fluffy. Slowly add the condensed milk, eggs, and milk. Continue to beat well. Sift the flour and baking powder together. Lower the speed on the mixer to low and incorporate the flour.

Heat the sour cream and baking soda together in a small pan until it is very warm but not hot.

Put the mixer on medium speed and blend the sour cream into the flour mixture. Beat well.

Turn the mixer to low speed, and slowly mix in the lime juice, the smooshed bananas, and vanilla. Pour into your prepared mold.

Bake for 40 minutes. Cool 10 minutes, and remove from the mold to a cooling rack. The cake can be eaten warm or cold.

Plantains with Honey
Plátanos con Miel

6 servings

There is no actual honey in this recipe, but when the sugar dissolves, it gives a honey flavor. If you are not familiar with plantains, you can look them up in the "Ingredients" section for complete information. As a brief explanation, they look like bananas but do not have much in common with sweet bananas. Plantains are almost always eaten cooked, and although they get sweeter when cooked, they do not necessarily get as soft as a banana. They have more of a dense texture and a peach color on the inside. A few recipes in this book use plantains, so try them. They have a great flavor and are easy to prepare.

Ingredients

6 plantains
12 teaspoons sugar (2 teaspoons for each plantain)
1 Tablespoon ground cinnamon (½ teaspoon for each plantain)
100 grams (7 Tablespoons) butter in slices
½ cup whipping cream, unsweetened

Preheat the oven to 200°C/400°F.

Butter an oven-proof dish with one of the tablespoons of butter.

Wash the plantains. Cut off both tips and cut a slit down the skin on opposite sides, being careful not to cut through the plantain. Peel off the skins; they will come off in 2 sections.

Place the whole plantains in the prepared dish. Sprinkle each plantain with 2 teaspoons sugar and ½ teaspoon ground cinnamon.

Dot the plantains with the remaining 6 tablespoons of butter. Bake uncovered for 30 minutes. Remove from oven. Serve immediately, bathed with the whipping cream.

Chicken in Orange Sauce
Pollo en Naranja

6 servings

A very interesting and tasty combination of ingredients, you can taste the saltiness of bacon, the fresh flavor of the oranges, and sweetness of the raisins. Mix that with the crunch of almonds and the creaminess of hard-boiled eggs, all in a tomato sauce—whew! And that just describes the sauce! Chicken is very inexpensive in Mazatlán, so many cooks have invented their own version of *101 Ways to Cook Chicken.* This is just another example of ingenuity when trying to stretch a peso.

Ingredients

water, as needed
1 chicken, cut in pieces, skin removed
salt and pepper to taste
1 onion, cut in quarters
500 grams (1 pound) tomatoes
2 Tablespoons oil for frying
50 grams (2 ounces) bacon, cooked and crumbled
4 oranges, juiced
50 grams (⅓ cup packed) raisins
30 grams (¼ cup) almonds, chopped
4 eggs, cooked and chopped
8 jalapeños chiles, canned in vinegar, sliced

Put the chicken, salt, pepper, and onion in a pot. Cover with water and boil until the chicken is cooked through, about 15–20 minutes.

Char the tomatoes in a large, dry, heavy frying pan until they have a few black char marks. Purée the tomatoes in a blender. Heat the oil in the pan you just used to char the tomatoes. When it is hot, pour in the puréed tomatoes, and fry for 3 minutes.

Add the chicken and bacon. Stir in the orange juice, a ladle of the chicken broth (chicken cooking water), the raisins, chopped almonds, eggs, and salt and pepper to taste. Simmer this stew for 5 minutes. Remove from the heat. Place the chile slices on top and serve.

Make sure to always have fresh tortillas on hand. You won't want to waste any of that wonderful sauce!

Tuna Salad with Avocado
Ensalada de Atún con Aguacate

4 servings

Even with the smoky flavor of the tuna, the flavors of the Worcestershire and salsa Maggi still come through. None of the flavors overshadow the others. The lettuce has no dressing, but with the other individual stronger flavors, no dressing is needed. A spritz of lime is added to the cucumber spears.

Ingredients

300 grams (10½ ounces) smoked tuna
1 avocado, peeled and seed removed
1 teaspoon Worcestershire sauce
1 teaspoon salsa Maggi
Salt and pepper to taste
lettuce
cucumber spears
fresh limes

Chop the tuna and avocado in cubes. Add the other ingredients, and mix very well.

To serve, arrange the tuna salad on a bed of lettuce, with a spear of cucumber spritzed with a little fresh lime juice and baked tortilla chips.

Shrimp Creole
(Mexican Style)
Camarón Criolla

6–8 servings

This is a ten-minute meal, start to finish! Keep some cleaned shrimp in your freezer so you can make this any time you need a meal that says *Wow*! I love living in a city where I can eat shrimp every day if I choose. It is inexpensive and always fresh and delicious. This is another example of Mexican ingenuity—take a few simple ingredients, and Ricky has invented a new dish. *Olé!*

Ingredients

1 kilo (2.2 pounds) shrimp, peeled and deveined
3 Tablespoons butter
3 large tomatoes, seeds removed, diced
1 onion, diced
2 serrano chiles, seeds removed, finely diced
250 grams (8 ounces) mild sour cream
1 Tablespoon powdered chicken bouillon
250 grams (8 ounces) Manchego or Chihuahua cheese, shredded

Cook the shrimp in boiling salted water, about 2–3 minutes, until they *just* turn red. Remove them to a bowl to avoid over-cooking.

Melt the butter in a pan. Add the tomato, onion, and serranos, and cook about 3 minutes. Incorporate the sour cream, bouillon, and shrimp. Bring to a slight boil; then sprinkle the cheese over top, remove from the heat, and allow the cheese to melt.

Serve with white rice and vegetables.

Shrimp Salad with Avocado
Ensalada de Camarón con Aguacate

6 servings

There is enough filling in each avocado half for a complete meal-size serving. It makes a great luncheon entrée or midnight snack! Scoop out some avocado with each bite and you have myriad textures and flavors. It's another one of those ten-minute meals that I hope you try. Good food, *fast!*

Ingredients

1 kilo (2.2 pounds) shrimp, cleaned, deveined, and cooked
½ head romaine lettuce or butter lettuce
3 tomatoes, seeds removed
1 onion
1 cucumber, seeds removed
3 eggs, hard-boiled
mayonnaise to taste

---

salt and pepper to taste
fresh lime juice to taste
3 avocados, cut in half and seed removed (leave skin on)

Dice the shrimp, lettuce, tomatoes, onion, cucumber, and eggs, and put in a bowl. Add mayonnaise, salt, pepper, and lime juice, to taste. (Start with 3–4 tablespoons of mayonnaise and adjust from that point.)

Divide the salad into 6 portions, and spoon some salad to overflowing into your seedless avocados.

Karina Ann Betlem

JOSUÉ

Meet Josué Antonio Muñoz Villa

Josué (Ho-*sway*) is a very quiet young man who just loves to cook and bake. He is from the small town of Tayotita (today's population is about 3,700) in the state of Durango. His family moved to Mazatlán when he was three years old, so he considers this to be his true home.

His family often returned to Tayotita to visit his uncles. Josué enjoyed these visits because he was intrigued by their work as bread-makers. On these visits, the family would make bread the entire time they were visiting, so naturally, Josué acquired the knowledge and his love of baking. In fact, bread and pastries seem to be in the blood of his family, as evidenced by the fact that he also has another uncle in Michoacán, one in Mazatlán, and a brother who all are pastry chefs.

Although he loved to bake, he wanted to learn more about cooking. As a teenager, he found employment at a local hotel as a kitchen assistant. Because of his young age, that was all the kitchen work he could find. Josué was fine with that, as he considered it a paid education. Josué continued at the hotel until he felt he had learned all he could and began looking for a higher level of employment.

The next step in his culinary education took him to a local seafood restaurant, where he was hired as a chef's assistant—a huge step up from his last job. He was now learning about the actual recipes and their ingredients, safe handling of seafood, and how to purchase good quality seafood. Josué was in heaven! This was his dream job, at least for a while. He loved going to work and stayed long hours to acquire as much knowledge as he could.

The pay was better too, enough so that he could now marry the love of his life, Gaby. They could not afford a real wedding, so they had a civil ceremony to unite them in marriage. He and Gaby both enjoyed working in the kitchen, teaching each other many new culinary dishes. Gaby taught Josué the more traditional dishes, while Josué taught Gaby all about seafood.

Josué now works as a chef at another local restaurant, where they not only serve fresh seafood but also more traditional Mexican dishes.

Josué's story is one of determination—he was determined to reach a goal that he set for himself many years ago and was not afraid to work for it. We all should follow his lead.

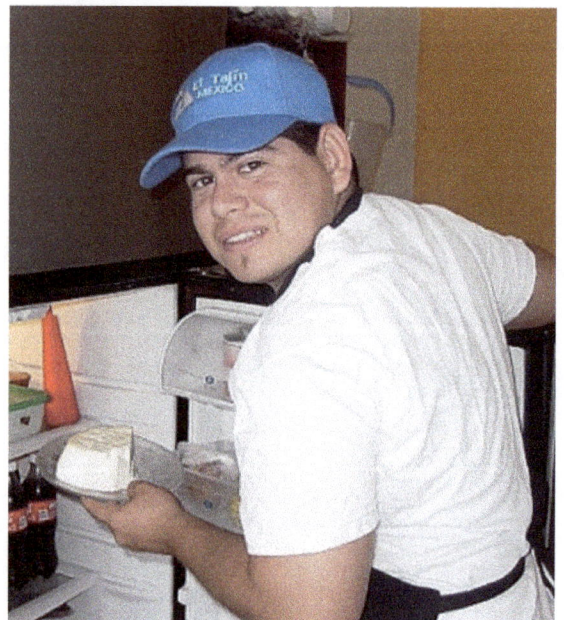

Karina Ann Betlem

Piña Colada

1 serving

You all know what a piña colada is—and now you can make them at home! Although Josué always makes a blended piña colada, you can have yours on the rocks if you prefer. A word of warning about the blended version: sip slowly, or you will get brain freeze! (Sorry, no pineapple garnish in this photo. We ate all the pineapple while we were chatting!)

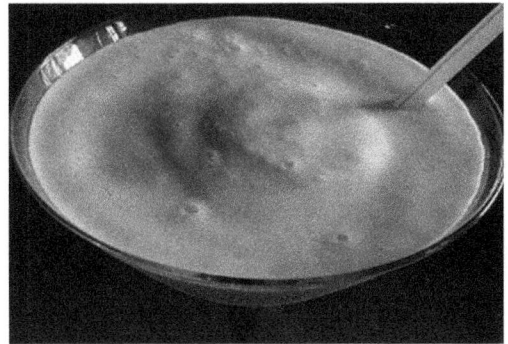

Ingredients

1 to 1½ ounces white rum
2 ounces crème de coco (Coco Lopez)
2 ounces pineapple juice
1 cup ice, crushed into large chunks (not shaved ice)

A shot glass is 1 ounce, so use a shot glass to measure your ingredients, and look like a pro!

Blend all the ingredients in a blender until smooth. Pour into a glass. Garnish with a triangular slice of pineapple and/or a maraschino cherry, and enjoy!

Note: For a non-blended version, mix all the ingredients, including the ice, without the blender, and pour into a glass.

Cabbage Salad
Ensalada de Col

8 servings

An excellent version of a traditional barbecue side dish. Note that the mayonnaise used is from Mexico and is preserved with lime juice. Since the recipe does not call for additional lime juice, but you want the authentic flavor, squeeze ½ lime into the mayonnaise before you mix it in. The addition of sour cream and vinegar will lighten up the mayonnaise and make the sauce thin, not heavy. Try this cole slaw the next time you make burgers on the grill. (By the way, let me know what time dinner is, and I will try to be there … don't I wish!)

Ingredients

1 head red cabbage, finely chopped
50 grams (2 ounces) raisins
2 cups mayonnaise
3 carrots, peeled and shredded
½ cup apple cider vinegar
¼ cup sugar
½ cup sour cream

Put all the ingredients into the bowl that you will use to serve the salad. Mix everything well. Place in the refrigerator at least 30 minutes to cool and allow the flavors to blend.

French Toast
Pan Frances

6 servings

French toast in Mexico always includes vanilla extract in the batter. Remember the cinnamon toast of your youth? Very similar, but this goes a huge step further. There is just something about that warm butter and vanilla scent that fills the kitchen and makes you salivate. When the hot bread is covered with the sugar and cinnamon mixture, you will harken back to the good old days. If you only eat a piece or two, you can round off breakfast with some fruit, eggs, bacon, and *viola!* You have a complete breakfast.

Ingredients

1 loaf white bread, your choice
3 eggs
½ cup milk
2 teaspoons vanilla extract
3 teaspoons ground cinnamon
¼ cup sugar
butter

Whisk the eggs, milk, and vanilla together in a bowl that will fit a slice of bread. In a separate flat dish, mix the sugar with the cinnamon. Dip the bread slices in the egg mixture.

In a hot skillet or grill pan smeared with butter, put as many bread slices as you can. When they are browned on one side, turn them over and brown the other side.

Dredge the hot cooked bread slices in the sugar/cinnamon mixture. Cut each slice in half on a diagonal, and put on a plate. Serve with syrup or crushed fruit.

Mexican Fruit Dessert
Escamochas

8 servings

In this recipe, you can pick your favorite fruits. Josué uses grapes, strawberries, apples, melon, mango, bananas, or pineapple, because the flavors blend well. He buys a crunchy granola to mix up the textures. This is a no-fuss dessert, and the variations are only limited by your imagination.

Ingredients

1 kilo (2.2 pounds) various fresh fruits (see note above)
1 can sweetened condensed milk
200 grams (7 ounces) shredded coconut, fresh or dried
200 grams (7 ounces) granola (your favorite)
100 grams (3.5 ounces) raisins

Chop the fruit into bite-sized cubes. With a potato masher, slightly mash the fruit—don't pulverize it; just squish it a bit. Add the rest of the ingredients and stir well. Serve in individual bowls or tall glasses garnished with more granola or coconut.

Baked Potatoes
Papas al Horno

6 servings

This is a very basic recipe for baked potatoes. If you are in the habit of baking them in your microwave, try this simple method. There is no comparison between the microwave version and the oven baked! Use *real* bacon, not imitation bacon bits. Again, there is no comparison between the two. You are only using 1 tablespoon on each potato, so don't skimp. Food is about flavor and quality.

Ingredients

6 large white potatoes with skin, scrubbed
1 Tablespoon oil
6 squares aluminum foil
6 Tablespoons butter
6 Tablespoons sour cream
6 Tablespoons bacon, fried crisp, drained and crumbled

Preheat the oven to 200°C/400°F.

Grease the potatoes with the oil, and wrap them in the aluminum foil. Place the wrapped potatoes in the oven for 1 hour.

Carefully squeeze one of the potatoes to make sure it is tender. It will give in to the pressure of your squeeze. Remove the potatoes from the oven, and leave the aluminum foil wrapping on them.

Cut a cross or X into the top of each potato. Give them a firm squeeze to open the X, ready for the goodies to go on top. Serve each potato with 1 tablespoon each of the butter, sour cream, and bacon.

Mashed Potatoes
Puré de Papas

6 servings

How many ways are there to make mashed potatoes? Who knows? This is another one I never thought of, and oh my goodness, you will love this one. It is so mouth-wateringly cheesy. (That phrase definitely fits these potatoes!)

Ingredients

1 kilo (2.2 pounds) potatoes, peeled and cooked
¾ cup butter, room temperature
3 Tablespoons salt
1 Tablespoon ground black pepper
500 grams (1 pound) medium cheddar or manchego cheese, shredded*, at room temperature
6 large chives, finely chopped

Preheat the oven for 15 minutes at 120°C/250°F.

Peel the potatoes, cut into chunks, and cook in *unsalted* water until tender.

Mash the potatoes with a potato masher until they are smooth. Then with a mixer or whisk, beat the butter, salt, pepper, cheese, and chives into the potatoes until they are fully incorporated.

After all the ingredients are mixed in, place them in a greased dish, and bake uncovered for 20 minutes.

*Josué prefers cheddar cheese but it is not always available here. His alternate choice is a manchego-type cheese.

Cream of Spinach Soup
Crema de Espinaca

6 servings

Josué uses either the evaporated milk or cream, depending on what he has on hand. I prefer the evaporated milk. Cream makes it a very heavy soup. In addition, if you use cream, you won't get the flavor the evaporated milk imparts. I have tried it both ways, and vote for the evaporated milk option, as it just adds more flavor. Make sure to grind the nutmeg over the soup before you dig in. The warm nutmeg scent enhances the other flavors.

Ingredients

750 grams (26 ounces) fresh spinach
50 grams (3½ Tablespoons) butter
½ white onion, very finely minced
2 cups chicken stock
2 cups evaporated milk or cream
salt and pepper to taste
freshly ground nutmeg

De-stem and wash the spinach leaves one by one. In a large pan, melt the butter and sauté the onion. Chop the spinach slightly and put into the pan. Cover the pan, and let the spinach cook in its own juices over a very low heat. Once it is cooked, put the spinach and onions into a blender, blend well, and return to the pan. Add the chicken stock and the milk or cream. Season with salt and pepper. Stir well and heat thoroughly. Serve in bowls, with a pinch of nutmeg over the top.

Fillet Tips
Puntas de Filete

6 servings

Thin slices of steak in a tomato and onion sauce—*yum!* The steak is tender and juicy; the sauce is simple and a perfect complement to the steak. By slicing the steak prior to cooking, each piece will be quickly and perfectly cooked. Make sure to pat each meat slice dry with a paper towel before adding it to the pan, or it will not brown. (Gray meat just isn't appealing!)

Ingredients

¼ cup oil
1 onion, finely minced
1 kilo (2.2 pounds) beef fillet tips, in slices
3 cans tomato purée (210 g/7.4 ounces each)

1 Tablespoon chicken bouillon
ground black pepper to taste

Heat the oil in a large frying pan. Sauté the onion until it is soft but not browned. Add the meat to the pan and brown. Remove and reserve the juice from the meat as it accumulates to allow the meat to brown. Once the meat has browned, return the juice to the pan, along with the tomato purée, bouillon, and pepper. Continue to cook over low heat for 5 minutes. Serve.

Enchiladas in the Oven
Enchiladas al Horno

6 servings

True enchiladas are never covered in cheese or swimming in sauce; rather, the sauce and cheese are simply accents to the flavor of fresh tortillas and the filling (chicken in this recipe, for example). Tomatillos give the green color and a tart flavor. If you cannot find tomatillos in your area, you can buy them canned from the Mexican food aisle, or try growing them yourself. One plant does not take up much space, and it will produce an abundance of fresh tomatillos. Fresh corn tortillas, if you can find them (or make them), are far superior to the prepackaged ones.

Ingredients
250 grams (8 ounces) tomatillos, papery skin removed and discarded
2 jalapeño chiles
1 slice onion
1 clove garlic
salt to taste
5 stems cilantro
lard for frying (or you can use olive oil or other flavorful shortening)
12 corn tortillas
2 cups chicken, cooked and shredded
150 grams (5¼ ounces) Chihuahua cheese, shredded
4 Tablespoons butter
sour cream, for topping

Preheat the oven to 180°C/350°F.

Put the tomatillos into a pan of boiling water with the chiles. Cook them until they are soft and have changed to a dull green color. Drain thoroughly and place the tomatillos and chiles (remove the stems) in a blender jar with the onion, garlic, salt, and cilantro. Purée until smooth.

In a skillet, melt 2 tablespoons lard until very hot. Carefully pour the tomatillo mixture into the hot lard or oil. Fry it until it has heated all the way through. The sauce should be liquid without being runny. Pour back into the blender jar.

Grease an oven-proof dish with the butter.

Heat more lard in the frying pan. You don't need too much, but the amount will depend on the size of your pan. Dip each tortilla into the hot lard for 3 seconds on each side, put on a plate, and place some of the chicken in a line on one side of the tortilla. Roll the tortilla around the chicken, and place it seam side down in the greased dish. Repeat with all the tortillas (enchiladas).

Pour the sauce on top of the rolled enchiladas, making sure to cover them completely. Sprinkle the cheese on top. Dot with bits of butter. Bake for 10–15 minutes until the cheese is melted and browned.

Serve the enchiladas with a drizzle of sour cream over the top, if you wish.

Queen's Chicken Breast
Pechuga Reina
(There is no better translation, so just call it Pechuga Reina)

4 servings

Pronounced *pay-chu-ga ray-na*, it probably is delicious enough for a queen. The filling of *panela* (fresh cheese) and spinach, wrapped in bacon, and a sauce flavored with Worcestershire is definitely a keeper. Cooks in Mazatlán love to stuff chicken breasts to enhance or change its basic flavor and appearance. This recipe does both!

Ingredients
1 kilo (2.2 pounds) boneless, skinless chicken breasts
salt and pepper to taste
1 small bunch fresh spinach, chopped fine
500 grams (1 pound) panela (fresh cheese), sliced
200 grams (7 ounces) bacon slices, uncooked (or 1 slice for each breast)
2 Tablespoons butter or oil

For the Salsa:
1 Tablespoon butter
500 grams (16 ounces) mild sour cream
2 Tablespoons powdered chicken bouillon
¼ cup Worcestershire sauce

Salt and pepper the chicken breasts. Slit open the breasts to make a large pocket. Fill the pocket with chopped spinach and slices of cheese. Wrap the stuffed breasts with strips of bacon.

In a large pan, melt the butter or oil. Carefully place the stuffed and wrapped breasts in the hot oil. Place a heavy pan on top of the chicken to weight them down and flatten them a bit while they cook. Occasionally, spoon some of the butter or oil from the pan over top of the breasts to baste.

When the bacon is cooked, turn the breasts over in the pan, continue cooking, and repeat with the weight and the basting.

Preparation of the salsa:
Melt the butter in a small pan. Add the sour cream and bouillon. With a whisk, beat very well while heating through. Pour in the Worcestershire sauce, and adjust the salt if needed. Heat for 1 minute.

Serve the breasts, and bathe them with the cream sauce.

Fish Rolls
Rollos de Pescado

6 servings

This has become one of my all-time favorites! A simple sauce like tomato purée mixed with sour cream makes all the difference between an ordinary stuffed fish fillet and an incredibly succulent fillet. I made it for my husband, and his eyes actually lit up as he made those "yummy" sounds—you know, those sounds a person makes when he just can't believe his taste buds are getting such a treat. Josué and I both used red snapper fillets, but any other mild fish will be good. I wish I could be there to see your face when you take your first bite!

Ingredients

6 thin fish fillets (snapper or similar fish)
2 limes, juiced
salt and pepper to taste
6 thin slices Chihuahua cheese
15 green olives, pits removed, chopped
sliced jalapeños in vinegar, to taste
½ cup mild sour cream
½ cup tomato purée (boxed or canned)
1 Tablespoon parsley, chopped

Preheat oven to 175°C/350°F.

Rinse the fillets and pat dry. Rub each fillet with lime juice, salt, and pepper. On top of each fillet, put one slice of cheese, ½ teaspoon chopped olives, and slices of jalapeños. Adjust the number of slices, depending on your tolerance for heat.

Roll up the fillets carefully to keep all the goodies inside. Secure with a toothpick.

Mix the sour cream with the tomato purée.

Place all the rolls in a greased oven-proof dish. Bathe them with the sour cream/tomato sauce.

Sprinkle the rolls with the remainder of the olives and the parsley.

Cover the dish with aluminum foil and bake for 30 minutes.

Zarandeado-Style Fish
Pescado Zarandeado

6 servings

There is no translation for the title of this amazingly delicious fish. What is it? A whole fish seasoned and stuffed with goodies, wrapped tightly in aluminum foil, and roasted on hot coals. The fish is split lengthwise, keeping the head, tail, and all the bones intact.

The meat is moist, with hints of all the flavors of the seasonings. The presentation is traditionally Mexican. It is served on a platter in one piece, still on the foil. The diners help themselves to the fish using their own forks. They fill their tortillas with the succulent fish and veggies and then spoon some salsa over top. Zarandeado is an event, so plan to spend time enjoying the food and visiting with your friends!

Ingredients

For the Fish:
1 fish, 4½ pounds (about 2 kilos), traditional robalo (snook) or snapper
salt and pepper to taste
1 Tablespoon Worcestershire sauce
3 Tablespoons butter to cook the garlic
2 cloves garlic, very finely minced or crushed
3 Tablespoons mayonnaise
1 Tablespoon mustard
2 tomatoes, cut in slices
1 cup red bell pepper, cut into strips or diced
½ onion, cut in slices
2 Tablespoons butter, for dotting the fish

For the Salsa:
3 tomatoes, charred
1 clove garlic
2 serrano chiles, charred
¼ cup cilantro
1 slice onion

Start your coals or preheat your barbecue. You will need very hot coals to cook this fish.

Open the fish down the entire belly side from head to tail, almost to a butterfly cut. If necessary, have your fishmonger do that for you. Do not remove the bones; they are an essential part of the flavor.

On the inside, cut very small slits in the meat, making sure you do *not* cut all the way through to the outside of the fish. Into the slits, spread salt, pepper, and the Worcestershire sauce.

In a small pan, melt the butter, and sauté the garlic until it is soft. Spread this butter/garlic mixture all over the inside of the fish.

Mix together the mayonnaise and mustard. Spread this over the inside of the fish.

Remember that you are building flavor layers, so do not be tempted to add all these ingredients together to save time.

Over the inside of the fish, evenly sprinkle the tomatoes, onion, and red bell pepper. Close by folding the fish over on itself, and dot with the butter on the outside.

Wrap the fish in a huge piece of aluminum foil so that the juices don't escape when you turn it.

Place the fish close to the coals. Cook for about 10 minutes on one side. Carefully, flip the fish to the other side. (I use a large tray.) Cook for another 10 minutes.

It is served in the foil, whole. Have a basket of fresh corn tortillas on the table to make your fish tacos. Drizzle with the salsa.

For the Salsa:

Roast the tomatoes and serrano chiles in a dry cast-iron skillet until they have char marks all over. They should not be totally blackened.

Place all the salsa ingredients in a blender and purée until it is smooth. Pour into a bowl.

Special Shrimp in Garlic Sauce
Camarónes al Mojo de Ajo Especiales

4 servings

The tender shrimp have a very slight tang, but the flavor is such that you cannot pinpoint the exact ingredients. (I think we need to do more "testing" on this one. Here, shrimpy shrimpy …)

Ingredients

10 fresh large shrimp
garlic salt
2 teaspoons apple cider vinegar
3 Tablespoons mayonnaise
1 Tablespoon mustard
3 Tablespoons olive oil (or a combination of olive oil and butter)

Peel the shrimp. Devein the shrimp by cutting them open on the back side in a butterfly fashion, without cutting them in half. Rinse out the vein.

Mix the garlic salt, vinegar, mayonnaise, and mustard. Marinate the shrimp in this mixture in the refrigerator for 1 hour.

Heat the oil in a frying pan. Remove the shrimp from the marinade and shake off the excess. Carefully place each shrimp in the hot oil. Make sure to have each shrimp opened flat when you sauté them. Cook until they turn white, about 2 minutes on each side. Depending on the size of the shrimp, it could be a bit longer in the pan. Remove them from the pan to a paper towel and serve.

Shrimp Fajitas
Fajitas de Camarón

6 servings

This fajita dish doesn't use a sizzling platter—that's a north-of-the-border flare. This simple but delicious dish is ready in about 10 minutes, and you will have a *wow!* meal to impress everyone at your table. Make sure the table is set, and all drinks ready before you start, because the food will be ready in a flash. Serve on a warm platter, and let everyone help themselves to succulent shrimp and stir-fried veggies.

Ingredients

1 kilo (2.2 pounds) shrimp, peeled and deveined
2 green bell peppers
2 onions
100 grams (3½ ounces) fresh mushrooms, sliced
1 tomato
½ cup Worcestershire sauce
salt and pepper to taste
¼ cup butter

Slice all the vegetables into large slices, about 6 mm / ¼ in. wide.

In a large frying pan, melt the butter. Add the onion and green pepper slices. When these begin to change color, add the shrimp. When the shrimp just begins to turn color, add the mushrooms, tomato, Worcestershire sauce, salt, and pepper. Cover and cook until the shrimp is cooked through. This only takes about 3–4 minutes, so keep a watchful eye.

Serve with fresh tortillas, *or* you can make quesadillas with this rich mixture.

To make quesadillas: in a dry, *hot* frying pan, place one flour tortilla. Immediately place some of the fajita mixture on the tortilla. Spread it around to within ½ inch of the edges. Top with a bit of shredded Chihuahua cheese; then cover this whole thing with another flour tortilla. When the bottom tortilla is crisp, slide the tortilla out of the pan onto a flat plate. Then invert the plate so the uncooked side is down, and slide the quesadilla back into the frying pan. When that side also is crisp, slide it out to a cutting board. With a large knife, cut into quarters. Arrange on a plate.

JUANA

Meet Juana Rodriguez Carrillo

Is this smile not contagious? Even when Juana—known as Juany—is having a difficult day, you would never know it by her outward demeanor. She always is ready with a big smile, a hug, and genuine happiness to see her friends, regardless of what her personal circumstances might be at the moment.

Juany says that she learned to cook by watching her mom in the kitchen but also admits that she was a terrible cook. Despite her attempts to help her mom, Juany was usually chased from the kitchen so she "wouldn't ruin another meal." She even tried to pick up some cooking hints from her friend's mothers, but somehow it just didn't stick (unlike the food in her pots and pans).

When she was twelve years old, Juany's family moved from Michoacán to Mazatlán. She now had all new friends' mothers to tap for information on cooking, but her reputation followed her wherever she went, and soon she was not welcome in their kitchens either. (Once, she actually exploded hot dogs all over a friend's kitchen, and to this day nobody knows how that could have happened!)

Unable to advance her hands-on culinary skills in the kitchen, Juany started watching a famous Mexican chef on TV, and little by little, some of his techniques and recipes started to sink in. She watched him diligently for years. In addition to the TV shows, cooking magazines were beginning to appear in the stores, so whenever she had a few extra pesos, Juany would purchase and study those as well.

By the time she was twenty-one and married, Juany was able to prepare meals that were deemed acceptable, but she still had to rely on friends to help with her recipes. Over the years, she practiced and perfected her cooking skills to the point that now she is an exceptional cook!

Vanessa and Angel

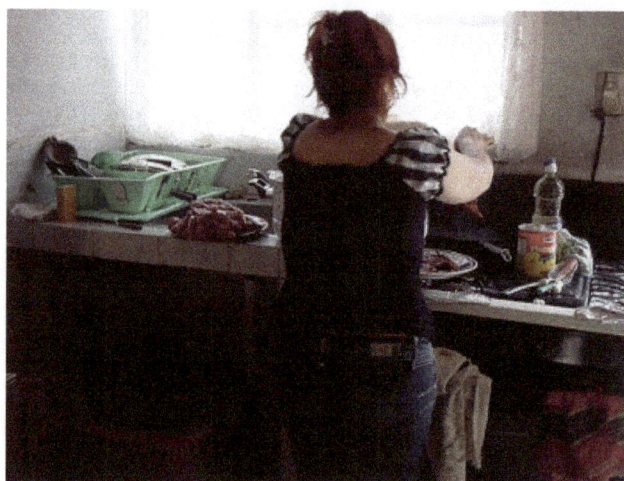

Until approximately four years ago, Juany had never worked outside of her home. When she became a single mom, however, it became necessary to find outside employment. Juany was not skilled in any particular field of employment but fortunately, Rosie, to whom this book is dedicated, provided Juany with the opportunity to attend beauty school. Being a beautician in Mazatlán is a good profession and one that does not take long years in school to become licensed. Juany needed work, and tips during the tourist season are excellent. Juany completed beauty school, obtained her license, and now works full time in Rosie's establishment.

When asked what she does in her spare time, Juany simply laughs. "What spare time?" she asks. Unfortunately, there is no spare time for her, as she supports her three children, helps them with their

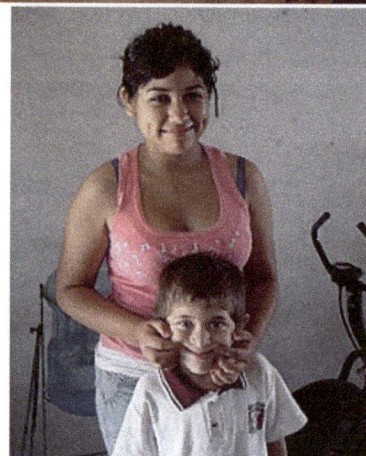

No counters—to use a blender, she places it on a chair in the living room near an outlet.

homework, cleans house, prepares meals, and awaits the start of another day.

Juany and her three children now live in a darling one-bedroom home. Although quite small, her home is very comfortable and clean. More important, it is filled with lots of laughter and Juany's exceptionally good nature.

Brussels Sprouts a la Parisian
Coles de Brucelas a la Parisien

6 servings

The people in Mexico love their Brussels sprouts. They are very seasonal, though, and are not available frozen, only fresh. Cut them in half after cooking but before sautéing so that there is more surface to brown. The browning gives off an amazingly fragrant buttery flavor that will please even those in your family who don't like Brussels sprouts. I never did like them until … now. Using this recipe, I cook (and eat them!) them several times a week during the season. Who would have thought?

Ingredients

750 grams (1½ pounds) fresh Brussels sprouts
2 onions, sliced
3½ Tablespoons butter
1 Tablespoon parsley, chopped

Cook the Brussels sprouts in boiling salted water until they are fork tender but not soft. Drain well. Cut each in half.

Melt the butter in a large frying pan and sauté the onions. When they begin to change color, add the Brussels sprouts to the onions and cook 10 minutes, stirring, allowing them to brown.

Remove to a serving bowl, and garnish with chopped parsley.

Stuffed Eggs, Mireia-Style
Huevos Rellenos "Mireia"

4 servings

This is a Mexican version of deviled eggs. I love deviled eggs but had never tried them with the anchovies called for in this recipe. At first, I really wasn't sure if I wanted to do this, but it was a tasty surprise for me! The combination of all the ingredients, including the tiny dollop of good mayonnaise on top, makes this a unique addition to your deviled egg repertoire.

Just a word about anchovies before you begin: the taste is more nutty than fishy. If you have ever eaten a marinara sauce at an Italian restaurant, chances are that sauce had anchovies in it. You have probably been eating them for years, but just didn't know it. (Caesar salad uses anchovies too.) If you're not familiar with anchovies, you may be pleasantly surprised too!

Ingredients

4 eggs, room temperature
2 anchovy fillets, finely minced
salt and pepper, to taste
1 teaspoon apple cider vinegar, or to taste
½ teaspoon oil
1 Tablespoon heavy cream
mayonnaise, for garnish (optional)

Place your room-temperature eggs in a pan of cold water; cover with a lid. Bring the eggs to a full rolling boil. Turn off the heat—do not remove the lid—and let the eggs sit in the hot water for 10 minutes until they are hard boiled. Place them in ice water to cool; this also helps release the shell. Peel the eggs, and slice them in half lengthwise. Remove the yolks, and place them in a shallow bowl. Mash the yolks with a fork and add the anchovies, salt, pepper, vinegar, oil, and heavy cream. Mix until it forms a paste. Fill the eggs and garnish with a dab of mayonnaise.

Note: Depending on the type of anchovies you use, you may not need to add the salt or the oil. You can purchase tins of anchovies in olive oil with no salt, or salted. Juany buys whatever is available when she wants to make this recipe. Sometimes they are salted, sometimes not. It really doesn't matter which you use, but adjust the oil and salt as necessary. For example, I use anchovies in olive oil with no salt added, so I use a bit of the oil from the anchovies, and add the salt myself.

Chilaquiles with Cream
Chilaquiles ala Crema

4 servings

Chilaquiles is a traditional Mexican dish, usually served with breakfast or brunch and sometimes topped with shredded chicken or eggs. Juany's version has neither. There is no translation for the word *chilaquiles*, but the description of it is simple: leftover corn tortillas, fried, and then cooked in a sauce. Fresh corn tortillas are only eaten "fresh" on the day they are made and purchased. Day-old tortillas make their way into chilaquiles, tortilla soup, and fried tortilla chips.

Ingredients

10–12 day-old corn tortillas, cut into squares or triangles
1 Tablespoon oil
1 box tomato purée (210 g/7.4 ounces)
1 pinch chicken bouillon powder
½ teaspoon salt
½ onion, small dice
200 ml (6.75 ounces) mild sour cream
190 g (6.7 ounces) cream cheese

The tortillas should be well air-dried so they are hard and break when bent. Do not use packaged tortilla chips; they already have been cooked and will not absorb the oil or sauce.

Have all your ingredients measured and ready to put in the pan at the same time.

Heat a large pan with the oil to super-hot but not blazing. Add the tortillas, and immediately stir in all the other ingredients. Continue stirring the tortilla mixture for 10 minutes, and serve while the chilaquiles are hot.

You can serve these as they are or with a topping of salsa (either fresh or roasted*), cheese, shredded chicken, or eggs.

*See Rogelio's Salsa.

Flour Tortillas
Tortillas de Harina

Makes 12 tortillas

Warning: These are addictive and so easy to make that you will never buy those gummy tortillas in the grocery store again. Roll them as thin or thick as you like.

Ingredients
1 kilo (4½ cups) all-purpose flour
250 grams (1¼ cups) solid white vegetable shortening
1½ teaspoons salt
1 cup cold water

Put the flour, salt, and shortening in a large bowl. Knead very well with your hands until all the shortening is dispersed, and you have a coarse meal consistency. Add the water, and continue kneading with your hands until you get a soft dough. More water can be added by tablespoons if needed. Let the dough rest for 10 minutes.

Heat a *comal*, cast-iron pan, or griddle on the stove to medium hot.

Form 12 balls with the dough. Roll out as thin as you can with a rolling pin, or use your hands to flatten the dough. Rubbing your hands or the rolling pin with more flour will keep the dough from sticking. Cook the tortillas on each side for 15–20 seconds. Place on a cloth napkin, and keep covered so they stay warm while you cook the others. Store any leftover tortillas, wrapped in plastic, in the refrigerator. To reheat, place in a pre-heated, dry cast-iron pan or griddle.

Slices of Chile to the Queen
(literal translation)
Rajas de Chile a la Reina

8 servings

Another variation of rajas: slices of chiles. The wonderful grassy flavor of poblanos mixes with the smooth flavor and texture of the cheese, and it all binds together with eggs and milk. This has all the ingredients of oven-baked chiles rellenos without the fuss of stuffing the chiles. Try this side dish for any meal, from breakfast to dinner.

Ingredients
8 poblano chiles
150 grams Chihuahua cheese, grated
2 eggs
1 can evaporated milk

salt and pepper, to taste
butter for greasing the pan

Heat the oven to 190°C/375°F.

Char the chiles, and put them in a covered dish to steam. Peel and remove the stems, veins, and seeds. Cut into very thin slices (not chopped). (See the "Chile" section for more detailed instructions on charring and peeling poblano chiles.)

Grease an oven-proof pan or dish with butter. Layer the chile slices, then the cheese, creating several layers, ending with cheese.

Whisk together the eggs, evaporated milk, salt, and pepper.

Pour the egg/milk mixture over the chiles and cheese in the pan. Place the pan in a bain-marie* or hot-water bath, and carefully place in the oven. Bake for 35–40 minutes until it has set. Insert a knife; if it comes out clean, it is done. If not, continue to bake for another 5 or so minutes.

Serve hot.

* See "Author's Notes."

Vegetable Soup Supreme
Caldo de Vegetales Supremo

4 servings

This soup is a very smooth, thick, blended purée that gets its light green color from the split peas. It is a hearty soup that tastes creamy without the addition of cream. When cooking the beans, do not add so much water that the beans float, or you will have to drain them—this will cause them to lose much of their flavor. Add only enough water to allow them to cook without scorching but still having enough to aid in the blending. The level of water after the beans are tender should just touch the top of the beans.

Ingredients

3 quarts water
1 Tablespoon salt
100 grams peas, dried
100 grams white beans, dried
100 grams lentils, dried
100 grams fava beans, dried**
50 grams butter
1 guajillo chile, toasted cut into thin strips (for garnish, optional)

Rinse and sort the peas, beans, and lentils, discarding any stones and wrinkled beans. Place all of them in a large pot. Pour in the water, and add the salt. Cook on medium heat until the beans are almost a thick purée, about 2 hours. If you need to add more water, do so, but do not add more than a cup or so at a time.

Place the contents of the pot into a blender with the butter, and blend until you have a very smooth purée. Adjust the salt and serve.

** Dried fava beans look similar to dried lima beans, except that they are large and yellow. You should be able to find them on the grocery aisle or on the Mexican aisle labeled as "Habas Secas" (dried favas). If you cannot find them, use large dried lima beans, which are not a true substitute but an acceptable one.

Green Bean Soup
Sopa de Ejote

6 servings

Ever want a new idea to use up all those green beans from your garden? Juany has the answer—a simple soup with a lot of flavor. The butter finishes the soup in the same way you would put a pat of butter on warm green beans. Juany knows some people prefer beef broth, but she uses chicken broth because she says beef broth covers up the flavor of the beans. You decide.

Ingredients

500 grams (1 pound) tender green beans
salted water for cooking the beans
50 grams (3.5 Tablespoons) butter
1 liter (4 cups) chicken or beef broth (homemade, canned, or boxed)

Clean and chop the green beans. Cook them in boiling salted water until they are tender. Strain the cooked green beans, keeping 1 liter (4 cups) of the cooking water. To the cooking water, add the chicken or beef broth. Heat them together. Then return the strained green beans to the liquid, and add the butter. Heat through, adjust salt if necessary, and serve.

Farm-Style Onion Soup
Puré Campesino

8 servings

Campesino means "farm- or rural-style." This is a very rustic dish that is a favorite of the farmhands on the ranchos. It is very inexpensive to make, very filling, and very tasty. It is always served with fresh tortillas.

Browning the onions before you begin cooking them in the broth makes them very sweet. They lose that "rough" onion flavor you can find in other onion soups. The delicate threads of egg yolks adds a filigree look to the soup. Pretty enough for company!

Ingredients

4 medium onions, small dice
2 Tablespoons oil
2 liters broth, beef or chicken
2 egg yolks
¼ teaspoon red wine or apple cider vinegar
salt and pepper to taste

Heat the oil in a deep saucepan. Add the diced onions, and brown, stirring occasionally. When they are well browned, add the broth. Season with salt and pepper. Simmer for 2 hours, until the onions turn to a purée. Just before serving, briefly beat the two yolks into the vinegar and quickly stir into the broth. Immediately you will see strands of egg separating while cooking into the broth.

Brazilian Salad
Ensalada Brasil

4–5 servings

When eating this dessert, you will find the rice is almost invisible because it is overpowered by the sweet freshness and texture of the pineapple. No added sugar is necessary if you have a well-ripened pineapple. If you do not know how to pick a ripe one, ask your produce manager for assistance. At our grocery stores in Mazatlán, they will cut fruit open so that customers can taste for ripeness. Ask if your store will do the same for you.

Ingredients
100 grams (½ cup) white rice
½ fresh pineapple, peeled and cored
½ cup whipping cream, whipped, unsweetened
small pinch of salt
1 lime, juiced

Cook the rice in water (unsalted) until it is tender. Pour it into a bowl and allow it to cool, stirring occasionally with a fork to keep the grains from clumping.

Peel and core the pineapple; then cut the fruit into bite-sized pieces. Mix with the cooled rice, keeping the rice loose. Add the whipped cream, pinch of salt, and the lime juice. Stir gently. Serve.

Cream of Pineapple and Banana
Crema de Piña y Plátano

6 servings

Yes, there really are purple bananas. They are smaller and sweeter than regular bananas and get even sweeter if heated. I have been told that these have become quite popular in other countries, so do try to find them. Although a regular plantain is not a real substitute, you can use them if you cannot find the purple bananas. You will have to cook it a bit longer, however, and it will taste totally different but still will make another sweet dessert.

Ingredients
½ fresh pineapple
3 purple bananas
30 grams (1 ounce) raisins
400 grams (14 ounces) sugar
300 grams (10.5 ounces) pine nuts (toasted) or shredded coconut (toasted)

Clean the pineapple by cutting off the exterior shell. Remove core, and grind the fruit in a food processor, leaving some smaller chunks—do not purée. Place in a large warm pan.

Peel the bananas and immediately add to the pineapple, along with the sugar. Cook over low heat, stirring constantly until the sugar has dissolved and the bananas have softened.

Empty onto a serving plate, and garnish with the raisins and pine nuts or coconut.

Baked Caramel Custard
Flan

12 servings

Almost like Mom used to make! It just pops right into the oven, no bain-marie (hot water bath) needed. The caramel comes from the sugar, and when it is baked, the flavor permeates the custard. Other than the baking time, it takes longer to melt and caramelize the sugar than to put this wonderful dessert together. Normally, these are made in pie plates with slanted sides, but this recipe makes more than a pie plate can hold, so Juany uses a bundt pan. It is not the traditional mold, but it definitely is the traditional flan.

Ingredients

6 Tablespoons sugar
1 can sweetened condensed milk
1 can evaporated milk
1 can media crema
1 cup milk
1 teaspoon vanilla extract
5 eggs

Preheat oven to 250°C/475°F.

Heat the sugar slowly in a frying pan to caramelize (keep an eye on it so that it does not burn, or it will become bitter). When caramelized, it should be golden in color. Pour into the mold you will be using for the custard, and rotate the mold so the entire bottom is covered. Let it cool while you prepare the custard.

Beat the eggs in a large bowl. Then mix in all the other ingredients, and blend very well. Gently pour this over the cooled caramelized sugar.

Put in the oven and bake for 35–40 minutes. Let it cool completely, and then invert onto a serving plate with sides to catch all the caramel.

Fruit Custard
Flan de Frutas

6 servings

An interesting version of the traditional flan. With the fruit cocktail blended in, you get a light fruity flavor throughout the custard. This fruit flan is always eaten with special cookies; in this case, ladyfingers.

Ingredients

2 cups milk, whole or 2%
2 eggs
4 egg yolks
1 can (850 g/30 ounces) fruit cocktail, strained, liquid discarded
¾ cup sugar, divided (¼ cup for caramel, ½ cup for custard)
12 ladyfingers, 2 for each serving
12 cherries

Preheat oven to 175°C/350°F.

Boil a pot of water to use in the bain-marie* (hot water bath).

Heat the sugar slowly in a small pan to caramelize (keep an eye on it so that it does not burn or it will become bitter). When it is caramelized, it should be golden in color. Pour into the oven-safe mold you will be using for the flan. Let it cool while you prepare the custard.

Blend the milk, eggs, yolks, fruit cocktail, and ½ cup sugar.

By now, the caramelized sugar should be cool. Pour in the milk and fruit mixture.

Place the filled custard dish into a bain-marie*. Bake in the pre-heated oven for 60 minutes or until set. A knife inserted in the middle should come out clean when it is done.

Before serving, turn out the flan onto a plate, and decorate with cherries and the ladyfingers.

* See "Author's Notes."

Cocktail of Fruits
Coctel de Frutas

10 servings

This is my kind of fruit cocktail—sweet and fruity in a frozen milky layer. The fruit sinks to the bottom of the mold during freezing so when it is unmolded, the fruit is at the top. Juany uses a large glass bowl to get that rounded-igloo effect. To unmold the iced milk, run a little cool water over the bottom of the bowl and have a small plate to catch it as it releases. You can serve it with or without Chantilly cream or sweetened whipped cream.

Ingredients

1 egg, slightly beaten
2 liters (8.5 cups) milk
1 Tablespoon fine sugar
1 can sweetened condensed milk
1 can media crema
1 large can fruit cocktail (850 g/30 ounces)

Beat the egg and milk together in a pan over low heat. Heat the milk to almost boiling, stirring constantly to keep it smooth. Remove the pan from the heat, and add the sugar, sweetened condensed milk, media crema, and fruit cocktail. Stir well. Pour into a mold or bowl and put in the freezer until it is frozen.

This can be served with Chantilly cream* or sweetened whipped cream.

*Chantilly cream is a stabilized form of whipped cream. In our hot and humid climate, regular whipped cream does not hold up. The recipe for Chantilly cream is as follows:

1 cup heavy whipping cream (cold)
½ cup powdered sugar (*not* granulated sugar)
½ teaspoon vanilla, liquid or powdered

Beat the whipping cream until the peaks do not disappear. Using a sieve to strain out any lumps, add the powdered sugar to the whipped cream, and whip until stiff peaks form. Add vanilla, and continue to whip until it is incorporated and the cream remains stiff. Refrigerate as you would regular whipped cream—it will not lose volume in the refrigerator.

Veal Tongue ala Florenciana
Lengua de Ternera "Florenciana"

8 servings

I'll bet many of you have eaten veal tongue without realizing it. I know I had—and imagine my surprise! Ask your butcher to order this for you if he does not have one on hand. It is a wonderful dish for a buffet or as hors d'oeuvres. Juany laughs, because she has only been able to purchase veal tongue once—all the other times it has been a small cow's tongue. She likes the sound of the name of this recipe, so she hasn't changed it.

Tongue is a meat that is popular in many cultures and is on many buffet tables. On Greek buffets, for example, tongue is sliced and served with bread to make a sandwich. The flavor has a strong beef flavor, similar to a good chuck roast, and it has a grain similar to a brisket.

Ingredients
1 veal tongue; if unavailable, a small cow's tongue works well
2 hard boiled eggs
1 head lettuce
mustard and mayonnaise, equal amounts

Boil the tongue in salt water until tender, about 2 hours. Peel the skin off, and chill the meat in the refrigerator. When it is cold, place it on lettuce leaves, garnished with slices of hard-boiled eggs. Cover the tongue with a mixture of ½ mustard and ½ mayonnaise, and slice it, thin or thick (your choice).

Serve on rolls.

Spaghetti Bolognese
Espaguetti a la Boloñesa

8 servings

There are many versions of this same dish. This sauce is very meaty and very light on the tomato sauce. The addition of diced carrots seems to be a common ingredient, and they add a slightly sweet flavor. Because there is so much meat in the sauce, you do not need to load it on your pasta. Just a small fork full with a bit of pasta is all you need to satisfy your palette.

Ingredients

400 grams (14 ounces) spaghetti
1 Tablespoon butter
½ medium onion, finely minced
(¼ onion for the spaghetti, ¼ for the meat sauce)
2 cloves garlic
1 kilo (2.2 lbs.) ground beef
1 Tablespoon oil, to brown the ground beef if it is very lean (optional)
1 carrot, diced
1 box tomato purée (210 grams each/7.4 ounces each)
2 cans mushrooms, chopped (184 grams each/6.5 ounces each)
salt and pepper
1 pinch oregano
Parmesan cheese, grated

Cook the spaghetti in boiling salted water for about 15 minutes. Drain the cooked spaghetti, and place in cold water.

Melt the butter in a pan, and sauté 1 clove of garlic and half of the onion. Cook until the onion is translucent; then add the spaghetti and stir. Remove from heat.

If you are using oil, heat it now in a large pan on medium-high heat. Add the ground beef, the other half of the onion, 1 clove of garlic, and pepper. Stir the beef until it is partially cooked, and add the diced carrot, salt, and tomato purée. When the beef and carrots are cooked, add the mushrooms and oregano.
Heat through and serve.

Serve the spaghetti topped with the meat sauce, and then grate Parmesan over all.

Breaded Pork Chops
Chuletas Empanizadas

4 servings

This is one of those quick-and-easy recipes that always looks like you spent more time in the kitchen than you actually did. Juany is a mom with three kids and also has a full-time job. Time is very precious to her, but having a good meal for her family is just as important. The parsley and lime juice under the breading adds just a hint of flavor to the pork chops. Purchase chops that are a bit thicker than you need. Pound them to a uniform thickness, and you will be tenderizing them as well.

Ingredients

4 large pork chops, deboned
2 limes, juiced
¼ cup parsley, finely chopped
salt and pepper
1 egg, slightly beaten
1 Tablespoon milk
2 cups bread crumbs
oil for frying

Pound the pork chops until they are equal in thickness. Sprinkle them on both sides with the lime juice, finely chopped parsley, salt, and pepper.

Mix the egg and milk in a bowl large enough to hold one chop. Add one chop at a time to the egg, and then dip into the bread crumbs. Place each coated pork chop on a plate while you dip and coat the others.

Heat the oil to hot in a frying pan large enough to hold all 4 pork chops. Fry on both sides, turning them only once, until they are golden, and the pork is cooked to your taste. Serve immediately with mashed potatoes and vegetables.

Meat Tacos with Pineapple
Tacos al Pastor

Serves 12 people, with several tacos each

If you love tacos, you will thank me one thousand times for sharing this recipe with you. When you have the ancho and pineapple sauce cooking into the meat, you can smell the sweet and savory aromas, along with the searing pork. You just have to try this!

This makes a ton of meat—enough for a large family gathering or a taco party. If you don't want to feed a large group of people, you can prepare everything, marinate the meat, and then freeze it. Or just reduce the amount of meat and sauce. I prefer to make the whole recipe and then freeze the meat in portions for my small family—I do all the work once, and then next time, I just have to defrost and cook the meat.

Ingredients

2 kilos (4.4 pounds) boneless pork leg, sliced very thin (less than 6 mm / ¼ inch)
6 ancho chiles
½ head garlic, peeled
3 teaspoons salt
1 large can sliced pineapple (1.7 pounds/820 grams)
⅓ large onion
oil (small amount for searing the meat)
warm corn tortillas (lots of them)

For the Salsa:
8 tomatoes

6 serrano chiles
9 tomatillos
½ clove garlic, peeled
1½ Tablespoons onion, finely chopped
⅓ cup finely chopped cilantro

In a small pan of boiling water, add the ancho chiles. When they are soft, about 5–10 minutes, remove them from the water. When they are cool enough to handle, remove the stems, seeds, and veins. Place the cleaned chiles in a blender jar with the garlic, 3 teaspoons salt, onion, juice from the canned pineapple, and enough water to cover the chiles. Blend until very smooth. Pour into a wide pan or dish.

In a hot skillet or grill pan, drizzle 1 tablespoon oil. Heat until it is very hot. Dip the meat slices into the ancho sauce, then carefully place them in the hot pan. Since the meat is very thin, it will cook in about 3–4 minutes on each side (depending on the thickness you have). When the meat is done, remove it to a plate. Scrape the scraps from the pan after each piece of meat is cooked and discard so you don't have any burned sauce on the next piece. Add more oil, 1 tablespoon at a time, as needed, and repeat the cooking process with as much of the meat as you wish to cook.

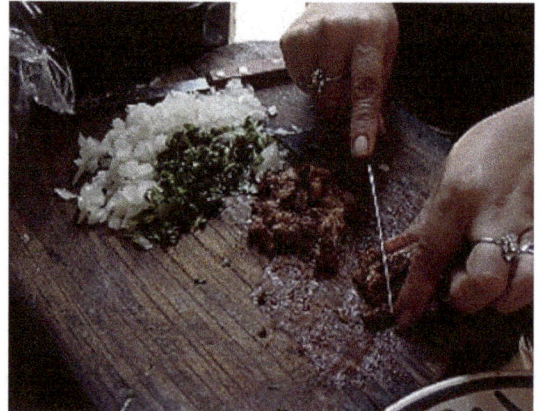

Dip the pineapple slices into the sauce, and sear them on both sides.

Chop the meat into bite-sized pieces and put on a large plate. Chop the pineapple into chunks, and place alongside the meat on the plate. Each person can make his or her own tacos from this serving plate.

Spoon the meat and pineapple into warm tortillas. Eat the tacos with the salsa, below.

For the Salsa:
In a medium-sized pan with boiling water, gently drop in the tomatoes, serranos, and tomatillos. Cook the tomatoes until the skins split, and they are a bit soft but not squishy. They will cook faster than the tomatillos and chiles, so remove them first. Cook the tomatillos and chiles until the tomatillos are a dull green color. Drain and discard the water.

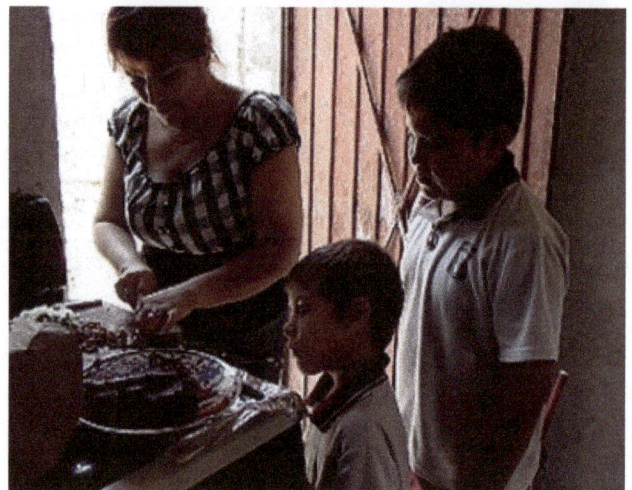

The hardest part for Angel and Marco is waiting

Put the tomatoes, tomatillos, garlic, and salt in a clean blender jar. Add a little fresh water to assist in blending. Less water for thicker salsa, more for a thinner salsa—your preference. Roughly blend. Pour ½ of the blender contents into a bowl. To the remainder of the blender ingredients, add the serranos. If you are not sure about the heat from the chiles, add them one at a time. Roughly blend. Pour these contents into a separate bowl. Sprinkle the chopped cilantro and onion over both bowls. You now have a mild and a hot salsa.

Fish Fillets with Asparagus
Filete de Pescado con Espárragos

Karina Ann Betlem

4 servings

This simple meal is light and interesting with the addition of asparagus. The asparagus is heated separately from the fish, so it retains its own flavor. The fish we used is mahi mahi (dorado), a common and inexpensive fish caught locally. It is much thicker and more dense than snapper or halibut, but it still cooks quickly, which makes this another 15-minute meal!

Ingredients

1 can white or green asparagus
50 grams (3.5 Tablespoons) butter, melted
4 tomatoes, seeds removed, then diced
4 large fish fillets (mahi mahi, snapper, halibut, etc.)
salt
2 Tablespoons all-purpose flour
2 Tablespoons oil
2 limes, one juiced and one sliced
2 Tablespoons parsley, finely minced

Preheat the oven to 175°C/350°F.

Place the asparagus spears side by side, with tips all facing the same direction in a shallow oven-proof baking dish. Lightly drizzle a little bit of the melted butter over the tips to keep them from over-browning. (It does not matter how much of the butter you use. The remainder will be added to the oil to fry the fish). Place the dish in the oven, and allow the asparagus to get very lightly browned.

Squeeze the seeds and juice from the tomatoes; then cut into small dice. Sprinkle them over the lightly browned asparagus, drizzle more butter over the tomatoes, and sprinkle a pinch of salt on them. Place back in the oven to heat the tomatoes. About 5–7 minutes.

Salt and flour the fish fillets on both sides. Heat the remaining butter with the oil in a large frying pan. Carefully place the fish in the hot oil/butter, and cook on both sides until they are golden brown. Squeeze one lime over the cooked side of the fish after you have turned it. Sprinkle the parsley over the lime juice.

Fish cooks very quickly, so you need to determine when the fish is cooked through, depending on the thickness of your fillets.

Arrange the fish on a platter, with the asparagus and tomatoes over and around the fish. Garnish with thin lime slices from the remaining lime.

Smoked Tuna Paté
Paté de Atún Ahumado

8 servings

I hope you can find smoked tuna in your area, because there is no substitute for the moist texture and smoky fish flavor. Juany usually makes this for fiestas or parties. Many fiestas have more than one hundred people attending, so she makes several bowls of this creamy paté to satisfy the hungry crowd before dinner is served. If you plan on a crowd this size, you will need to double or triple the recipe. By the way, no one brings food to these fiestas; it is all prepared by the hostess or host and their family.

Ingredients

2 cups smoked tuna
570 grams (21 ounces) Philadelphia cream cheese, softened
½ large onion
3 Tablespoons mayonnaise
1 pinch ground black pepper

Place all the ingredients in a blender and blend well. Chill in a bowl or mold.

If you use a mold, after chilling it, unmold it onto a plate. Adorn with celery leaves or cilantro. Serve with crackers.

Stuffed Fish
Pescado Relleno

6 servings

The fish we prepared here is mojarra, a type of talapia. It has a fleshy body, and the bones are large, so you don't have to strain the meat through your teeth. The skin is edible, but if that is not what you like, it comes off easily in large pieces. These fish are sold cleaned but with the heads and tails still attached. You don't eat the heads or tails, so if you like, have your fishmonger remove them for you. The fish is steamed so the meat is flaky and juicy, with the added flavors of the stuffing throughout. We used fish weighing 400 grams each (14 ounces). One fish was a perfect portion for each person.

Ingredients

6 small fish (mojarra talapia, red snapper, etc.), cleaned but left whole
(400 grams/14 ounces each, with heads)

1 Tablespoon oil
½ cup onion, finely diced
3 cloves garlic, finely minced
2 tomatoes, chopped
1 fish fillet, raw, chopped (any type you like; we used snapper)
salt and pepper to taste
1 lime, juiced
2 avocados, smooshed

Heat the oil in a pan and sauté the onion, garlic, tomato, and the chopped fish. Season with salt and pepper. Stir well.

Wash the whole fish and open them up. Sprinkle the fish with salt, pepper, and lime juice, inside and outside. Fill them with the sautéed fish and vegetable mix.

Wrap each stuffed fish individually in aluminum foil. Place the wrapped fish in a steamer or large pan fitted with a rack. Steam them for about 30 minutes. Remove each fish from the aluminum and put on individual plates. Cover them with smooshed avocado, salt, and more lime juice.

Serve them with white rice and carrot sautéed in butter.

Octopus Veracruz Style
Pulpos a la Veracruzana

8 servings

Are you ready for a new experience? This may be it. Cleaning and cooking a whole octopus is not something most of us do on a regular basis, but it is not complicated. If you prefer not to clean it yourself, your fishmonger will do it for you.

Always keep the uncooked octopus cold. It spoils very quickly. While you are working with it, keep a bowl of cold or iced water handy.

To clean: Cut the head off just above the eye section. Cut the legs off just below the eye section. Discard the eye section now completely removed from the head and the legs. Carefully slit open the head by inserting your knife into the opening and slicing upward to fully expose the inside. Remove the ink sack and entrails (guts). There will be three hard "spines" (not really spines, but that is a good description) that hold the entrails to the inside of the head. Pull them loose and discard; then rinse it thoroughly, inside and out, under cold running water. Turn the leg section (they are all still connected) inside out, and push in the middle to remove the beak. You will be able to feel the hard beak when you do this. Just pop it out and discard. Rinse. (Note: the head has a skin on it that can be removed before or after cooking.) Juany removes the skin after cooking, but don't forget to remove it; it is quite rubbery.

You can find videos and step-by-step photo instructions to follow on the Internet, if you want more specific hands-on instructions.

Ingredients

1 kilo (2.2 pounds) fresh octopus
3 onions, diced
3 tomatoes, diced
½ cup (or more) tequila
2 Tablespoons oil
salt and pepper to taste
small corn tortillas (*horneadas*)

Rinse the octopus at least 3 times in a bowl of water before you begin to clean the octopus. Either have your fishmonger clean it for you, or use the instructions above to remove the unwanted guts, beak, and ink sack.

Boil a pot of water and slowly add the cleaned octopus. This size octopus cooks in 45 minutes to the tender stage. Start checking at 30 minutes with a small sharp knife. Poke it as you would a baked potato for doneness. If the knife goes in without much resistance, it is done. Remove it from the pot, and place in cold water. This stops the cooking process. When it has cooled sufficiently to handle, cut it into small pieces (yes, including the head).

Heat the oil in a frying pan, and sauté the tomatoes with the onions, smooshing them softly while they cook. When the onions are translucent, add the octopus pieces. Pour in the tequila, add the salt and pepper, and continue to simmer over low heat, only until the octopus is reheated.

LETICIA

Meet Elva Leticia Figeroa Tostado

I had the good fortune to meet Leticia many years ago when she was still a young teenager. For many years she worked in a local beauty shop, doing pedicures for about 100 pesos a day in salary and tips (that is about $9 US). She saved as much money as possible from this meager income so that she and her boyfriend could purchase clothes wholesale to sell at the weekly flea market. With this extra money and help from her boyfriend's family, beauty school became a reality. She has developed into a very competent professional hairdresser. She also became a wife, mother, and exceptional *cocinera* (cook) along the way. That boyfriend, by the way, is now her husband. His family is as proud of Leticia as they would be of their own daughter.

Don't let her pretty smile fool you! She definitely has an impish side, and when we are together, there are always lots of jokes and laughter, often at my expense!

Notice the rock and stick keeping the faucets turned off.

Leticia laughs somewhat sheepishly about how she learned to cook. Growing up, she stayed out of the kitchen, almost running from it, hoping that her mother would not ask her to help. When she was ten years old, however, she decided to make her first meal. Having secretly watched Mom make it and over again, she just knew she could make it herself. She made *Sopa Verde* and, as it happened, it turned out wonderfully. She made this repeatedly with great success.

A couple of years later, Leticia, pumped up and ready to take on the culinary world, decided to venture back into the kitchen. Her second meal was *Marlin en Estofado* (Marlin stew). The recipes had never been written down, so she made the recipe from memory. She had watched her mother make it many times, so off she went into the kitchen to surprise her mom. The whole family still laughs today about the outcome. The flavor was so bad that it had to go in the garbage— there was just no way to save it. Almost nothing goes in the garbage,—certainly not food—so you can draw your own conclusions regarding the meal. Over the next several months, she practiced the recipe, adjusting the ingredients, until finally it was the way she wanted it. She never asked Mom for help. This was *her* recipe. Leticia still loves to watch her mother and grandmother cook, because she always learns something new. Let's give credit where credit is due, shall we? *Thanks, Mom and Grandma.*

White Rice
Arroz Blanco

10 servings

This recipe is a dressed-up version of plain white rice. It is wonderful with chicken, pork chops, ribs—gosh, I can't think of anything it wouldn't be good with. The fresh aroma of poblanos cooking with the rice and bouillon fills the kitchen. It reminds me of homemade chicken and rice soup, with that warm, inviting smell. You will want to make this often, just for that scent!

Even though this dish does have poblano slices in it, there is no spicy heat, only a grassy poblano flavor. Throughout the book you will see what appear to be duplicate recipes. They are not. Each cook has her own version of many of the same titled dishes, but they are all different. Try the different versions, and choose the one (or more) that you prefer. You cannot make a bad decision.

Ingredients

2 Tablespoons oil, vegetable or canola
2 cups long-grain white rice
3 Tablespoons fresh poblano, sliced, no seeds (not necessary to char first)*
3 cloves garlic, peeled but left whole
¼ medium onion, sliced
5 cups water
3 teaspoons powdered chicken bouillon
130 grams (4½ ounces) can whole kernel corn (quantity is drained)**
1 teaspoon salt, or to taste

Heat the oil in large frying pan. When it is hot, add the rice, poblano, garlic, and onion. Cook, stirring constantly, until the rice is golden, not brown. Add the water and bouillon. Stir to combine. Cook uncovered over low heat until almost all the water is absorbed, about 15 minutes. Add the corn, and cover with a lid. Turn off the heat, and let the pan sit covered for 5 minutes. Serve.

* The fresh poblano in this recipe can be used without peeling. If you have some in the freezer already peeled, use them instead.

** You can use frozen corn instead of canned, but add it with the water and bouillon so it will defrost.

Cold Chiles Rellenos with Escabeche
Chiles Rellenos en Frio

10 servings
(one chile per serving)

These are not the typical chiles rellenos (ray-*yay*-nos) with which you might be familiar. They are not breaded, fried, or loaded with cheese. They are peeled, stuffed, and refrigerated. The chiles actually cook during the peeling process. When they are chilled, they are served smothered with a carrot, onion, and oregano mixture called escabeche (es-ca-*bay*-chay). You may have seen this term, "*en escabeche*," on a can of pickled jalapeños—jalapeños with carrots and onions. This is a quick and easy meal that can be made up to a day ahead and kept in the refrigerator. Store the stuffed chiles and escabeche separately in the refrigerator, so the flavors don't blend.

To make 5 servings (5 chiles), just reduce the ingredients by half.

Ingredients

10 poblano chiles
6 carrots, peeled, cut into tiny dice
4 potatoes, peeled, cut into tiny dice
5 cans good-quality tuna, drained (5 to 6 ounces each)—*1 can for 2 chiles
6 Tablespoons mayonnaise
180 ml (¾ cup) mild sour cream
¼ teaspoon ground black pepper
1 teaspoon salt

Prepare the poblano chiles. (See complete instructions for poblano chiles in the "Chile" section). Set the chiles aside to steam in the bowl while you prepare the carrots and potatoes.

In a large saucepan, bring about 2 quarts of salted water to a boil. Add the diced carrots and cook until *almost* tender, about 6 minutes. Remove with a slotted spoon to large bowl. Set aside to cool. Put the diced potatoes in the same boiling water you used for the carrots. Cook the potatoes until just tender, about 4 minutes. Drain and add the cooked potatoes to the carrots. Place them in the refrigerator while you clean the chiles.

Remember the gloves! Under slowly running water or a bowl of water, remove the outer charred skin from the chiles. Make a long slit in the side of the chile, being careful not to cut all the way through to the other side. These will be served open-face. Remove the seeds, but leave the stem attached. Rinse and drain. Set aside while you clean the other chiles the same way.

Prepare the filling: Drain and discard all the liquid from tuna, flake it, and put in the bowl with the carrots and potatoes. Add the mayonnaise, sour cream, salt, and pepper. Stir gently but well.

On a plate or board, stuff the peppers with 2–3 large spoonfuls of the carrot/tuna mixture. Add more to the peppers if you have any filling left over. Cover and chill until cold.

Another note: Instead of tuna, Leticia at times has used shrimp, ground pork, or chicken.

Escabeche
(es-ca-*bay*-chay)

Makes enough to top 10–12 chiles

Although some escabeches contain vinegar, this one contains all the ingredients without the vinegar. The flavors complement the other ingredients perfectly. This also makes a delicious side dish.

Ingredients

2 Tablespoons oil, vegetable or canola
3 large carrots, peeled
2½ white onions, thinly sliced
2 teaspoons Mexican oregano
½ teaspoon salt

Heat the oil in a large frying pan over medium to medium-low heat.

Shred the carrots lengthwise with a potato peeler, so that the shreds are wide and long. Add the carrots and onions to the hot pan. After 2 minutes, add the salt and oregano. Rub the dried oregano between your hands to crush it and release the flavor. Let this mixture cook until the onions are very soft. Remove from the heat. Place the escabeche in a covered dish, and let it chill in the refrigerator until you are ready to serve the chiles.

To serve: Place one chile relleno on a plate, and cover it with the escabeche. Leticia serves this with the Arroz Blanco (white rice)—her recipe on page 124.

Poblano Slices in Cream
Rajas en Crema

8 servings

Rajas means "slices." The chiles and onion are sliced (not chopped) and cooked. I had these for breakfast with the ladies and a couple of their husbands at Gabby's beauty shop one cold morning. We sat outside in our coats and ate them with fresh, warm corn tortillas. It warmed our innards quickly and was a surprisingly good breakfast. Add a hot cup of coffee and enjoy!

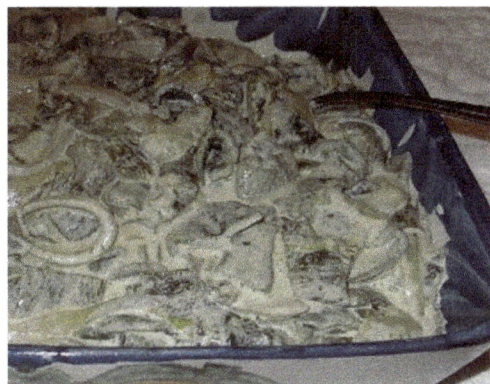

Ingredients

2 kilos (4½ pounds) poblano chiles
3 Tablespoons oil
1 onion, cut in half, then sliced
3 cloves garlic, very finely chopped
335 ml (11 ounces) media crema (table cream)
1 teaspoon salt, or to taste

Char the chiles. Remove the peel, seeds, and veins. (See complete instructions in the "Chile" section for poblano chiles.) Slice the chiles into 6 mm / ¼ inch-wide slices. The direction of the slices does not matter. You can slice them lengthwise or crosswise.

In a very large frying pan, heat the oil, sauté the onion until translucent, and then add the garlic. Cook for 1 minute. Add the poblano slices, media crema, and salt. Stir while it heats through.

Serve over white rice for a main dish. For breakfast, wrap the rajas in a warm tortilla.

Note: The creamy rajas are a wonderful base for adding shredded or chopped cooked chicken. Then serve over rice.

Pasta Cooked in Green Sauce
Sopa Verde
Literally: Green Soup

4 servings

Sopa Verde is the recipe that started Leticia on her journey of culinary experiments. This delicious green pasta is easy to make and delightful to eat. The green color comes from the poblano chiles. Remember that poblanos do not add much heat, just flavor and color. The addition of sour cream to the sauce adds a wee bit of tartness, while the cheese rounds out the flavor. In less than 15 minutes (you do have to cook the macaroni), you will have a delicious and filling meal. I serve it to guests, and they are always impressed by the amount of time they think I must have spent in the kitchen.

Ingredients

1 liter (4 cups) water
½ Tablespoon oil
1 cube chicken bouillon
1 teaspoon onion, finely chopped
200 grams (7 ounces) small elbow macaroni
3 poblano chiles
1 cup mild sour cream
2 Tablespoons butter
200 grams (7 ounces) Chihuahua cheese, grated
salt to taste, if necessary

Boil the water with the oil, bouillon, and onion. When the onion is cooked, add the macaroni. When the pasta is cooked, drain, discarding the water. Set aside.

Char the chiles. Place them in a covered bowl and let steam for 10 minutes. Slip the skins off under slowly running water. Remove the stem, seeds, and veins. For more detailed instructions, see the "Chile" section. Purée the chiles in a blender with the sour cream.

Melt the butter in a large pan. Pour in the puréed chiles, and heat to a low boil. Add the macaroni and stir well to coat with the sauce. Sprinkle the grated cheese over the top, and allow it to melt on top of the pasta.

Cream of Mushroom Soup
Crema de Champiñones

4 servings

This soup is loaded with mushrooms. It is by far the best mushroom soup I have ever made or eaten. It is so quick—it takes longer to slice the mushrooms than to actually make the soup. (Good-bye, canned mushroom soup!)

The first time I made it, my husband and I ate the whole pan at one sitting. I must confess: the second time I made it, we did the same thing—it is *so* delicious.

If you have unexpected guests and have the mushrooms in the fridge, invite them to stay for a hearty meal. This is great for a soup course and also as a main course with a salad and crusty bread.

Ingredients

300 grams (10½ ounces) mushrooms
4 Tablespoons butter, divided usage
1 onion, finely diced
4 Tablespoons flour, all purpose
3 cups hot chicken broth

½ cup mild sour cream
ground white pepper, to taste
salt, to taste

Clean and cut the mushrooms into thin slices. (Leticia slices by hand; I use my food processor's thick-slice disk for this.)

Over low heat, melt 2 tablespoons of the butter in a large pan. Sauté the onion for 5 minutes—do not allow it to brown. Add the sliced mushrooms to the onions, and cook until no white remains on the mushrooms.

In another pan, melt the remaining 2 tablespoons butter. Add the flour, whisking and cooking until it is golden in color. Continue to whisk rapidly as you slowly pour the hot chicken broth into the butter/flour mixture (this prevents lumps—the same process you use to make gravy). Cook for 1 minute.

Season with salt and pepper. Stir the "gravy" into the cooked mushrooms; then add the sour cream. Heat thoroughly, approximately 2 minutes. Serve.

Pineapple Gelatin
Gelatina de Piña

Makes about 16 servings

Even if you are not a gelatin aficionado, you will enjoy this dessert. Pineapple makes it very refreshing, while the media crema makes it creamy, and the large quantity of nuts makes it very crunchy. There will be a flavor explosion in your mouth. The pretty yellow color is inviting and makes a perfect summer dessert.

You can substitute any other type of crunchy *unsalted* nuts for the pecans and almonds, or use a combination of your favorites.

Ingredients

1 liter (34 ounces) pineapple juice
2 large (6-ounce size) boxes pineapple gelatin
1 small (3-ounce size) box pineapple gelatin
450 ml (15 ounces—2 cans) media crema (table cream)
1 large can (800 grams/28 ounces) chunk pineapple in juice (or syrup)
300 grams (10½ ounces) chopped walnuts or pecans
300 grams (10½ ounces) chopped almonds

Drain the pineapple, and use that juice plus more canned pineapple juice to make 1 liter.

Heat the juice so it is very hot, without actually boiling. Stir in the gelatins and allow to dissolve completely. Place this gelatin mixture in a large bowl in the refrigerator until it is medium set.

Add the media crema, pineapple chunks, nuts, and almonds to the medium-set gelatin. Stir *gently* to mix. Pour into a 9 x 13 pan. Return to the refrigerator until it is completely set.

Note: Make sure you *do not* add fresh pineapple, because the gelatin will not set.

Lime Dessert
Pastel de Limón

6–8 servings

The refreshing taste of lime is evident in every bite!

This is a perfect dessert for the kids to make—no cooking or baking, only assembly. The cookies keep their shape, absorbing the sweet, lime-flavored milky pudding. (Dibs on the spatula!)

Leticia and her mom, Elva, use this same recipe. I wonder who invented it?

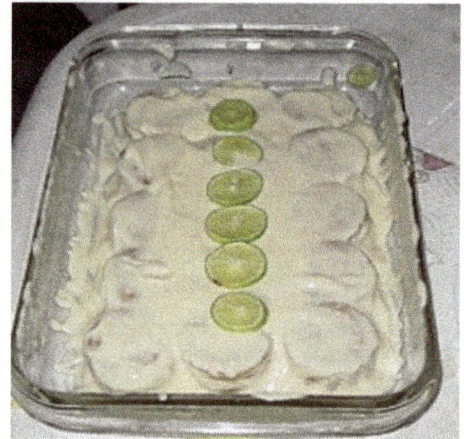

Ingredients

2 packs Maria's Cookies* (170 grams each/6 ounces each)
7 limes, juiced
1 can evaporated milk (378 g/12 ounces)
1 can sweetened condensed milk (397 g/14 ounces)

Place a layer of cookies in a 9 x 13 baking dish. Mix the lime juice, evaporated milk, and sweetened condensed milk in a blender. The milks will increase in volume and get thicker.

Use a tablespoon to spread about 2–3 spoonfuls of mixture over the cookies, making sure each cookie is covered. Place another layer of cookies on top of the original layer to make a stack. Repeat with the milk mixture and layers of cookies, until you are out of cookies. (If you have any extra cookies, you should eat them at this point.) Pour the remaining mixture over the top layer. Smooth it out over the cookies and down all sides of the stacks. Cover and refrigerate for at least 1 hour. Serve on plates or in bowls.

Note: This dessert already has a wonderful fresh-lime flavor, but a few berries on the plate would be a nice complement and dress it up.

* Maria's are a flat vanilla-flavored cookie and can be easily stacked. They should be available in the Mexican section of your grocery store. Look for the bright orange wrapper. If you cannot find Maria's cookies, you can use any other vanilla-flavored flat cookie.

Pulled Pork
Cochinita Pibil

8 servings

Cochinita Pibil is a very famous Mexican dish from the Yucatan. Traditionally, the pork is wrapped in banana leaves and cooked in a pit. Leticia's recipe is not the classic preparation but a more simplified version, because she doesn't have a yard in which to dig a pit! Again, almost every cook in Mexico has her/his own version. The most common similarity is the addition of achiote paste as a main ingredient, mostly for its color. See the "Ingredients" section of this book for more information on achiote paste.

Ingredients

½ cup orange juice
½ box achiote paste (1 box is 100–110 grams)
1 clove garlic
4 whole peppercorns
1 purple onion
5 Tablespoons apple cider vinegar
1 kilo (2.2 pounds) pork leg or shoulder, without bone
salt to taste

Liquefy the orange juice, achiote, garlic, peppercorns, ¼ of the onion, and the vinegar. Pour this mixture into a large pan with the pork. Cook the meat on low heat until it can be shredded, approximately 2–2½ hours. Shred the meat and put it in a bowl. The sauce will have thickened and will coat the meat. Top with slices of purple onion.

Serve with refried beans and fresh warm tortillas.

This is great on hamburger rolls too. I once made this for Leticia and added a little brown sugar to make it more like a barbecue sauce. She occasionally makes it that way now too. Of course, she tells everyone she thought it up—the rascal!

Beef with Potatoes
Carne con Papas

6 servings

This is actually a type of hash but with a lovely, light broth. Serve over a baked potato, mashed potatoes, or rice. It is also a great dish for breakfast, served with eggs. By itself, it can be loaded into a tortilla, and you'll have a fast lunch. The recipe is easily increased for a crowd.

Note: Cooking the brisket in a pressure cooker assures that you will have a rich-tasting broth because it does not need much water to cook. If you are "pressure cooker challenged," cook it in a crockpot or tightly covered on the stove top.

Ingredients

500 grams (1 pound) beef brisket
2 cloves garlic, divided usage
1 teaspoon salt
2 cups beef broth
4 roma tomatoes
¾ teaspoon ground cumin
1 Tablespoon oil
1 medium potato, peeled and cut into very small dice
ground black pepper to taste

Cook the beef in a pressure cooker with about 2.5 cm/1 inch of water, 1 clove of garlic, and salt for 30 minutes. Alternatively, it can be cooked in a crockpot (follow manufacturer's instructions) or on the stove top in a pot with the same 2.5 cm/1 inch of water, garlic, and salt for 2 hours. Check the water level after 1 hour. Add more if necessary. If the meat does not shred easily, cook it longer, checking after 15 minutes for tenderness. Remove the meat from the liquid and shred.

Pour the broth from the pressure cooker or pan into a measuring cup, and add more beef broth to make 2 cups.

Boil some water in a small pot. Drop in the tomatoes, and cook until the skins split, about 3 minutes. Drain the tomatoes with a slotted spoon, discarding the tomato cooking water. Put the tomatoes in a blender with the beef broth, 1 garlic clove, and cumin. Blend until very smooth.

Heat the oil in a frying pan. Fry the shredded beef slowly until the oil is absorbed; then slowly add the tomato/broth mixture and the potatoes. Continue to cook on low to medium-low heat, uncovered, for 10–15 minutes, until the potatoes are tender. Season with pepper, and adjust the salt if necessary.

Breaded and Stuffed Fish Fillet
Filete de Pescado Empanizado y Relleno

4 servings

Leticia loves to stuff things, and she is an expert at it. Mahi mahi (dorado) fillets are stuffed with thin slices of cheese and then breaded and fried. The Chihuahua cheese is a perfect choice for the stronger flavor of this fish. If you have never eaten mahi mahi, run to your local fish market and get some today. In restaurants, this fish is quite expensive, but cooked at home, it is easily affordable. After you have tried stuffed mahi mahi, experiment with other varieties of fish. This recipe might become one of your favorites.

Ingredients
4 thick fish fillets, such as mahi mahi, with a slit in the side for filling
½ Tablespoon powdered chicken bouillon
4 slices Chihuahua cheese, thinly sliced
¼ cup flour
1 egg, slightly beaten
1½ cups bread crumbs
oil, as necessary to reach halfway up the fish fillets

Rub the powdered chicken bouillon on the outsides of the fish. Open the fish, and put one piece of cheese in each cavity. Dredge the fish with flour. Put the fish in the egg; then roll it in the bread crumbs.

Heat the oil in a large frying pan. When the oil is hot, carefully place the fish in the oil and cook on both sides. They will be golden brown and the cheese will be melted. Remember that fish cooks more quickly than beef or chicken. Remove the fish to a paper towel, and serve with white rice and a green salad.

Stuffed Chicken Breasts
Pechuga Rellena
(pay-*chew*-ga ray-*yay*-na)

4 servings

What a rascal Leticia is! When I asked where this recipe came from, she left the room! When she returned, she pretended not to have heard me. I finally found out that it was from her aunt Lorena and her grandmother. So again, thanks go to the women in Leticia's family for sharing their recipes with her.

The term *rellena* or *relleno*, such as Chile Relleno, only means "stuffed." In this case, stuffed chicken breasts.

This particular stuffed chicken has become a regular in our house—easy to prepare, quick cooking, and very filling. The aroma of the melting cheese with the ham, and the corn flake crumbs toasting to a perfect crispness in the hot oil—it makes my mouth water just thinking about it!

Ingredients

4 chicken breasts, boneless, skinless
salt and pepper to taste
corn oil, 13 mm / ½ in. depth in pan
2 eggs
½ to ¾ cup evaporated milk
½ cup all-purpose flour
2 cups corn flake crumbs
4 slices ham
4 slices American cheese

Pound the chicken breasts to 6 mm / ¼ inch thick—the thinner the better—without breaking the meat. If you can buy *milanesa*-style chicken, it will already be pounded for you and will save a ton of time. Rub both sides of the chicken liberally with salt and pepper.

In a large frying pan, begin heating the corn oil to **very hot** but not smoking.

Whisk the eggs and evaporated milk together in a large, flat bowl.

Put the flour on a separate plate. Pour the corn flake crumbs onto another plate.

You will make these in a small assembly-line fashion, so line them up in this order: flour plate, egg bowl, crumb plate.

Lay out each chicken breast flat on a board or plate. In the middle of each breast, place one slice of ham and one slice of cheese. Fold over the sides and ends of the chicken to make a pouch.

Lightly dredge each chicken "pouch" with flour. Dip in the egg/milk mixture; drain the excess back into the bowl. Immediately place the pouch on the corn flake crumbs, and cover completely, pressing the crumbs into the chicken. Set the completed chicken pouch aside on another plate or board while you prepare the other breasts.

Place the coated pouches into the hot oil, and fry on each side until golden brown. This only takes about 5 minutes on each side because the chicken is so thin. If your chicken is a bit thicker, you will need to cook it a minute or two longer. Remove the cooked breasts from the oil, and place on layers of paper towels to absorb the excess oil.

Serve with cooked vegetables, mashed potatoes, and a green salad.

Chicken with Vegetables
Pollo a la Verduras

4 servings

This meal takes less than 30 minutes to prepare! Definitely Mexican comfort food.

Ingredients

2 whole chicken breasts, skinless and boneless
salt and pepper, to taste
3 Tablespoons butter
4 tomatoes
½ onion
1 clove garlic
3 cups chicken broth
2 potatoes, cut into 13 mm / ½ inch cubes
4 carrots, 6 mm / ¼ inch sticks, about 5 cm/2 inches long

Season the chicken breasts with salt and pepper. Melt the butter in a large frying pan. Brown the chicken in the butter for 3 minutes.

Cook the tomatoes in boiling water until the skins split. With a slotted spoon, remove them from the water and place in a blender, along with the garlic and onion. Discard the water. Use some of the chicken broth to thin the tomatoes so that they will purée completely. Add this mixture, plus the remaining broth, to the chicken.

Carefully position the potatoes and carrots in the liquid around the chicken. Cook until the vegetables are tender and the chicken is cooked through. This should be about 10–15 minutes.

To serve, cut each breast into 3 or 4 pieces. Plate with the potatoes and carrots, drizzling a bit of broth over the top. Serve warm flour tortillas to sop up that wonderful broth.

Marlin Stew
Marlin Estofado

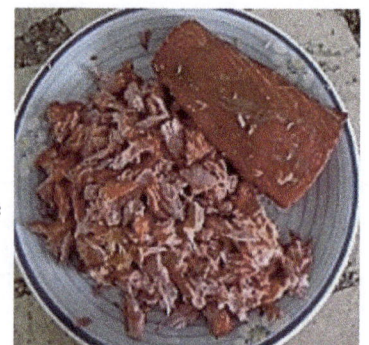

4–6 servings

The flavor of this stew is rich and meaty. I expected a fishy taste, but by using the smoked fish, that issue is eliminated. The marlin, which is really tuna (see the section "Is it Smoked Marlin or Smoked Tuna?"), is smoky and moist. If you do not have smoked tuna available in your area, choose a moist smoked salmon as your substitute. The smoked salmon is not a perfect substitute, but please use it instead of flipping past this recipe. It is well worth the effort!

Ingredients

8 large roma tomatoes
¼ medium onion
4 cloves garlic, crushed (divided usage)
4 Tablespoons oil, vegetable or canola
500 grams (1 pound) smoked tuna, broken into bits
2 bay leaves
500 grams (1 pound) carrots, peeled and diced
250 grams (9 ounces) Mexican squash, diced
250 grams (9 ounces) fresh green beans, cut into small pieces
1 cube shrimp bouillon
1½ cups Clamato juice
1 teaspoon salt, or to taste
12 fresh medium-sized shrimp, cleaned and deveined
100 grams (½ cup) cilantro, including stems
Lime juice to taste

Boil the tomatoes in hot water, about 3 minutes, until the skins burst. Drain and put them in a blender with the onion and 1 clove of garlic. Purée until smooth. Set aside.

Pour the oil into a large pan over medium-low heat. When the oil is hot, add the broken pieces of tuna, the remaining 3 garlic cloves, and bay leaves. Stir until the tuna is hot. If it begins to stick to the pan, add one more tablespoon of oil. Add the carrots, squash, green beans, tomato mixture, bouillon cube, Clamato, and salt. Cook uncovered on low heat until the vegetables are almost tender, about 15 minutes. Stir in the shrimp and cilantro. Continue to cook until the vegetables are cooked through but not mushy.

Serve in bowls with a squeeze of fresh lime juice on top. Usually half a lime per bowl is a good ratio. Have plenty of warm tortillas to sop up the broth.

Note: Mexican squash is similar to zucchini but not as fragile when cooked. The flavor is almost the same.

Shrimp Ceviche with Chiles
Camarónes en Aguachile

6 servings

Ceviche is a seafood dish—shrimp, in this case—marinated in fresh lime juice. It is not cooked with heat but "chemically cooked" with the acid from the limes. It is not the same as sushi, which many times is raw. Ceviche is *not* raw. The most common addition to shrimp ceviche is cucumber, which complements the flavor very nicely. Whether in a restaurant or at home, every cook in Mazatlán thinks her/his recipe is the best.

Ingredients

1 kilo (2.2 pounds) raw, medium-sized shrimp, cleaned and deveined
3 large cucumbers, seeds removed and sliced
½ medium onion, thinly sliced
ground black pepper, to taste

salt to taste

6 serrano chiles

1 clove garlic, peeled

500 grams (1 pound) fresh key limes (approximately 20 limes)

The shrimp can be previously frozen but *not* cooked. While you are cleaning and deveining the shrimp, cut almost all the way through the body so that they lay flat on a plate, butterfly-style. There are enough shrimp and cucumbers to fill 3 dinner/serving plates. Keep the shrimp in ice water while you clean them.

Place the cleaned shrimp on a cold plate and arrange the cucumbers in between each shrimp, first around the outside of the plate and then a second circle inside and overlapping each shrimp a bit. Cover with the onion slices, reserving one slice for the chile salsa. Sprinkle liberally with ground black pepper. Add salt to taste, if preferred.

Purée the whole chiles, one onion slice, and the garlic clove in a blender. A small amount of water can be added to make it blend more easily, but the salsa should be thick. Drizzle this salsa over the shrimp and refrigerate. This can be done up to an hour prior to serving. If you will not be serving this dish within an hour, store the salsa separately in the refrigerator. Pour over the shrimp closer to serving time.

At least 20–30 minutes *before* serving, juice the limes directly over the shrimp, so that all the of shrimp have been *bathed* by the lime juice. This will be the "cooking" process, or "lime time." Let them sit in the refrigerator for 20–30 minutes until you are ready to eat.

Serve with corn tortilla chips.

Note: Medium-sized shrimp work beautifully, but if you cannot find them, go smaller, not larger. Larger shrimp do not work well in this recipe.

Serrano chiles are very spicy, especially with the seeds. For milder salsa, remove the seeds and veins of the serranos before puréeing.

For an hors d'oeuvre, cut the medium-sized shrimp into 2 pieces and the cucumbers into smaller pieces as well. The "lime time" will remain the same.

Leticia knows that non-Mexicans are always in a hurry and usually want to eat immediately. Her suggestion is to relax and enjoy your friends and family while this marinates. If you just cannot do that, and you plan on eating immediately after preparing, she recommends placing the cleaned shrimp in a bowl and pouring the lime juice directly onto the shrimp. Refrigerate the shrimp while you prepare the cucumbers and salsa. After the shrimp has marinated for 20 minutes, remove them from the lime juice and arrange on the plates, as described above. You can use some of the lime juice to sprinkle over the cucumbers and onions.

Shrimp Paté

Paté de Camarón

6 servings

Cool and refreshing is how I would describe this paté. I can barely stop eating this creamy shrimp. It can be used on crackers or to stuff celery or cherry tomatoes. With only a little imagination, you will find numerous other healthy ways to eat this—other than by the spoonful!

Ingredients

2 cups beef broth, chilled
2 envelopes unflavored gelatin
1 kilo (2.2 pounds) cooked shrimp, cleaned and deveined
225 grams (8 ounces) cream cheese, room temperature
canned chipotle chiles, to taste**
1 pinch salt

Pour ¼ cup of the cold broth into a small bowl, and sprinkle the gelatin over top to hydrate. Wait 5 minutes; then heat it for 20 seconds in a microwave or on the stove top until it is very warm but not hot. Add this plus all the other ingredients to a blender, and purée. Refrigerate until it is ready to use.

Serve with assorted crackers or sliced baguette.

*Note: **Chipotles are very hot and spicy, so start with a small amount, about ½ teaspoon for mild, more for hotter. Please do not omit them from the recipe; just be cautious if chipotles are new to you. The smoky flavor of chipotles is a natural complement to the shrimp.*

MARIA (GRISELDA)

Meet Maria de Los Angeles Soto

Maria was born and raised in Durango, Mexico, where her eighty-five-year-old mother still lives. As long as Maria can remember, her mother has called her Griselda. She has no idea why she has the nickname, but her mom still calls her that today. All of her friends call her "Gris" for short. Imagine my confusion when I got a stack of recipes from Maria de Los Angeles Soto. Perhaps the early nickname came because Mom needed something more unique than "Maria" to remember her by, especially considering that Gris is one of eleven siblings. We will never know for sure.

Her mom worked as a seamstress to help support the family, which meant that she did not have time for regular household chores. Fortunately, Gris's aunts also lived with them and tended to the children and housekeeping duties. When Gris was about seven years old, she discovered the kitchen. Gris would come into the kitchen and plop herself down on a chair to watch and ask questions of the aunts as they cooked. Seeing her interest and willingness to help them, the aunts gave her small duties in the kitchen. As she mastered these small duties, the aunts would add greater responsibilities. By the time she was twelve years old, Gris was cooking the entire family meals by herself.

In 1982, Gris moved to Mazatlán to seek employment as a maid in the resort hotels. Being a single mother of five children has not been an easy task for Gris. But she made sure all of her children got an education so that they could have a better life. She still has children at home and is also raising one young grandson. Gris still finds the time to travel by bus to Durango every two or three weeks to check in on her mother, who is almost blind and lives by herself. Gris would love for her mom to move to Mazatlán, so she could care for her, but Mom is stubborn and won't leave Durango.

By the way, Gris also finds time to manage all the women volunteers at the local church in Colonia Pancho Villa. She says her life would not be as full without her volunteer work.

What a beautiful heart she has. I am honored to know her.

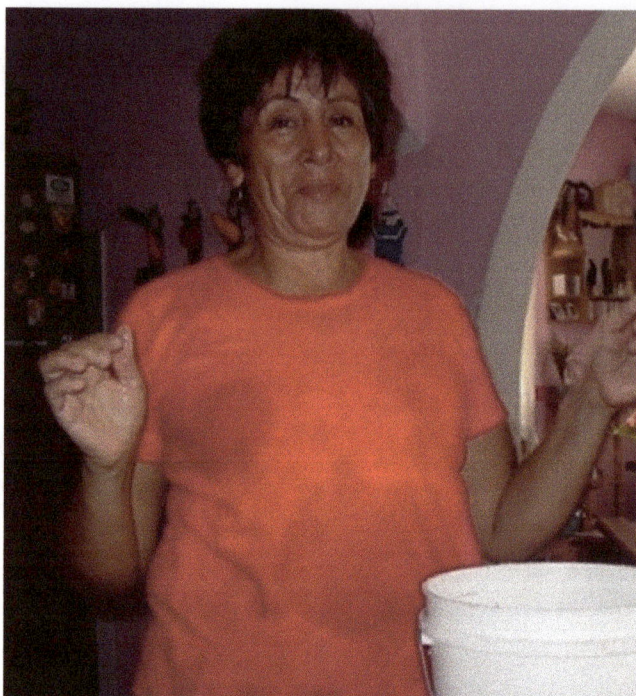

Karina Ann Betlem

Hibiscus Flower Water
Agua de Flor de Jamaica

2 liters/2 quarts

Jamaica (ha-*my*-ka) is a tart herbal drink made from red hibiscus flowers. It is a favorite in Mazatlán and is in the category of *aguas frescas*—fresh waters. Although carbonated drinks are popular, jamaica is often the drink of choice. The flavor is similar to cranberry juice. For Mexican Independence Day, this red drink is a must for the traditional Mexican fiesta!

Jamaica flowers are available all over the world in health food stores or in the Mexican section of your grocery store.

Ingredients

1 cup loose-pack jamaica (hibiscus) flowers
1 cup granulated sugar
2 liters/2 quarts water
ice

Make a simple syrup by heating 1 cup water until it is very warm but not hot. Add the sugar to the warm water; then stir to dissolve the sugar. Set aside to cool.

Put the dried jamaica flowers in a strainer with small holes. Rinse the flowers under cool water to remove any dust. (The flowers are not cleaned before packaging, but the only thing you need to remove is dust.)

Place the rinsed flowers in a pan with 1 liter/1 quart of water. Bring the water to a slow boil, cover the pan, and allow it to slowly simmer for 10 minutes. Strain the jamaica water into a pitcher; add the simple syrup and enough water to make 2 liters/2 quarts. Stir, and add ice. Discard the used flowers.

Sweet Griselda
(Frozen Pineapple Layered Dessert)
Dulce Griselda

6–8 Servings

This is one of Griselda's inventions, so she named it after herself. Sweet Griselda is another dessert recipe that is quick and easy to prepare. Pineapple-infused milks make up the ice cream layers, while chopped pineapple lingers between each cookie for a frozen fruit crunch. The vanilla-flavored cookies add just a hint of cake-like texture once the milky solution is absorbed. I have just one last word for this sweet treat: *yum!*

Ingredients

1 can evaporated milk
1 can sweetened condensed milk

2 cups pineapple, fresh or canned, chopped into large chunks
2 packages Maria's Cookies (170 grams each/6 ounces each)
1 cup pineapple, fresh or canned, finely chopped

Liquefy both milks and the large chunks of pineapple in a blender. Place a layer of cookies in a 9 x 13 baking dish. Pour some of the milk mixture over the top of the cookie layer, and then sprinkle on a bit of the finely chopped pineapple. Place another layer of cookies on top of the original layer to make a stack. Repeat with the milk mixture and layers of cookies until you are out of cookies. Finish with the milk mixture. You should have 5 layers of cookies, but if you have extra cookies, just eat them. Freeze for 4 hours. Serve one or two stacks as a serving.

Mosaic Gelatin
Gelatina de Mosaico

10 servings

This is a classic, very festive Mexican gelatin dessert. It takes time to make, but the vibrant colors and flavors make it all worthwhile. In this dessert, you have 3 different fruit flavors accentuated by a creamy gelatin that is mixed throughout, holding the mosaic together. Use any 3 different colored gelatins that you like. In our area of Mexico, we cannot always get the exact flavors of gelatins we want, so the *mosaicos* are quite often a different flavor each time it is prepared. The ingredients call for 3 specific flavors, but Gris made the one in the photo with grape, orange, and pineapple flavors. The flavor selection is just a guideline, not a rule.

Also note that if you want to make a smaller batch, use 85 gram/3 ounce boxes of gelatin, and reduce the water. For instance, the instructions on the 6-ounce boxes specifies 2 cups boiling water and **2 cups cold water**. We have used 2 cups boiling water and **1 cup cold water**. Use the same ratio when reducing the size boxes of gelatin by using the specified amount of boiling water and reducing by half the cold water in this recipe. Do not follow the box instructions. The resulting gelatin sets up quite firm, sort of like "jigglers." Keep all the other ingredients the same.

Ingredients

1 large box (170 grams/6 ounces) strawberry gelatin
1 large box (170 grams/6 ounces) lime gelatin
1 large box (170 grams/6 ounces) pineapple gelatin
12 cups water
3 packets unflavored gelatin
1 can evaporated milk
1 can sweetened condensed milk

Empty each flavor gelatin into a separate bowl, keeping each flavor separate. Pour 2 cups of hot water into each bowl. Stir until dissolved. Add 1 cup cold water to each bowl. Pour into square or rectangular bowls, and refrigerate for at least 6 hours or overnight. (Mine set up faster, so I only had to wait 2 hours.)

Sprinkle the unflavored gelatin over the top of 1 cup cold water. Allow it to sit and hydrate for about 5 minutes. Meanwhile, heat the last 2 cups of water until very hot. Pour the hot water into the hydrated gelatin and stir. Mix in the milks, and chill in the refrigerator until the flavored gelatins are completely set, and you are ready to assemble. Do not allow this milky gelatin to set up. It needs to be pourable. If it starts to set up, remove it from the refrigerator and allow it to "un-set" on the counter.

You can use a large mold or trifle dish for this. Cut each flavor gelatin into 2.5 cm /1 inch squares. Place one handful of each flavor in the mold or dish and continue alternating colors until they have all been placed in the dish. The purpose is to make it very colorful, so make sure you separate the colors. Pour the milk mixture over the gelatin squares. Refrigerate until completely set. Serve by slicing, so that all your guests can see the mosaic effect.

Beef with Coke
Carne a la Coca

10 servings

This beef stew seems to have all the flavors you can imagine, from the sweet Coca-Cola to the salty olives, surrounded by an herb and chile sauce with a hint of vinegar. These ingredients are simple and inexpensive, yet when they are put together, they create a finely blended aromatic stew that compares to no other I have ever tasted. You will definitely need to make this recipe so you can taste that difference for yourself. Note: Do not be hesitant about using 6 chiles. Guajillos only add flavor and color, not heat.

Ingredients

1 kilo (2.2 pounds) beef, sirloin or other tender cut of beef
ground black pepper to taste
3 teaspoons chicken bouillon
4 large carrots, peeled, cut into chunks
4 large potatoes, peeled, each cut into 8 pieces
100 grams (3.5 ounces) green olives, pitted
6 guajillo chiles, stems, seeds, and veins removed
1 clove garlic
1 pinch oregano
1 pinch ground cumin
2 Tablespoons cider vinegar
1 liter (34 ounces) Coca-Cola

Cut the meat into bite-sized pieces, and place them in a large pot. Sprinkle with pepper and the bouillon. On top of the meat, add the carrots, potatoes, and olives.

Prepare the chiles: after removing the stem, seeds, and veins, place the chiles in a small pot of boiling water for 3 minutes. Drain and discard the water. Place the chiles in the blender with the garlic, oregano, cumin, and vinegar. Liquefy using a small bit of the Coke to help it blend. Pour over the meat and vegetables, and add the remainder of the Coke to the pot. Allow to simmer on medium heat for 1 hour.

Meat with Nopales
Carne con Nopales

The mild guajillos make a great broth for this nopales dish. Remember that guajillos are dried and have almost no spicy heat. The nopales are the main ingredient and ground beef has been added to make it more of a complete meal. I hope you live in an area where you can either pick or buy fresh nopale paddles. As with any food, fresh is always better than canned.

Ingredients

500 grams (1 pound) nopale paddles, diced
1 onion (divided usage)
500 grams (1 pound) ground beef
5 guajillo chiles, stems and seeds removed
1 clove garlic
1 cube chicken bouillon
pinch of Mexican oregano

Cook the nopales and ½ onion (keep the onion half as a whole piece) together in boiling water until the nopales are tender. Scoop out the onion and discard. Drain the nopales, discard the cooking water, and then put the nopales back in the same pan.

Put the guajillos in a small pot of water, and simmer them for 5 minutes until they are rehydrated and soft. Remove them from the hot water and place them in a blender with ¼ onion, the garlic, bouillon cube, oregano and 1½ cups of the chile cooking water. Liquefy the ingredients. Set aside.

Add the ground beef and the remaining ¼ onion, chopped, to the nopales, and cook until the meat is browned. Pour in the chile mixture, and simmer for 10 minutes. Serve on rimmed plates with refried beans and fresh tortillas.

Meat in Its Own Juice
Carne en su Jugo

10 servings

Beef is a treat for families in the colonia, because it is more expensive than other types of meat or fish. When beef is cooked, it is always something special to savor. This dish is no exception. The addition of so much bacon gives the *jugo* (juice) a rich, smoky, salty flavor. The serrano chiles only enhance the flavor and surprisingly do not add much heat. You can serve this over rice if you prefer, but Gris serves this in bowls with a side of refried beans and tortillas.

Ingredients

1 teaspoon oil
1 kilo (2.2 pounds) beef steak, flank or sirloin, cut into cubes
250 grams (½ pound) bacon, diced
1 onion, finely diced
5 serrano chiles, seeds removed, if you want
2 Tablespoons powdered beef bouillon

2 cups water
1 bunch cilantro, leaves only, finely chopped
1 bunch large green onions with green stems attached

Heat the oil in a large frying pan to very hot. Put the chopped meat into the pan to sear. When it is browned, remove it to a bowl.

In the same pan, fry the bacon until it is almost crisp; then add the onion and sauté with the bacon. Reduce the heat to low, and add the seared beef back into the pan.

Purée the chiles with the bouillon and water; then add to the meat mixture. Cook for 15 minutes on very low heat.

Meanwhile, char the green onions in a cast-iron skillet or grill pan. .

When the beef is finished, add the chopped cilantro, stir, and serve in bowls. Serve the green onions alongside the meat in the bowl

Spaghetti Bolognese
Espagueti a la Boloñesa

8 servings

The photo shows the sauce in the pan, rather than mixed with the pasta. The addition of squash makes a more interesting sauce. Mexican squash is firm when cooked, not mushy like zucchini. Although it looks a bit like zucchini, that is where the similarity ends. If you have access to a Mexican produce market or section of your grocery store, you may be fortunate enough to get one. To identify what it looks like, check the "Ingredients" section of this book.

Ingredients

400 grams (14 ounces) uncooked spaghetti
3 Tablespoons oil
1 white onion, finely chopped
¼ kilo (½ pound) ground beef
2 boxes tomato purée (210 grams each/7.4 ounces each)
1 carrot, finely chopped
1 squash, 15 cm/6 in. long
1 clove garlic, finely minced
2 bay leaves
½ teaspoon salt, or to taste
1 small can (184 grams/6.5 ounces) mushrooms, drained
¼ cup Chihuahua cheese, grated

Cook the spaghetti in an ample amount of salted water, per package instructions.

In a large frying pan, heat the oil. Sauté the onion and the meat together. Add the tomato purée, carrot, squash, garlic, bay leaves, and salt. Continue to cook until the carrots and squash are almost tender, about 10 minutes. Stirring occasionally.

Drain the spaghetti, and add to the meat mixture, along with the mushrooms. Stir gently. Sprinkle with the grated Chihuahua cheese. Cover the pan and heat on slow for 5 minutes.

Serve with flour tortillas or crusty bread.

Spanish-Style Fish
Pescado a la Vizcaina

10 servings

This is a traditional Mexican dish for *Semana Santa* (Holy Week, the week before Easter), with the green, red, and white colors of the Mexican flag. The mild flavor of sole and the tart saltiness of the olives bring this dish alive. It takes only 10–15 minutes to cook—it takes longer to slice the carrot and bell pepper!

Ingredients
1 kilo (2.2 pounds) fillet of sole
salt, pepper, and garlic powder to taste
1 carrot, peeled
1 red bell pepper
1 jalapeño chile
1 white onion, thinly sliced
1 jar green olives, pitted, sliced (240 g/8.5 ounces)
1 cup red wine
1 box tomato purée (210 g/7.4 ounces)

Season the sole with salt, pepper, and a pinch of garlic powder—only a pinch, as the sole is very delicate. You don't want to overpower it with garlic.

Slice the carrot, red bell pepper, jalapeño chile, and olives into thin matchsticks.

In a large frying pan with a lid, place the fish and then the carrot, red bell pepper, jalapeño, onion, and olive slices. Drizzle in the red wine. Cover and cook over low heat for 10–15 minutes. When done, add the tomato purée to the liquid, and let it heat slightly.

Serve with white rice.

Tuna Salad Stuffed Chiles
Ensalada de Atún en Chiles

6 servings

This is by far the best and most unique version of tuna salad I have ever eaten. The poblanos are crisp, and the filling creamy—a nice texture combination. Served cold, the chiles are a nice break from a hot relleno or a boring sandwich. If you purchase large chiles, serve one per person. When removing the charred skin on the poblanos, be careful not to split them up the sides. If you accidentally do split them, use a new chile that has not been split, and use the split one for rajas or another open-face type relleno. See the section on "Chile" in this book for complete instructions on charring and peeling the poblanos.

Ingredients

6 poblano chiles
2 Tablespoons oil
4 Tablespoons apple cider vinegar
4 bay leaves
2 cans tuna, water-packed, drained
1 can (225 g/7.9 ounces) whole corn, drained
1 cup mild sour cream, plus more for garnish
6 Tablespoons mayonnaise
salt and pepper to taste

Prepare the poblano chiles. See the "Chile" section for complete instructions.

In a large frying pan over low heat, put the oil, vinegar, and bay leaves. Allow to heat slowly for 5 minutes to leech some flavor from the bay leaves. Put the chiles in the pan, and let them warm through, turning once to coat both sides with the vinegar/oil combo, about 2 minutes. Remove the chiles and chill. (This can be done up to two days ahead.)

For the Salad:
In a bowl, mix together the tuna, corn, sour cream, mayonnaise, salt, and pepper. Stuff the poblanos neatly with the mixture. Put a dollop of sour cream on top to garnish.

Note: Gris suggests you try substituting cooked shrimp for the tuna—*delicioso!*

Stuffed Shrimp
Camarónes Rellenos

10 servings

Wrapped in bacon and stuffed with cheese—succulent shrimp at its best! Gris tells me the only reason she uses American cheese is for the color. For flavor, she prefers Chihuahua, but the white color of the cheese blends in with the color of the shrimp, so is not as visually appealing. Cooking the shrimp in the microwave assures that the bacon cooks thoroughly without overcooking the shrimp. The bacon we have available here is very good. It's flavorful without a lot of salt—yummy! Make sure to buy a good quality bacon to wrap around these little gems.

Ingredients

1 kilo (2.2 pounds) shrimp, medium or large
56 grams (2 ounces) American cheese or Chihuahua
½ slice of bacon, cut in half cross-ways for each shrimp
22.5 grams (2½ Tablespoons) butter
garlic salt, to taste
pepper to taste

Peel the shrimp. Devein the shrimp by cutting them open on the back side in a butterfly fashion, without cutting in half. Rinse out the vein and lay the shrimp open on a plate. Sprinkle with a pinch of garlic salt and pepper.

Slice the cheese into thin strips. and lay one strip on each open shrimp. Close the shrimp over the cheese. Wrap each shrimp in ½ slice bacon. When all the shrimp are wrapped, dot them with the butter. Put them in a microwave-safe dish or plate. Cover with a paper towel. Microwave on 90 percent for 13 minutes.*

* Time depends on the wattage of your microwave. Gris's microwave takes 13 minutes, but my microwave takes only 7 minutes to perfection. Check during the cooking process to make sure you are not overcooking the shrimp.

Shrimp Rolls
Rollo de Camarón

6–8 servings

These are a form of pinwheel, where the filling is rolled up inside bread—another example of using simple, inexpensive ingredients to make a very tasty and attractive hors d'oeuvre. These are most often served at family gatherings and fiestas. I have eaten these when the attendance at the event was over one hundred people. They are easy for the hostess to make and easy to serve. A double bonus for her! Normally, these rolls are sliced thin, but when we tested this recipe, we sliced them thicker—there were only a few of us, and we were hungry! Try these next time you have an hors d'oeuvre party.

Ingredients
500 grams (1.1 pound) shrimp
1 loaf white bread, crusts removed (16 slices of bread)
1 large potato, in small dice, cooked and cooled
1 carrot, shredded, cooked, and cooled
1 can peas, drained, or 1 cup frozen, thawed
1 can tuna, drained well and flaked
1 can red bell pepper, chopped
2 Tablespoons mayonnaise
1 cup mild sour cream

Clean and devein the shrimp. Drop the cleaned shrimp into boiling salted water for 3 minutes. Drain. Roughly chop the shrimp when it is cool enough to handle. Set aside in the refrigerator to cool.

Put a large square of aluminum foil down on the counter. Lay out the bread on top of the foil 4 slices across and 4 slices up and down to form a square. You will be using 16 slices. Make sure all the interior edges of the bread are touching so there is no space between them. Roll the bread with a rolling pin to flatten and join the seams.

Mix together the potato, carrot, peas, tuna, red bell pepper, mayonnaise, sour cream, and chopped shrimp. This will look like a wonderful salad!

Spread this salad mixture over the center part of the bread, keeping it away from the edges by about 2.5 cm/1 inch. Roll as you would a jellyroll. Wrap the roll in the foil, and refrigerate for several hours or overnight. Cut into slices to serve.

ROCIO

Meet Maria del Rocio Estrella

While putting this page together, I realized that the photo I took of Rocio (Row-*see*-yo) shows her head surrounded by stars. Her last name, *Estrella*, means star!

Every time we cooked together, we had to use a neighbor's kitchen, because Rocio has no kitchen in her own home. Her home is small but very clean and quite comfortable, just no kitchen. That will be added later on as they can afford to complete their house. Interest rates for home loans in Mazatlán are very high, sometimes more than 20 percent, so almost all homes in the colonias are built on the "pay as you go" method. It can take years, in some cases.

Rocio is from Mexico DF (*Distrito Federal*, or Federal District), much the same as Washington DC. It is also known as Mexico City, the largest city in Mexico and also the country's capital.

When Rocio was just thirteen years old, her mother thought Rocio should learn to cook, so she began teaching her the basics. Rocio was not very interested but out of respect for her mother, she did her best. Both Rocio and her mother cooked for the entire family, with Rocio performing the menial tasks, while her mom handled the more complex aspects of the meal. Following graduation from high school, Rocio went to work as a secretary. Cooking was put on the back burner (sorry!). Her job kept her away from the house during the week, so she only helped out in the kitchen on weekends.

Rocio always has loved to chat and visit. She is a self-proclaimed "Nosy Nellie"—she wants to know everything that is happening or being talked about when she is near. Once, as a teenager, she was secretly trying to hear a conversation between her mother and a friend, so she was not sufficiently focused on cooking the pasta for the family's dinner. She put raw pasta in a pot of cold water to save cooking time, so she wouldn't miss any of the conversation. When the pasta was done, it was like glue! Rocio then snuck out of the house and went to the local corner market for some new pasta. She had to promise to bring the money back later to pay, since she did not want her mom to know what she had done.

No countertops? No problem!

On another occasion, Mom did know what she had done when Rocio, once again, was "spying." This time, the pressure cooker exploded, and beans were everywhere! Apparently, pressure cooker explosions are common here, because so many people have a tale to tell regarding them. Please note that pressure cookers are only dangerous if you don't pay attention to them!

Rocio chatting with Elva Sanchez in the kitchen of Dulce Ibarra

Karina Ann Betlem

Rocio is the youngest of five children and was watched over very closely by her family. When she was seventeen years old, she met a man and fell in love. The problem: he was thirteen years older. Mom forbade Rocio to see him, but the ardent suitor was not to be deterred. For years, he tried to court Rocio. Each time he came to visit her, he would bring a gift. He brought flowers, teddy bears, dolls—anything that would show Mom that he was sincere. After four years, he had worn Mom down, and she gave in. He and Rocio married and shortly thereafter moved to Mazatlán, where they continue to be in love!

Beets with Grapefruit
Los Betabeles con Toronja

6 servings

The sweet flavor of freshly cooked beets with the tart citrus of grapefruit and finished with fresh mint leaves—wow! Beets are eaten frequently here because they are healthy and inexpensive. The common thought is that the combination of beets and grapefruit is good for your blood. Just about everyone here eats beets, because we have the dengue mosquito, and eating beets is thought to ward off dengue fever by boosting your red blood cells. I have no idea if this is true, but just in case, we eat them several times each week. The grapefruit will be cut in a way that's referred to as "supremes." They don't sing; they just look pretty and taste great.

Ingredients

4 medium to large beets
2 whole grapefruits
fresh mint leaves

If you have never prepared fresh beets, you need to be aware of one precaution: use gloves! If you don't, your hands will have a red color for a few days—the color does not wash off! Peel the beets with a vegetable peeler, and cut them into bite-sized squares. Put them in a pan and pour enough cold water to cover them completely. Over medium heat, cook them for 25 minutes or until fork tender. Drain and allow to cool.

Now you will make supremes. Cut off the top and bottom of the grapefruits with a knife. You want to see the fruit not the pithy white part. Sit the flat part of the grapefruit on a board, and with your knife, peel the rind and pith away from the fruit. There should be no pith showing, just naked fruit. Take the knife and cut between the fruit and the segments so that you end up with only the fruit and no membrane. Totally naked fruit segments is the goal here. While you are cutting the supremes, capture the juice from the grapefruit in a bowl.

Mix all the supremes and their juice with the cooled beets. Snip some fresh mint over top, and serve.

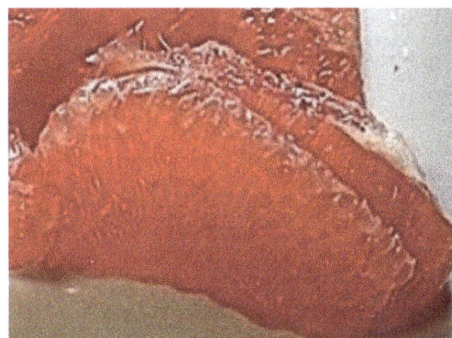

Potato Cakes
Tortas de Papa

6 servings

Potato cakes, unlike potato pancakes, are usually served with lunch or dinner and are much thicker than a pancake. The cotija cheese is a must-have ingredient, as there is no real substitute. Parmesan has been said to be an acceptable substitute, but I find this is not the case. Cotija cheese is quite salty and has a very mild, fresh-milk flavor, unlike the stronger aged flavor of Parmesan. (Cotija cheese is sprinkled on top of the potato cakes in the photo.)

Ingredients

1 kilo (2.2 pounds) potatoes, whole, unpeeled
3 eggs, slightly beaten
200 grams (7 ounces) cotija cheese, or Parmesan cheese (if you must)
salt to taste
1¼ cups oil

Scrub the potatoes and put them in a pot. Add enough water to cover the potatoes, and place the pot over high heat. Once the water boils, reduce the heat to medium, and cover the pot with a lid. Cook them in the boiling water until they are tender when pierced with a fork but not falling apart, between 15 and 30 minutes, depending on how large the potatoes are.

When they are cool enough to handle, peel and dice them into a large bowl. Add the eggs, cheese, and salt. Smash them all together. Heat the oil to very hot in a large skillet over low heat. Form the potatoes into thick "hamburger" shapes; then fry in the hot oil on both sides until they are golden, 3–4 minutes on each side. Remove to a warm plate. They are typically served with warm tomato sauce and a salad or refried beans.

Spinach Cakes
Tortas de Espinacas

8 servings

The spinach leaves are cooked whole and then wrapped around a chunk of cheese, dredged in flour, and fried in a whipped egg batter. If that isn't enough to tempt your taste buds, then they are cooked in a tomato broth to absorb even more flavor. The batter and the frying methods are exactly the same as the Tortas de Camarón that Dulce makes. Frying the spinach cakes does not melt the cheese inside, but boiling them in the broth does.

Ingredients

6 large bunches fresh spinach
2 small onions
3 cloves garlic
500 grams (1 pound) Chihuahua cheese

Karina Ann Betlem

10 tomatoes
1 serrano chile
2 cups flour
5 eggs, separated
oil as needed, to have a depth of 13 mm / ½ inch
salt to taste

Trim the spinach by cutting off the tough stems. Then wash the leaves one by one in water. Put the whole spinach leaves in a large pot, add 4 cups water, and cook with 1 onion, 1 garlic clove, and salt for 10 minutes or until the leaves are wilted. Drain well; discard the onion and garlic.

Cut the cheese into 2.5 cm/1 inch square cubes

While the spinach cooks, purée the tomatoes, serrano chile, 1 onion, and 2 cloves of garlic in a blender. Pour into a large pot and bring it to a boil. Rinse the blender with ½ cup water, and pour this into the pot with the tomato sauce. Add salt to taste.

When the cooked spinach has cooled enough to handle, take 2 or 3 of the cooked leaves and place a cube of cheese in the middle. Form the spinach around the cheese to make a "packet."

Dredge the packets in the flour, and set aside on a plate until all the packets are formed and dredged.

Whip the egg whites in a bowl until they form stiff peaks. One by one, add each yolk to the whites, beating well after each addition, until all the yolks are incorporated.

Dip a packet into the eggs, making sure each packet is totally covered with batter. With your hands, gently remove the packet from the eggs, leaving as much of the egg batter as possible on the spinach, and put in the hot oil. Fry on each side so that both sides are browned. This only takes a minute, so watch them carefully. When they are browned, remove them from the oil, and put them on a plate until all the packets are fried.

By this time, the tomato sauce should be boiling. One by one, gently drop the fried packets into the sauce. Allow them to boil for at least 5 minutes. Serve in bowls with plenty of the tomato sauce.

Wrap spinach around cheese   *Spinach dredged in flour*   *Battered and frying*

Fava Bean and Nopales Soup
Sopa de Haba y Nopales

6 servings

Preparing this soup may be an entirely new experience for you; it was for me. The soup is hearty because of the beans, with a light tomato broth, and nopales added to finish with a slight dill flavor. If you are fortunate enough to live in an area where you have fresh nopales, make sure to buy or pick them for this soup. Canned nopales should be available just about everywhere else.

Ingredients

2 Tablespoons oil
1 onion, minced
2–3 cloves garlic, minced
5 tomatoes (not roma), peeled and diced
salt to taste
2 cups dried fava beans**, sorted and rinsed
3 medium nopales, chopped and cooked (*see below)
1 chile guajillo, toasted and thinly sliced, for garnish

Sauté the onion and garlic in the oil until they are soft. Add the peeled and diced tomatoes with a little salt, and cook 5 minutes. Add 4 cups of water and the beans. Cook over low heat for 30 minutes. When the beans are soft, add the nopales, and cook for 5 minutes. Put in a bowl garnished with toasted chile guajillo. Serve this soup with warm tortillas, sliced baguette, garlic bread, crackers, or tortilla chips.

* To cook fresh nopales: If they still have spines on them, wear gloves and remove the spines by scraping with a knife or vegetable peeler. Dice them, and boil the nopales until they are soft. Drain completely, and let sit in the hot pan to evaporate the remainder of the moisture.

** Dried fava beans look similar to dried lima beans, except that they are large and yellow. You should be able to find them on the grocery aisle or on the Mexican aisle, labeled as *Habas Secas* (dried favas). If you cannot find them, use large, dried lima beans, which are not a true substitute but an acceptable one.

Napolitano-Style Flan
Flan Napolitano

8 servings

This style of flan is not quite as sweet as a Flan Casero, but it does have a light sweetness accentuated by the caramel topping. Both types are equally popular, but you will not find both types made in the same house. For instance, Rocio always makes Flan Napolitano, while Elva always makes Flan Casero. It is just a personal preference. It is my opinion that you should make both types and decide for yourself which you prefer. The decision is not as easy as you think!

Ingredients

75 grams (6 Tablespoons) granulated sugar
2 cans evaporated milk

1 can sweetened condensed milk
7 eggs
2 Tablespoons vanilla extract

To make the caramel: In a pan on very low heat, melt the sugar. Keep stirring gently until it is a golden brown. Take off the heat. Pour the caramel into a heat-proof bowl, and refrigerate until cold.

Blend the milks, eggs, and vanilla thoroughly. Rocio uses a blender, but you can use a whisk if you prefer.

Pour the custard over the cold caramel. Cover the dish with foil, and put in a bain-marie* on the stove top over medium-low heat for 45–60 minutes. Carefully remove the dish from the water bath, cool, and then refrigerate until set. Invert on a plate, and the caramel will be on top. Cut with a knife into serving sizes. Rocio likes to make round shapes, letting the kids nibble on the leftover scraps. I think I will get in line for those.

* See "Author's Notes."

Alambres

1 serving

There is no translation for the name of this corn tortilla dish. Literally, *alambre* means "wire," usually a skewer. In this recipe, the meat for the tortillas is not skewered but sliced in long, thin slices (thus resembling wire). The filling also includes vegetables and is covered with a layer of cheese. When these corn tortillas are filled and rolled, they will be bursting at the seams with this succulent meat and vegetable mixture.

Ingredients

1 Tablespoon vegetable oil
2 slices bacon, chopped
100 grams (3½ ounces) sirloin tip or chuck roast, cut into thin strips
½ large onion, diced
2 poblano chiles, diced (not charred)
½ cup large red tomatoes, seeds removed, cut into small dice
salt to taste
100 grams (3½ ounces) Chihuahua cheese, grated
2 or 3 corn tortillas
1 fresh lime (optional)

Fry the bacon in hot oil over low heat until it is crisp. Add the steak and brown it on all sides. Put in the diced onion, and cook until it is almost translucent. Then add the diced chiles and continue cooking until the chiles are cooked through. Stir in the chopped tomatoes and salt. Combine well.

Sprinkle the grated cheese on top; then cover it with tortillas, using them as a lid until the cheese is melted. This will also warm the tortillas.

To serve, put the warmed tortillas on a plate first and then the meat, keeping the cheese on top. Squeeze a small amount of lime juice on top for a zing.

Mexican Pot Roast
Cuete Mechado

8 servings

Cuete (*koo*-ay-tay), or boneless round roast, is one of the few cuts cooked as a whole roast. It is very lean and requires "larding." In this recipe, it is done with pieces of bacon. You will be using a pressure cooker for this recipe. Mexican cooks do not have hours to wait in a hot kitchen for the meat to cook, so almost all cooks have an *olla express* (pressure cooker). You can adjust the recipe to cook in the oven or your favorite method of cooking a roast of this type. Leftovers are great for beef tacos or as a topping on baked potatoes.

If you do not have a pressure cooker, you may want to invest in a good one—they are extremely handy!

Ingredients

1 kilo (2.2 pounds) boneless bottom round roast
250 grams (8–9 ounces) bacon, cut into large pieces
8 large potatoes, whole, unpeeled, scrubbed
2 Tablespoons oil
750 grams (1½ pounds) large tomatoes
2 chipotle chiles (from can) or to taste
10 bay leaves

1 liter (4¼ cups) water
salt to taste

Make 2.5 cm/1 inch deep incisions on all sides of the roast. Insert the pieces of bacon into each slit. Cut a slice in each potato, and insert a piece of bacon. Pour the oil into the pressure cooker. (Don't put the lid yet.) Heat the oil to medium hot. Add the piece of meat, and sear it on all sides.

Mix the tomatoes in a blender with the water and chipotle chiles. Put the potatoes in the pressure cooker, nesting them around and on top of the meat. Then add the tomato mixture. Now put the lid on the pressure cooker. Start the timing when the valve begins to rock, and cook slowly for 45 minutes. Turn off the heat, and let it sit to allow the pressure to release on its own. **Do not pour water over the pressure cooker to cool,** as that causes the meat to be tough. When the pressure has fully released, open the lid, and cut the meat into 8 portions. Put on individual plates with some of the broth and 1 potato.

Brisket Salad
Ensalada de Pecho

4 servings

This is a layered beef brisket and vegetable dish, covered with a fried sauce. Beef brisket has a rich flavor, and because it shreds well, it is the perfect cut of beef for a dish like this. The beef and potatoes can be served hot or warm. The sauce should be hot. Notice that there are no chiles in this recipe. (Yes, Virginia, there are some Mexican recipes without chiles!)

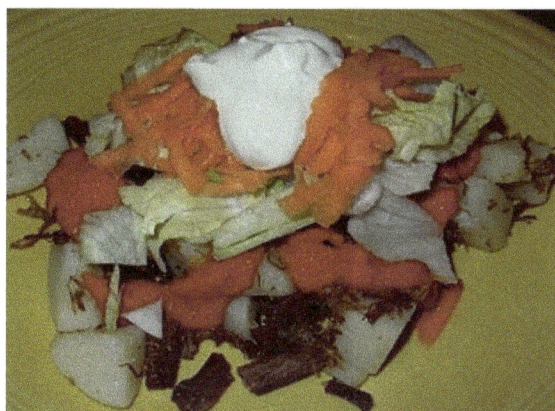

Ingredients

1 kilo (2.2 pounds) beef brisket
4 Tablespoons oil for frying the meat, 2 Tablespoons oil for frying the sauce
1 kilo (2.2 pounds) potatoes, peeled and cut into large dice
500 grams (1.1 pound) tomatoes
¼ teaspoon ground cumin
¾ onion
1 clove garlic
½ teaspoon salt
½ head lettuce, chopped
2 carrots, grated
1 cup mild sour cream

Cut the meat into large cubes and cook with 1½ liters (6 cups) water in a pressure cooker for 35 minutes. Heat 4 Tablespoons of the oil in a large frying pan. Drain the meat, and start to fry it in the hot oil, shredding it as it fries.

Cook the potatoes in water in a separate pan until they are tender. Drain, and add those to the meat. Continue to fry the potatoes and meat together.

Boil the tomatoes in water for 3 minutes; then drain and put them in a blender with the cumin, onion, garlic, salt, and the juice from the meat, and liquefy. Heat the 2 tablespoons oil in separate pan. Pour in the blended ingredients and fry, stirring often so it does not stick to the bottom of the pan. (This step evaporates most of the liquid and leaves all the flavors more concentrated.)

When the potatoes and meat and the blended ingredients have been fried, it's time to serve. Plate in this order: meat and potatoes; then the fried blended ingredients, chopped lettuce, and grated carrots; then a spoonful of sour cream on the top.

Meat and Sauce in One Pot
Mole de Olla

6 servings

A mole is literally a sauce. In this instance, the sauce is cooked with the meat in one pot (an *olla*) and served as one dish, instead of a sauce drizzled over the meat. If you have trouble finding spines (backbones) with meat, a good substitute would be pork ribs. The bones are the key to flavoring the broth. Remove the bones before serving.

Ancho and guajillo chiles combine here to give a light but somewhat smoky chile flavor to the sauce, without much heat. Fill a tortilla with this savory meat and sauce, drizzle some fresh lime over the top, add some beans on the side, and you'll have a most excellent meal!

Ingredients

1 kilo (2.2 pounds) pork spines (backbones) with meat or beef tail
3 liters (12.5 cups) water
2 teaspoons salt
8 guajillo chiles
3 ancho chiles
1 large pinch ground cumin
4 whole cloves
4 whole black peppercorns
¼ onion
150 grams (5.25 ounces) masa de maiz (dough for tortillas) **see note below
fresh limes (optional)

Cook the meat and bones in the salted water, 1.5 to 2 hours. The meat should be tender.

Remove the stems, seeds, and veins from the chiles. Put the chiles in a small pot of boiling water for 5 minutes. Drain and discard the water.

Put the chiles, cumin, cloves, pepper, onion, masa, and a bit of broth from the meat in a blender; liquefy. Strain the blended ingredients into the broth and the cooked meat. Simmer for 10 minutes. Adjust the salt, if needed. Stir constantly—the masa is a thickener.

Put on the plate (you can remove the bones as you do this), and squeeze fresh lime over the meat, if you want. Eat with corn tortillas.

** If you cannot buy the prepared masa, make your own using 7 Tablespoons Maseca (corn flour for tortillas), 6 Tablespoons warm water, and a pinch of salt. Or use 6 Tablespoons corn flour (*not* cornstarch) mixed with 6 Tablespoons cold water as a substitute. Rocio and I made the sauce both ways, and we agreed this is an acceptable substitute. Regular flour is not a substitute because it does not give an earthy corn flavor to the sauce.

Tamales

20 Tamales

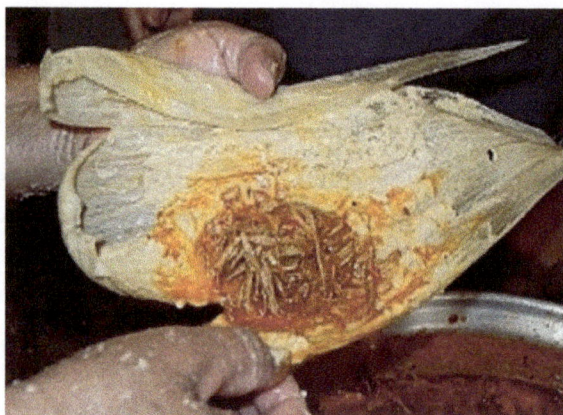

Tamale making is not something you do without some advance preparation. The first thing is to round up some friends to help. This is an assembly-line process. I was honored to be invited to be part of this assembly line to help make two hundred tamales for the children's catechism class at the local church. There are about a hundred children in the class, but more show up when they know good food is being served, and there is always plenty of food to share!

We used Señora Rocio's recipe, but made enough for two hundred tamales, not twenty. You should see the size of the steamer! A person could actually get inside, sit down, and still be able to close the lid.

Please do not be intimidated by tamale making. Use the proper ingredients (no substitutions), and your tamales will be delicious. Invite some friends over, make tamales, have a couple of margaritas or cervezas while you wait for the tamales to steam, and then sit down to a fabulous Mexican feast! Make sure to ask your friends to bring an authentic Mexican side dish to share at this feast.

Ingredients

For the filling:
500 grams (1.1 pound) pork roast or beef roast
3 liters (12.5 cups) water
2 teaspoons salt
¼ onion, finely chopped
1 clove garlic, minced
1 jar mole***

For the masa:
125 grams (4 ounces) solid vegetable shortening (Manteca, near the Crisco)
125 grams (4 ounces) pure pork lard (in the refrigerator section)
1 kilo (2.2 pounds) Maseca (corn flour for tortillas)
2 teaspoons baking powder
3 teaspoons salt
2 packages corn husks (you will need at least 20 good corn husks)

Cook the meat in 3 liters of water with the onion, garlic, and 2 teaspoons of salt. Simmer for about 2 hours. Check the meat at this time to make sure it is tender and shreds easily. Add the jar of mole, and stir so that it dissolves completely. Take the pan off the heat, and allow it to cool down while you prepare the masa.

Mix the shortening and lard with the masa, baking powder, and salt in a large dish. The dough needs to be a little salty. Using your hands, mix the dough very well so that there are *no* lumps. It must be very smooth. (This feels great on your hands, and when you are finished, your hands will be very soft!)

Rinse the corn husks to remove any dirt; then put them in a tub of hot water to soak for about 30 minutes, so they are pliable. They float, so make sure to weight them down with a plate or lid. When they are pliable, remove them from the water, and put on a plate to be used in the assembly line.

Hold the corn husk in your palm, with the thick end facing away from you. Put a big spoon of masa on the corn husk, and spread it around from side to side and about 1 inch from the thick end (top) of the husk and down about two-thrids of the way, leaving the bottom third of the husk empty. Put a tablespoon of the meat in the center of the masa, and add a tiny bit of its sauce. Imagine the meat being on one-third of the husk in the center. Fold the 2 sides over the meat, so you now have a long packet, one-third the size of the original husk. Fold the bottom section up over the middle to almost halfway. Turn the tamale over, and put it in a big steamer or tamale *olla*. (You can also tear off a small shred of husk, and tie it around the tamale to make it look pretty.)

Put enough water in the bottom of the pan under the steamer rack so that it does not touch the tamales but can make enough steam for 1½ to 2 hours. After 1½ hours, check the tamales to see if they are cooked. To do this, remove one of the tamales, and open it up. The masa will hold together like a pouch when it is done. Serve with refried beans. (Don't eat the husk!)

*** Jar of mole: There are several brands available just about everywhere. Doña Maria is one brand that is very good. A jar is about 235 grams/8.25 ounces. There are several flavors also; choose the one that says *mole*.

| Mixing the masa | Sorting the husks | Folding the tamales |

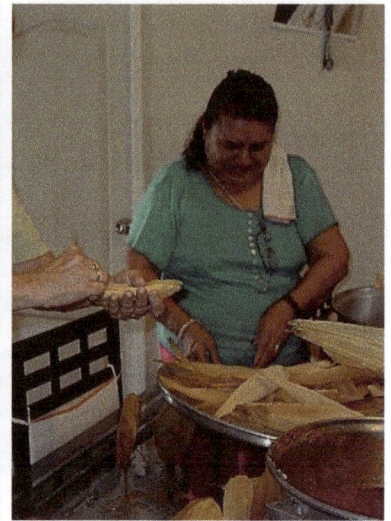

Purslane with Pork
Verdolagas con Carne de Puerco

5 servings

In Mazatlán, pork is one of the best meats you can buy. It is very lean and inexpensive—two great qualities! The tomatillo sauce has lots of heat because you use 6 whole serrano chiles, and serrano chiles are very spicy. If you like it less spicy, only add 1 or 2 chiles, and remove the seeds. Taste as you add them to the blender—you can always add more. The tomatillos add a different flavor to the sauce and blend exceptionally well with the *verdolagas* (purslane), as they both have a piquant, dill type flavor.

Ingredients

500 grams (1 pound) pork meat, pork shoulder, or boneless pork chops
2 Tablespoons vegetable oil
1 bunch verdolagas (purslane)
2 cloves garlic (divided usage)
salt to taste
500 grams (1 pound) tomatillos, papery husk removed
6 serrano chiles
5 stems cilantro

Boil the pork in a little salted water until it is tender (this depends on the cut of meat you have). As it gets tender, allow the water to boil and evaporate until the meat is almost dry. To the same pan, add the oil, and fry the meat.

Remove the thick stems of the verdolagas, but leave all the top part of the stems with leaves. Wash well, and then cut into 13 mm / ½ inch long pieces. Boil them in water with 1 garlic clove, and salt to taste.

In another pot, boil a small amount of water. Put the tomatillos in the water with the chiles. When they are soft, carefully remove them from the water using a slotted spoon (the tomatillos will be fragile at this point), and place in a blender. Remove the stems from the serranos, and add them to the blender with 1 more garlic clove and the cilantro, and blend. Put the verdolagas in with the meat, and pour the blended ingredients over the top.

MARIA

Meet Maria de Los Angeles Carrillo Chavez

Señora Maria is from the very old village of Zamora in the state of Michoacán. The village was officially founded in 1574 and is an interesting and beautiful city to visit. Maria still travels back to her roots by bus to visit family and enjoy the culture of Zamora, which is much more formal than the lifestyle in Mazatlán.

When Maria was just a small girl, she taught herself to cook when she was sent to work outside her home at a roadside cafe that catered to the truckers. She watched the owners of the cafe and did her best to learn from them. The cafe was very busy, so instruction was limited to what she could glean by watching.

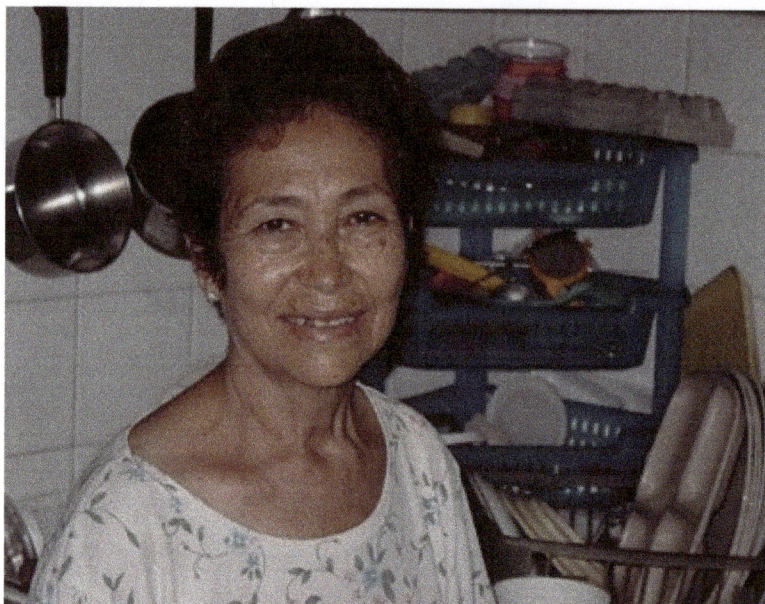

Maria's mother had many health problems and was unable to take care of her family. By the time Maria was ten years old, being the oldest daughter of eight children, it was now her responsibility to start cooking for her family. She got up very early each morning to cook the day's main meal for her family and then went to work.

When she was fifteen years old, she changed jobs and began working in private homes, where she says her cooking became much better. The women of the homes taught her the correct way to cook and even today, she is very thankful to those women who were so kind to her and enhanced her cooking skills.

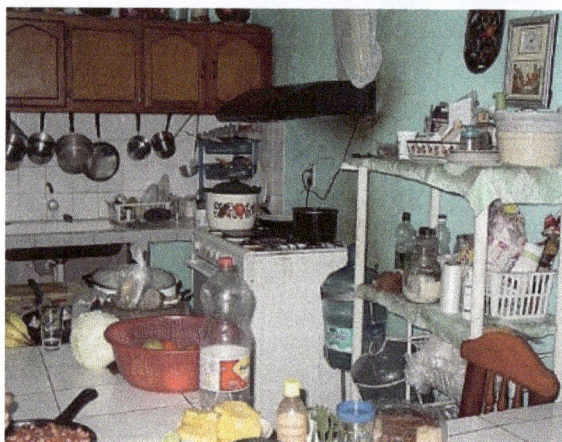

Maria still cooks three meals a day for her own family, even though they are grown and do not live with her and her husband. Walking into her kitchen is like walking into a restaurant kitchen, with its warm aromas of simmering pots of food. I have never been to her home when there were not at least two pots simmering on the stove. Her kitchen is open to the other parts of the house. It is very compact and always—I mean *always*—has bowls of fruit, vegetables, and meats on the counter for anyone stopping by to help themselves.

Stuffed Potatoes with Egg
Papas Rellenas con Huevo

4 servings

The eggs in these stuffed potatoes can be either baked with a loose yolk, like this one, or hard cooked. Both are very tasty with the tomato and onion salsa. Although the potatoes look more like a breakfast dish, they can be eaten at any meal. Maria makes them two different ways: one, like the photo, with the egg cooked inside a baked potato, and the other, by emptying the entire potato and re-stuffing it into the potato with the egg on top. The second version is more of a twice-baked potato.

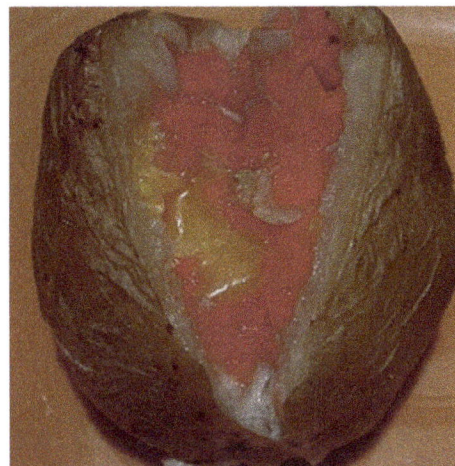

Ingredients

4 large potatoes
oil
4 eggs
2 tomatoes
1 small onion
salt to taste

Preheat the oven to 200°C/400°F.

Oil the skins of the potatoes, and bake them until they are tender. Carefully remove part of the cooked potato from the skin to make a bowl inside. Whiz the onion, tomatoes, and a pinch of salt in the blender, leaving medium-sized chunks, so you have a thick sauce. Inside each potato, put a cracked egg.

Put the potatoes on a fireproof dish or pan, trying to keep them level so that the egg does not spill out. Pour some sauce over the egg, and put into the hot oven until the eggs are done to your liking. Serve immediately.

Note: if you make the twice-baked version, after the potatoes are tender, remove as much of the cooked potato as possible. Mash it up and re-stuff it into the potato skin, making a well so the egg has a place to sit.

Tuna Cake
Pastel de Atún

18 servings

Tuna cake is a literal translation, but they are actually great little sandwiches. Maria makes these for fiestas and other family gatherings. You can cut them into small triangles or other fun shapes, if you like. Make sure to serve these with plenty of napkins, because they are very messy. The amount of chipotles in this recipe gives the filling a wonderful smoky flavor but also an intense heat. Add only a small amount of chipotles at a time, taste-testing as you go.

Ingredients

1 bag white bread (1 bag is about 20 slices)
1 can (105 grams/3.7 ounces) chile chipotle
190g/6.7 ounces Philadelphia cream cheese
1 can tuna, drained

½ cup sour cream
1 cube chicken bouillon

Mix all the ingredients except bread in a blender.

Cut the crust off the bread. In a square dish, place one layer of bread and then one layer of mixture. Do this so you have 4 layers. Refrigerate until cold. Slice into small triangles or squares for hors d'oeuvres.

Kisses
Besos

Makes about 48 cookies

Small one-bite shortbread type cookies, these are only slightly sweet. The big burst of sweetness comes from the powdered sugar coating. They taste just as good without the coating, but it would not be a true *beso* (kiss) without it. For those cooks who own ovens, this little delight is usually made around Valentine's Day, sometimes two cookies sandwiched with a filling of strawberry jam. Mexico is full of traditions, and this is a sweet one!

Ingredients

2 cups flour
½ cup granulated sugar
2 Tablespoons baking powder
1 Tablespoon vanilla extract
1 cup butter, or a combination of butter and solid vegetable shortening
powdered sugar for coating after baking

Preheat the oven to 175°C/350°F. Prepare a cookie sheet by greasing with shortening or lining with parchment paper.

Knead together all the ingredients except the powdered sugar until fully mixed. Form into small balls the size of hazelnuts. Place on the prepared cookie sheet. Flatten a little with a fork. Bake for 10 minutes. Remove from the oven, carefully remove cookies from the cookie sheet (they are fragile), and cover them in powdered sugar. Gently shake off the excess sugar, and cool on a wire rack.

Noodle and Milk Soup
Sopa de Fideos y Leche

4 servings

Fideos delgados are skinny little noodles, about 13 mm / ½ inch long. If you cannot find them, you can use capellini pasta, and break it into small, uniform pieces. Maria says you can use any type of milk, from low-fat (*not* non-fat) to whole. The milk makes this soup almost sweet tasting. By cooking the pasta in the milk, the starch from pasta makes the milk get thicker, like a cream soup. Try this one on a cool day.

Ingredients

1½ liters (6⅓ cups) milk
200 grams (7 ounces) thin noodles, cut or broken into 13 mm / ½ inch pieces
½ teaspoon salt

Pour the milk into a saucepan, and bring slowly to a boil. Do not let it scorch. When it is at a rolling boil, add the salt and the noodles. Cook for 10 minutes, and serve.

Wrapped Child
Niño Envuelto

6–8 servings

I love the Mexican names of their food dishes! *Niño envuelto* is a type of jellyroll (no child harmed in this recipe), this one with ham and tuna. There are many versions of niño envuelto, from main course through dessert.

The carrots you see in the photo are from the can of *jalapeños in escabeche*. They have a nice vinegar taste to perk up the mild flavors of the other vegetables. Normally, canned jalapeños are not too spicy, but use your own judgment, according to your tastes. You do not have to use the whole can!

Ingredients

28 slices white bread (a standard loaf is 20 slices)

250 ml (7.75 ounces) mayonnaise, more or less to your own taste
500 grams (1 pound) ham, sliced thin
1 can jalapeños en escabeche, drained (220 g/7.75 ounces)
1 can mixed vegetables, drained (215 g/7.5 ounces)
1 can peas, drained (215 g/7.5 ounces)
1 can tuna, oil or water-pack, drained

Note: weight of the canned jalapeños, mixed vegetables, and peas is *before* draining.

Cut the crusts off the bread, and discard the crusts. Place the bread slices side by side on a damp cloth, 2 rows of 7 slices each. Flatten the bread slightly with a rolling pin. You will have 2 layers of filling and 2 layers of bread. Using half of each ingredient, put a layer of mayonnaise, the ham, the chiles, vegetables, peas, and the tuna. Cover with another layer of bread and the remainder of the filling ingredients. Roll up into a type of jellyroll, using the damp cloth as an aid. Let the roll sit for about 10–15 minutes. Slice and serve with beans or a salad.

Mexican Bread Pudding
Capirotada

20 servings

Capirotada is a dessert made at Eastertime—a delicious combination of fruit, bread, and sugar, dotted with shredded cheese. There are a few variations, of course. This version comes from the state of Michoacán and uses hard white bread rolls instead of the Sinaloa tradition of using sweet raisin bread. The only accompaniment is a tall glass of milk or a cup of coffee.

Ingredients

90 grams (6½ Tablespoons) butter
20 large hard sandwich rolls (*bolillos*)
2 plantains
200 grams (7 ounces) raisins
200 grams (7 ounces) prunes
200 grams (7 ounces) peanuts, peeled
250 grams (8 ounces) Chihuahua cheese, shredded
7 large piloncillo cones (about 4 cups), crushed
2 cups water

Melt the butter in a large pan. Cut the hard sandwich rolls in slices, and fry them in the hot butter. After all the bread is fried and coated with butter, place half of the bread in a large casserole dish, covering the bottom. Put a layer of half of the sliced plantains, raisins, prunes, and peanuts. Then add the remainder of the bread on top in another layer. Then add the last layer of plantains, raisins, prunes, and peanuts. Sprinkle the cheese over the top. Boil the piloncillo with 2 cups water until totally dissolved. Pour over the top of the cheese/bread. Let it sit for 5 minutes.

Layering: first layer—bread, plantains, raisins, prunes, and peanuts. Second layer—bread, plantains, raisins, prunes, peanuts, cheese, and piloncillo.

Enjoy with a glass of milk.

Coconut Delight
Delicia de Coco

Makes 24 large cookies

Crunchy flourless cookies with a moist coconut center. Maria makes hers with fresh coconut, but she says it is perfectly fine to use *unsweetened* packaged coconut. You should see her face when she says not to use pre-sweetened coconut—it just does not taste like real coconut. These make a great afternoon treat with a cup of coffee or tea.

Ingredients

4 egg whites

1 cup granulated sugar
2 Tablespoons cornstarch
2 teaspoons baking powder
3 cups shredded coconut

If you are using packaged dried coconut, rinse it several times to remove any cornstarch or other additives. Make sure to drain it and dry it with paper towels before adding it to your batter, or the batter will absorb the moisture, and you will end up with flat, hard cookies.

Preheat the oven to 175°C/350°F. Prepare a cookie sheet by greasing with shortening or lining with parchment paper.

Beat the egg whites until stiff peaks form. Very slowly fold in the sugar and then the cornstarch and the baking powder. Finally, add the coconut. When it is totally mixed, drop by tablespoons of the mixture on the prepared cookie sheet. Bake for 30 minutes. Remove from the cookie sheet, and put on a cooling rack. Store in an airtight container to keep out all moisture and humidity.

Spanish Custard with Raisins
Natilla con Pasas

4 servings

A simple creamy stove-top custard, this sweet custard—more like a pudding—is infused with cinnamon and has the added touch of plump raisins. It's another quick dessert to tantalize the palate after a heavy or spicy meal.

Ingredients

1 cup granulated sugar
2 Tablespoons cornstarch
2 eggs
½ liter (17 ounces) milk
50 grams (⅓ cup, packed) raisins, seedless
1 cinnamon stick (small)

Mix the sugar, cornstarch, eggs, and milk together. Beat until they are very smooth and perfectly blended.

Pour them into a heavy-bottomed pan, and place over very low heat. Add the raisins and cinnamon stick. Cook, stirring constantly, until the pudding is thickened. Allow to chill. Remove the cinnamon stick and serve.

Beef with Rice
Morisqueta

5 servings

This traditional *morisqueta* (beef with rice) is from the state of Michoacán, and as with most traditional foods, there are many versions. Some have chorizo instead of the steak. Maria prefers this version and makes it often. It is very easy to prepare, so you can have this any time you need a quick meal. The meat and onions swim in the rich, roasted tomato sauce. Top it off with a roasted serrano to kick it up a notch!

Ingredients

500 grams (1 pound) rice, uncooked
2 liters (8.5 cups) water

1 teaspoon butter
3 Tablespoons oil
1 kilo (2.2 pounds) steak
1 onion, cut in half, then sliced
1 kilo (2.2 pounds) fresh tomatoes
2 cloves garlic
5 serrano chiles (more or less for garnish)
salt to taste
250 grams (8.8 ounces) dry cotija cheese, grated

Cook the rice with 2 liters of water, salt, and the butter, until all the water is absorbed and the rice is tender, 15–20 minutes.

While the rice is cooking, sauté the beef and onions in a frying pan with the oil. When the meat is cooked the way you like, remove it from the pan, and slice it into small serving sizes. Return it to the pan with the onions.

In a dry pan, roast the tomatoes, garlic, and serranos until they have brown marks. Remove the serranos, and set aside to use as garnish for the finished dish. Place the tomatoes and garlic in a blender with salt, and liquefy. No need to add water—the tomatoes will have enough liquid in them. Pour the tomatoes into the beef, and simmer on very low, just enough to heat the sauce.

To serve, put the steak with tomato sauce on top of the rice, and sprinkle with cheese. Place one serrano chile on each portion.

A good accompaniment is a chile relleno.

Liver with Green Sauce
Higado con Salsa Verde

4 servings

I am happy to say that I love liver! I often order it for breakfast and thankfully, most of the Mexican breakfast buffets have it on their table. This particular version is one of the best I have ever eaten. You can smell the onions and sherry all the way outside.

The trick to cooking liver while avoiding that strong scent and flavor is to cook it *slowly*. The cooking time of the liver may not appear to be long enough, but trust me, it is.

Remember how your mom used to cook the life out of liver, to the point that you could use it to re-sole your shoes? Please do not overcook it. Properly cooked liver only needs to be cooked enough so that no pink remains on the inside. If you are not sure how long to cook liver, periodically cut open a small piece and check the inside during the cooking process.

Ingredients

400 grams (14 ounces) beef or calves liver, sliced very thin (less than 6 mm / ¼ inch)
salt to taste
4 Tablespoons oil
1 large onion, diced
1 cup sherry
1 bunch parsley
bread crumbs

Rinse the liver, and cut it into serving-sized pieces. Blot dry. Sprinkle with salt.

Heat the oil over medium-low heat in a large frying pan, sufficient size to hold all the liver at once. Slowly sauté the liver with the onions. After 2 minutes, turn the liver over, and add the sherry. Turn the heat to low. Cook until the liver is almost done. About 3 more minutes.

With a mortar and pestle, mash the parsley with enough bread crumbs to make a paste. If you do not have a mortar and pestle, use a food processor with a teaspoon of water. Add to the liver, and let it cook 5 minutes. Serve immediately.

Roasted Potato
Papa Asada

10 servings

Maria makes this for a fiesta. Any excuse for a party is how we like to live here! *Olé!*

Look at all the goodies you get on top of this ultimate stuffed potato! You can bake the potatoes ahead; just keep them warm or reheat them. Although Maria serves the potatoes already dressed, you can make a potato bar for everyone to dress their own. Make sure the potatoes are big so you can load them up!

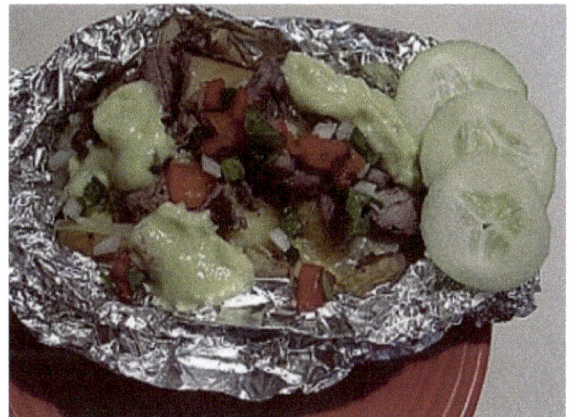

Ingredients

10 large potatoes
1 kilo (2.2 pounds) beef for grilling
salt and pepper to taste (for meat)
1 kilo (2.2 pounds) tomatoes
1 medium onion
10 sprigs cilantro, leaves and tender stalks only
20 serrano chiles (more or less, as you like)
3 avocados, peel and seeds removed
2 cucumbers, sliced
10 pieces aluminum foil to wrap potatoes
10 teaspoons butter
1 kilo (2.2 pounds) Chihuahua cheese, shredded, divided into 10 servings

Bake the potatoes ahead of time. Keep them hot. If you make them the day before, just make sure to pop them in the oven so they can reheat sufficiently.

Season the beef with salt and pepper; set aside.

Salsa Mexicana: Cut the tomatoes and onion in small dice. Cut the serranos and cilantro in very small dice, and mix with the tomatoes and onion. (Normally, you would also use lime juice, but Maria does not the like the lime with the potatoes.)

Put the avocados with ½ cup water in a blender, and blend until smooth.

Grill the meat on the barbecue to your liking. Chop the meat into very small dice.

Put one cooked potato in each piece of foil. Slice open, and crush the inside with a fork. Place 1 teaspoon butter and a portion of cheese on each potato. Place on the grill, and heat until the cheese is melted. Open the foil; add the meat, salsa, and avocado; and garnish with slices of cucumber.

Quesadillas
(kay-sa-*dee*-yas)

5 servings

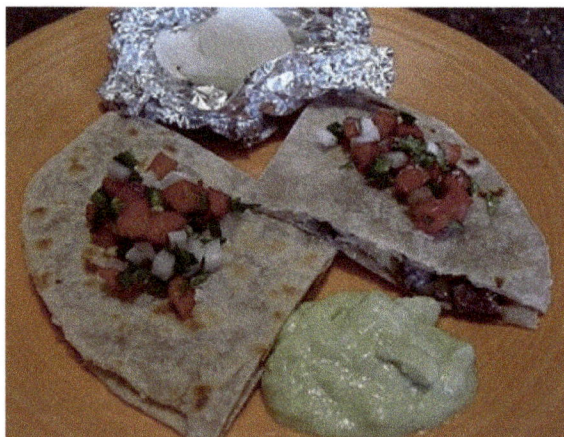

Freshly grilled steak with homemade or purchased flour tortillas is irresistible! A grilled onion on the side, along with avocado salsa and salsa Mexicana, provides you with all your food groups (except beer and chocolate—you can add those to round out the meal). Use any type of steak you prefer to grill. Maria uses a steak appropriately called *carne para asado* (meat for grilling). Make sure to serve these hot off the griddle while the cheese is melted, and the meat is tender and juicy.

Ingredients

1 kilo (2.2 pounds) beef steak for grilling
5 onions, cut in half, and both halves wrapped together in aluminum foil

1 kilo (2.2 pounds) tomatoes, finely chopped
1 onion, finely chopped (reserve 2 slices onion for the avocado salsa)
10 serrano chiles, seeds removed (if you want) and diced very small
½ bunch cilantro, chopped
2 limes, juiced
3 avocados, peel and seeds removed
salt to taste

1 kilo (2.2 pounds) Chihuahua cheese, shredded
2 packages flour tortillas (usually 12 tortillas in a package)

First, grill the meat. Let it rest, and then chop it into small pieces.

Wrap 5 onions in foil, and place on the hot grill to steam.

Salsa Mexicana: Cut the tomato, onion, and the serranos in small dice. Place in a bowl. Mix in the chopped cilantro and spritz juice from 1 lime over the salsa. Mix well and taste. If it needs more lime, squeeze more into the salsa.

Salsa of Avocado: In a blender, put the avocados with a ¼ cup water, salt, and onion. Blend until smooth.

To make the quesadillas: Heat a flat pan or griddle until it is hot. Place one tortilla in the pan and immediately place a handful of cheese and some of the chopped beef, and top with another tortilla. After the bottom tortilla has toasted, carefully flip it over to toast the other side. Slide onto a cutting board, and slice into 4 or 6 wedges. Serve 2 or 3 wedges on each plate. Place one steamed onion on each plate. Let everyone add his or her own salsa(s) to the quesadillas.

Smoked Tuna Ranchero Style
Atún Ahumado Ranchero

10 servings

This simple and versatile smoked tuna topping for chips also is good on top of scrambled eggs; then wrapped in a fresh tortilla. The ideas for this dish are only limited by your imagination!

Serve it in small bowls around the hors d'oeuvre table, and see how fast they need refilling. There is not much spicy heat from the chiles, so make sure to put some hot sauce on the table.

Ingredients

4 Tablespoons corn oil
500 grams (1 pound) smoked tuna, crumbled
1 clove garlic, minced
1 teaspoon whole oregano
¼ teaspoon ground black pepper
4 tomatoes, chopped
1 white onion, chopped
1 small poblano chile (stem, seeds, and veins removed), chopped
1 jalapeño chile, chopped
1 Tablespoon cilantro leaves, finely chopped

Heat the corn oil to medium hot, add all the other ingredients, and stir to combine. Sauté for 5 minutes for the flavors to blend. Serve with tortilla chips.

Smoked Tuna Salad
Salpicón de Atún Ahumado

6 servings

This delightful smoked tuna salad has a variety of colors, textures, and flavors that are so pleasing to the palate that it is difficult to stop eating. There were only three of us at Maria's house the day we made this *salpicón* (literally: a cold mixed salad), and we ate all six servings! If you use this for a main dish, add some sliced hard-boiled eggs and more veggies of any kind and just drizzle them with more lime juice.

Ingredients

3 poblano chiles, charred
3 tomatoes
½ head iceberg lettuce
500 grams (1 pound) smoked tuna
200 grams (7 ounces) purple onion, diced or sliced thinly
2 limes, juiced, or to taste
salt and pepper to taste
1 avocado, peeled and sliced

As you prepare and slice each ingredient, place it with the others in a large salad bowl.

Char and peel the poblano chiles as described in the "Chile" section. Slice the cleaned poblanos into thin rings.

Remove the seeds from the tomatoes, and slice the flesh into julienne slices.

Wash and dry the lettuce. Then cut into bite-sized pieces.

Crumble in the tuna and add the onions. Toss together.

Drizzle with lime juice and sprinkle with salt and pepper.

Place the avocado slices on top.

Small Dried Fish with Nopales
Charales Secos con Nopalitos

4–6 servings

Be brave, and give this dish a try—you may get addicted to it. This is a quick and deliciously interesting meal. The *charales* are mild-flavored and crunchy—surprisingly, they do not have much of a fishy taste—the nopales are a bit tart, and the tomato/serrano sauce adds a kick.

In the photo is a standard-size toothpick.

Charales (char-*ah*-lays) are little dried fish (minnows) about 5 cm/2 inches long, a bit smaller than sardines They are almost always found dried and should be available on your Mexican or Asian food aisle or specialty store. You also can eat them right from the package as a crunchy snack. In a Japanese market, you can buy these as a honey-coated or wasabi-coated snack; they are very tasty—yes, I have eaten them!

Ingredients

40 grams (1.4 ounces) little dried fish (minnows)
3–4 Tablespoons oil
250 grams (8 ounces) whole tomatoes
1 or 2 serrano chiles, stems removed (seeds removed, if you don't want the heat)
2 cloves garlic
2 Tablespoons cilantro leaves, finely chopped
¼ teaspoon salt
250 grams (8 ounces) small new potatoes, peeled and cooked
2 whole nopales (flat nopales), cut in small dice and cooked

Heat the oil in a large pan over medium heat. Add the minnows, and cook until they are golden. This also will make them more crunchy (pop one in your mouth and try one). Remove from the pan, and set aside.

Boil the tomatoes in a small amount of water until the skins split, about 3 minutes. Place the tomatoes and their water in a blender with the chiles and garlic; purée. Pour into the empty pan in which you just browned the minnows.

Over medium heat, bring the sauce to a slow boil, along with the cilantro and salt. Slowly boil the sauce for 15 minutes to evaporate most of the water. Add the minnows, potatoes, and nopales. Heat through and serve.

Breaded Squid
Calamares Rebosados

6 servings

If you have never cooked squid, you are in for a treat. The squid cooks in about 1 minute—not much longer or you will be chewing rubber. You can buy the squid uncleaned and clean it yourself, or just buy some that already has been cleaned. I have even seen it cleaned and frozen but not cooked. There is no excuse for not trying this simple recipe!

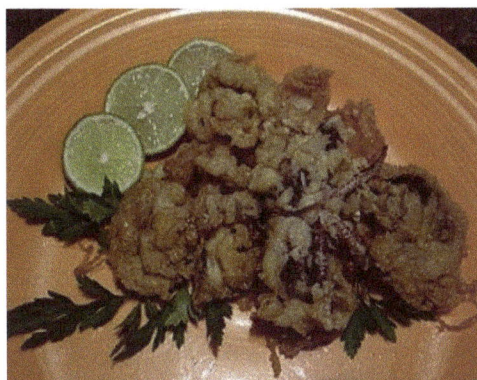

Ingredients

500 grams (1 pound) small squid
oil for frying
flour, for dredging
1 egg, beaten
1 lime, sliced
parsley sprigs for garnish

Clean the squid. Peel the bodies, and remove the quill (the transparent spine). Rinse under water.

Cut the squid bodies into strips, or if they are small, like the ones in the photo, leave them whole but remove the tentacles to fry separately. (Be sure to use the tentacles—they are the best part!)

Pour oil 13 mm / ½ inch or more deep in a pan. This is enough oil to avoid having to turn the squid. Heat until it is very hot (about 200°C/395°F).

Dredge the squid in flour. Then dip it into the beaten egg, and place in the hot oil. Cook the squid for no more than 1 minute. Use your eyes as the guide to cooking. When the batter turns color, they are done.

Serve accompanied by sliced lime and parsley sprigs.

If you like, you can serve with a dipping sauce of your choice.

Shrimp Ceviche
Ceviche de Camarón

8 servings

A good ceviche is fresh and flavorful. This recipe is an example of that. To remind you, ceviche is not raw but chemically cooked in the lime juice, which is extremely acidic. (You will see by the pink color of the shrimp after its marinated that it is not raw.) Add the tomatoes, onion, and cucumber, and you will have made a first course.

The addition of the *pico de gallo* (fresh salsa) adds another flavor layer. I make my fresh salsa with a ratio of 1 jalapeño to 1 tomato, or 1 serrano chile to 2 tomatoes. That may be a bit too spicy for you, but as you begin to train your taste buds to accept a little heat, you will find that this is a nice contrast to the soft texture and flavor of the tomatoes. Try using serrano chiles, if you dare! If you don't care for cilantro, you can leave it out, but this dish won't taste the same.

Ingredients
1 kilo (2.2 pounds) medium-sized raw shrimp, no heads
½ cup fresh lime juice
2 red tomatoes, chopped
1 large onion, finely diced
4 cucumbers, peeled and sliced thin
salsa pico de gallo (fresh salsa), recipe below
salt to taste

The shrimp must be fresh and kept cold. (Fresh seafood has a nice fresh scent, If it smells strong or fishy, do not buy it.) Peel and devein the shrimp; rinse thoroughly. Slice the shrimp lengthwise into thin slices; then place them in a container and pour the lime juice over the top. Refrigerate while it marinates for 6–8 minutes.

After the shrimp has marinated for the 6–8 minutes, add all the vegetables, salsa, and salt to taste. Stir well.

Serve with tostadas (small, round, crunchy tortillas) or saltine crackers

Salsa Pico de Gallo (salsa cruda—raw salsa)
Mild Version:
6 ripe roma tomatoes, seeds removed
2 jalapeños or serranos
½ white onion, finely diced
½ cup cilantro leaves, minced
2 limes

Chop the tomatoes into a medium-sized dice. Remove the seeds as you go—they add no flavor, just unwanted moisture.

Get your gloves on! Remove the stem end from the chiles, stand the chile on the flat end, and carefully slice down the chile between the flesh and the seeds—this is actually the easiest method to remove those pesky seeds—and then dice the chiles into very tiny squares.

Combine all the tomatoes, onion, cilantro, and as much of the chiles as you want. Then squeeze the juice from the 2 limes over the salsa and gently stir to combine.

Under *no* circumstances should you add salt! Salt will cause your salsa to swim in a pool of watery tomato juice, very unappetizing!

MARTHA

Meet Martha Patricia Valenzuela Zataraín

Have you ever known anyone who could smile at you and brighten your whole day? This lady has that effect on me. She always has a big grin, accompanied by a hug.

Martha (pronounced Marta) is known to her friends as Martita (little Martha) because she is very short! Conversely, her giving heart and personality are not short at all. Martita works full time during the week and teaches catechism at the local Catholic church to some of the poor colonia children on the weekends.

She is from El Concepción, Concordia, a small *puebla* (village) of about nine hundred people, located on the outskirts of Mazatlán. The youngest of six children, Martita moved to Mazatlán with her husband, Freddie, but still travels back to El Concepción often with her mom to see her family.

When she was young, Martita wanted her mother to teach her how to cook but the response was always, "No, you are too small and will get burned." This frustrated Martita very much. To get around her mother's objections, she began just hanging out in the kitchen when Mom cooked. She stared intently at what was being prepared and handed Mom the ingredients when it was time to use them. Still, she was too small to cook.

Martita began to sneak into the kitchen when her mom was absent and prepared meals by herself. In her own words, she began to "lose the meals"—meaning they were really bad and had to be saved by Mom. Over the years, through lots of practice, her cooking improved, and now she is a very accomplished cook. Her meals are always flavorful and creative. "Losing meals" is a thing of the past!

Today, her mom is almost ninety years old and still tells Martita how to cook! Señora Magdalena is a true mom, through and through, barking instructions as if no one had ever made the recipe before. When I visit her home, I am given a glass of *limonada* and instructed to sit down and watch. Of course, I do just that. She bosses me around too, for goodness sakes!

Cucumber Water
Agua de Pepino

12 servings

Cucumber water is only one of the many vegetable and fruit waters made here, especially in the summertime, when it is imperative to drink lots of water. The flavor is slightly cucumber with a bit of sweetness. It is not considered a sweet drink; the sugar just enhances the flavor of the cucumber. After you have tried this light concoction, try some others, like melon or carrot. We have juice bars all over town, where you can get just about any flavor of *aguas* you like at any time of the day. These are much healthier and cost much less than soft drinks or energy drinks.

Ingredients

500 grams (1 pound) cucumbers
4 Tablespoons sugar or to taste
3 liters (12½ cups) cold water

Peel and remove the seeds from the cucumbers. Roughly chop the cucumbers, and put them in the blender. Add the sugar and some of the water; liquefy totally. Empty this into a pitcher and add the remaining water. Taste and adjust the sugar if needed. Serve over ice.

Dessert Fruit Salad
Antojillo

6 servings

Martita invented the name of this recipe, so there is no translation available. It is a luscious, smooth dessert with a crunch of chocolate chips. I could eat this practically all day. The dessert is sweet but not overly sweet, because the sour cream balances out the sweetness of the condensed milk. It thickens to a semi-thick pudding without having to cook it. Mix all the ingredients, pop it in the refrigerator, try to wait the 3 hours for it to chill and thicken, and dig in!

Ingredients

1 large can fruit cocktail in syrup (850 g/30 ounces)
1 can sweetened condensed milk
500 grams (17½ ounces) sour cream
½ bag (6 ounces) chocolate chips

Pour the fruit with its syrup and all the other ingredients into a glass bowl. Mix well. Place in the refrigerator for 3 hours to chill. This is a stand-alone dessert or sweetened fruit salad. You also can serve it with cookies or a slice of cake.

Sweet Cow's Milk
Dulce de Leche de Vaca

6 servings

A thick vanilla pudding with a hint of zesty lime. The blender does most of the work for you; then you cook it on the stove for a couple of minutes to thicken, pour into a bowl or pretty glass, and place it in the refrigerator. How simple is that? I find that I make more desserts now than I ever did, because they are so easy and so flavorful. You may find yourself doing the same thing!

Ingredients

1 liter (4¼ cups) whole milk
1 cup sugar
½ cup flour
2 egg yolks
1 Tablespoon vanilla extract
zest of one lime

Slowly heat the milk to very warm but not hot.

In a blender, liquefy the sugar, flour, and egg yolks, adding the milk to this mixture while continuing to blend. Strain into a pan. Heat and stir until it begins to boil. Add the vanilla and lime zest. Continue cooking for 2 minutes. Pour into individual molds or custard cups and refrigerate.

Cooked Milk
Leche Cocida

6–8 servings

Because of the masa*, this is a very thick pudding that you can actually cut with a knife into servings. The first time I had this, I thought the pudding was a bit too starchy, but I was somehow compelled to keep eating. Before I knew it, my plate was clean, and I was asking for seconds! The moral here is, don't concentrate on the starchiness but on the flavors—it is very addictive! Martita and I like it with whipped cream.

For this pudding, Martita used a large shallow dish to allow her pudding to set up. If you want the pudding to have thicker slices, use a smaller dish, such as a pie plate.

Ingredients

250 grams (8 ounces) masa, raw (corn flour mixed with water into a dough) *
2 cups water
2 large piloncillo cones, hammered to break up (**see note below)
2 Tablespoons granulated sugar
1 can evaporated milk
3 Tablespoons cornstarch dissolved in 1 cup additional water
½ teaspoon vanilla

Place the prepared masa in a medium-sized saucepan. Add 1 cup water and mix until no lumps remain. (Martita and I use our hands to stir while breaking up the lumps. Remember: your hands are your best tool.) When it is smooth, add 1 more cup water, and stir again. Strain this masa liquid through a fine mesh strainer or cheesecloth, discarding all the solids. Put the liquid back into the pan.

Add the broken piloncillo, sugar, and evaporated milk to the masa liquid. Turn on low heat stirring constantly so it does not burn. When it is hot and the piloncillo is dissolved, add the cornstarch/water mixture and continue stirring until it is thick. Remove from heat. Add the vanilla and stir. Pour into a long pan or pie plate. Chill in the refrigerator until it is totally set. The pudding will be so thick that you can cut it with a knife. (This is a good thing.)

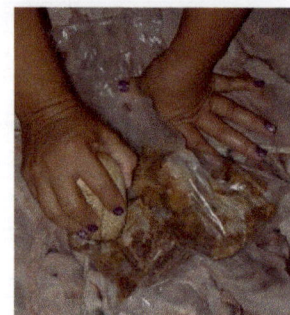

* Masa dough (see photo) can be purchased pre-made at a store that makes corn tortillas (*tortillerias*) or made yourself by mixing Maseca (corn flour for tortillas) with water to form a dough. If you have a favorite Mexican restaurant, you can probably purchase some there as well.

Hammering the piloncillo: Here, Martha uses a rock and the kitchen floor to break up the hard sugar in a thick plastic bag. She does not own a hammer, so she keeps a clean rock in her kitchen for these types of jobs.

Mango Snow
Nieve de Mango

12 servings

This really does look like mango-colored snow. Three types of milk plus fresh mango gives this frozen dessert a complex flavor that no one would ever guess is so simple to prepare. Removing from the freezer and allowing it to thaw before refreezing eliminates almost all of the ice crystals usually found in iced milks. Oh, I'll bet this would be good with some chocolate chunks on top!

Ingredients

500 grams (1 pound) mangoes, peeled and de-seeded
2 cans sweetened condensed milk
2 cans evaporated milk
2 cups milk, whole or 2%

Purée all the ingredients in a blender. Pour into a bowl, and freeze for 2 hours. Remove from the freezer and allow it to thaw and liquefy. Return it to the freezer, and allow to freeze again for 3 hours.

Green Soup
(literal translation)
Sopa Verde

5 servings

This soup is not really green but rather a lovely greenish tint; it's a light cream soup with a thin layer of butter on top. The cream part comes from mild sour cream, so it is not a heavy soup. The green comes from a poblano chile but without the spicy heat, just a hint of that grassy poblano flavor.

Ingredients

2 liters (2 quarts) water
1 Tablespoon oil
3 bay leaves
1 pinch salt
200 grams (7 ounces) small elbow macaroni
1 poblano, charred
250 grams (9 ounces) mild sour cream
1 Tablespoon chicken bouillon powder
3½ Tablespoons butter

Put the water in a pot to boil with the oil, bay leaves, and salt.

Once the water is boiling, add the elbow macaroni and cook until it is *almost tender.* Drain the pasta and reserve the liquid in a bowl. (You will be boiling the pasta again for 5 more minutes later on, and you do not want to overcook it.) Discard the bay leaves.

Char the poblano on the stove. Place it in a covered bowl for at least 10 minutes to steam. Remove the charred skin under slowly running water. Remove the stem, seeds, and veins, and purée in a blender with the sour cream and the bouillon.

In a separate pot, melt the butter. Add the drained macaroni and stir for about 2 minutes. Add the pasta liquid and chile/cream mixture. Heat, stirring constantly for 3 minutes. Serve immediately.

Serve with beef or chicken as a main dish.

Chipotle Chicken
Pollo ala Chipotle

4 servings

Using canned chipotle chiles is a shortcut to an amazing sauce that can be as spicy or non-spicy as you like. When Martita makes this dish for her family, she uses the entire can of chipotles but tells me when she makes it for company, she only uses half that amount. The sour cream counteracts some of the heat in the sauce but not all. Chipotles have a wonderful smoky flavor that makes a perfect pairing with chicken or shrimp.

Chicken is a main staple of the diet here in Mazatlán. There are so many wonderful sauces for chicken, and all so very different. I can live with chicken as a staple in my diet too.

Ingredients

1 chicken, cut into pieces, with skin and bones
butter and oil combination for browning the chicken
1½ cups V8 juice
2 cups mild sour cream
1 small can (105g/3.7 ounces) chipotle chiles
½ teaspoon ground pepper
¼ onion, finely diced
4 carrots, peeled and cut into thick sticks

Brown the chicken well on all sides in the butter/oil.

Purée the V8 juice, sour cream, chipotle chiles, and ground pepper in a blender.

When the chicken is well browned, add the onion, carrot slices, and blender ingredients. Cover and cook 45 minutes over medium-low heat until the chicken is tender and cooked through.

Chicken ala Monterrey
Pollo ala Monterrey

4 servings

This is one of those dishes that I would classify as comfort food. It is fresh tasting because of the bell peppers and has a richness that makes you say, "M-m-m, can I have some more, please?"

I serve this for my guests who either don't like spicy dishes or whose tummies just can't tolerate chiles. There is absolutely zero spiciness here. It is beautifully colorful and invites you to dip right in!

Need more for a larger crowd? Just double all the ingredients and you can serve 8, and so on.

Ingredients

6 Tablespoons butter
800 grams/1¾ pounds chicken breasts, no skin or bones
¼ teaspoon ground white pepper
1 teaspoon salt
4 small green bell peppers, sliced into strips
1 onion, thinly sliced
1 cup mild sour cream
250 grams (9 ounces) Chihuahua cheese, shredded

In large pan, over medium-low heat, melt the butter, but do not let it brown. Cut the chicken into large bite-sized chunks. Add them to the pan along with the pepper and salt.

Cook until the chicken is white on the outside but not cooked all the way through, about 3–5 minutes. Add the sliced onion and green peppers. Cover and cook until the chicken is cooked through but still juicy. This should take about 5 more minutes; then turn the heat to low.

Stir in the sour cream and half of the shredded cheese. Adjust the salt at this time. When that cheese is melted, add the remainder of the cheese on top, but do not stir it in. Cover the pot and remove it from the heat. When the cheese is melted on top, it is ready to serve. Serve with white rice.

Marinated Chicken
Pollo Adobado

4 servings

The addition of Coke, a meat tenderizer, makes this chicken melt in your mouth. Don't be afraid to use all 12 chiles. Guajillos are very mild, so they do not add much heat, and they balance out the sweetness of the Coke. In this instance, the chiles add not only flavor but also a tremendous amount of color. Although the chicken cooks for 1½ hours, it is not hands-on time. It is simple to make and will delight your taste buds.

Ingredients

12 guajillo chiles
4 cloves garlic
1 teaspoon Mexican oregano
½ teaspoon ground coffee
½ liter Coke
1 chicken, cut in pieces, skin removed
2 teaspoons butter, melted
½ teaspoon ground pepper

Preheat the oven to 190°C/375°F.

Remove the stems, seeds, and veins from the chiles. Don't worry if a seed or two remains in the chile—the next step will remove them. Boil a small pot of water, and add the cleaned chiles to rehydrate, about 5 minutes. Remove them from the water (discard the water), and place the chiles in a blender with the garlic and oregano.

Purée to a smooth consistency. Use some of the Coke if you need to thin it out for blending. Then add to this the coffee and the remainder of the Coke. Blend well.

Put the chicken pieces in a covered casserole dish. Drizzle with the butter, the pepper, and blended ingredients. Cover and put in the preheated oven, 1½ hours.

Pozole

12 servings

Although Rosie doesn't think this is the "real" pozole, I love this one! It is rich tasting, full of meat, and a flash to make. Martita knows that some people do not like the pigs feet so she does not incorporate them into the main soup but instead serves them on the side. This is definitely one recipe to make on a cool autumn or winter day.

The key to this recipe is to make sure the pork you buy is still on the bones. Like making a good beef or chicken broth, the bones add more flavor than the meat.

Ingredients

2 kilos (4½ pounds) pozole corn (whole hominy)
2 kilos (4½ pounds) small pork ribs
2 kilos (4½ pounds) pork back bone with meat
3 large purple onions (divided usage)
4 kilos (9 pounds) pig's feet or pig shanks (optional)
6 dried chile guajillo, stems, seeds, and veins removed
2 cubes tomato bouillon
1 head garlic, peeled
1 Tablespoon oregano
½ teaspoon ground black pepper
½ head cabbage
6–8 fresh limes, cut into quarters
salt in a small bowl
tortilla chips

In a large soup pot or Dutch oven, put the corn, the ribs, backbones, and 1 onion, finely diced. Cover with cold water, and cook for 3½ hours. If you choose to cook the pigs feet, place them in a different pot filled with cold water, and cook those for 3½ hours.

After 3½ hours, turn the heat down to simmer. In a separate pan with boiling water, drop the chiles in, and allow to boil for 5 minutes. Drain the chiles (discard the water) and place them in a blender with the bouillon cubes, ¼ cup clean water, all the garlic, oregano, and pepper. Purée until very smooth—no lumps. More water can be added to the blender if necessary. Pour this into the soup and stir to combine. Allow to simmer for another 5 minutes for the flavors to meld.

Very finely shred the cabbage and the 2 remaining onions. Place them in separate serving bowls.

Serve the pozole in soup bowls with the bones, meat, corn, and broth. Pass bowls of cabbage, onions, lime, salt, and tortilla chips for everyone to dress up their own soup.

Note: I prefer not to have bones in my finished pozole bowl. After the meat is cooked, I remove the bones from the soup, putting any meat that was still attached to the bones back in the pot. Place the meatless bones on a separate plate. It is amazing how many people like to place a bone in their pozole while they eat.

Marlin Stew
Marlin en Estofado

6 servings

We all know by now that the fish in these "marlin" recipes is not marlin at all but smoked tuna. Read more about this in the "Is It Smoked Marlin or Smoked Tuna?" section.

This stew has a thick sauce, and the ingredients differ from the recipe by Leticia. Try them both to see which you like best. Both recipes are rich and flavorful, with bright vibrant colors to tempt the palate and the eyes. The smoked tuna blends into the tomato broth and imparts a fish taste that is pleasant and not overpowering.

Ingredients

6 tomatoes, cooked
6 guajillo chiles
4 cloves garlic
1 box (210 g/7.4 ounces) tomato purée
2 cubes tomato bouillon

500 grams (1 pound) smoked tuna
4 carrots, medium dice
250 grams (8 ounces) green beans, cut into 2 cm / ¾ in. pieces
1 bottle (240 g/8.5 ounces) green olives, pits removed, cut in half
3 bay leaves
1½ Tablespoons oregano

Note about the size of packaged ingredients: In your area, the sizes of cans, jars, or boxes may be slightly different from here in Mexico. This is not a problem on recipes of this type. Close is good—you can easily be off 14 grams or ½ ounce, more or less, and still have a successful recipe. As in all recipes, use your own judgment.

Prepare the tomatoes: Put the tomatoes in a small pot of boiling water until the skins split, 5 minutes. Drain and discard the water.

Prepare the chiles: Remove the stems, seeds, and veins from the guajillo chiles. In a small pan of boiling water, boil the chiles for about 5 minutes to rehydrate them. Drain (discard water), and put in a blender jar with the cooked tomatoes, garlic, tomato purée, and the bouillon cubes. Blend until very smooth—no bits remaining.

Break the fish into small pieces and put in a large pan. Add the diced carrots, green beans, olives, bay leaves, oregano, and the blender ingredients. Stir and begin to heat on medium to medium-high, stirring occasionally to keep the stew from sticking to the bottom of the pan. Let it cook for 45 minutes until the vegetables are cooked.

Serve in bowls over white rice with fresh tortillas to sop up the tomato broth.

MARY ELENA

Meet Mary Elena Villa Falcón

Mary Elena's nickname is China (pronounced *Cheena*), which means "curly hair." For years I had no idea what her real name was. When I met her about five or six years ago, she was extremely shy and barely uttered a word to anyone. Since then, she has come out of her shell. Now married with a beautiful little girl named Emily, she is funny and rarely quiet—I think that is a good thing!

Born and raised in Mazatlán, China is the oldest and only girl of five children. (Maybe having four brothers made her so quiet.)

A self-taught cook, she began learning to cook when she was in secondaria (junior high or middle school). Twice a year, her mom would leave for extended periods to travel to the state of Durango to visit China's grandmother. Dad and brothers, choosing not to go on the trips, stayed at home. China, being the only girl, was enlisted to do the cooking. At this point, she had no practical knowledge of cooking.

China started experimenting with a variety of ingredients and found that she had an aptitude for food preparation. She began inventing meals that were quick, easy, and well received by the family. (I think it was because they didn't want to learn to cook.)

As time went on, she became more and more interested in food and the various types of preparation methods. Being a health-conscious woman, her recipes are usually low-fat and low-sugar but very tasty. Today, she is still learning about healthy foods and is passing that knowledge on to her friends. Several days a week after work, she encourages—no, drags—friends and coworkers to join her for long power-walks or jogs on the beach. She's a very long way from that shy little girl of a few short years ago.

Broccoli Salad
Ensalada de Brócoli

6 servings

Fresh vegetables are an important part of the Mexican diet. Salads like this one are invented on a daily basis to highlight the season's bounty. This recipe is for a primavera (spring) salad with a light olive oil dressing. The broccoli is pre-cooked a bit to remove the harsh raw taste and then chilled before mixing with the other vegetables and dressed. Very fresh-tasting and simple to prepare.

Ingredients
1 kilo (2.2 pounds) broccoli, cut in florets, cooked
8 tomatoes, cut in halves

1 onion, sliced
2 cucumbers, diced or sliced
2 Tablespoons olive oil
2 Tablespoons apple cider vinegar
2 Tablespoons water
1 Tablespoon mustard
2 cloves garlic
½ Tablespoon salt
1 Tablespoon red onion, finely chopped for garnish

Cook or steam the broccoli florets until the surface can be pierced with a fork, no more than 5 minutes. Drain; then run cold water over the broccoli to cool.

Toss the broccoli, tomatoes, onion slices, and cucumbers in a salad bowl.

Blend together the remaining ingredients *except* the red onion. Pour the dressing over the broccoli mixture and toss. Dust with the red onion.

Black Bean Salad
Ensalada de Frijoles Negros

12 servings

Either homemade or canned black beans can be used for this hearty salad. Consider making them yourself; they are easy to cook, and you don't get any of that industrial strength sludge that usually comes at the bottom of a can. The colors are inviting but foremost, there are different textures, from soft beans and cheese to crunchy bell peppers and onions. No one will be able to resist this salad!

Ingredients

500 grams (1 pound) black beans, cooked
500 grams (1 pound) corn kernels, canned or frozen
1 green or yellow bell pepper, diced
½ cup onion, diced
1 cup Manchego cheese, shredded

For the dressing
½ cup fresh salsa (salsa Mexicana or pico de gallo)
2 Tablespoons cilantro, minced
1 Tablespoon garlic, minced
½ Tablespoon ground cumin
¼ cup olive oil

Place the beans, corn, green or yellow pepper, onion, and cheese in a salad bowl. Mix well.

Whisk together all the dressing ingredients in a bowl. Pour over the salad and toss.

Hearts of Palm and Surimi Salad
Ensalada de Palmitos y Surimi

6 servings

Surimi is available just about everywhere. It is imitation crab meat made from white fish. The salad is fresh and combines several different flavors and textures. Make sure to buy a good-quality surimi to accentuate the mango and hearts of palm. Hearts of palm are canned here, the same as you would find in your grocery store. The addition of cinnamon may be a surprise, but it only enhances the flavor of the mango. This entire salad only takes about 3 minutes to prepare. Slice the ingredients, whip up the dressing, and enjoy. How easy is that?

Ingredients

1 kilo (2.2 pounds) surimi, sliced
2 mangoes, peeled and cut into cubes
500 grams (1.1 pounds) hearts of palm, sliced (1 large can, drained)
2 Tablespoons olive oil
1 Tablespoon honey
2 Tablespoons fresh lime juice
2 Tablespoons pecans, finely chopped
½ teaspoon ground cinnamon

In a salad bowl, combine the surimi with the mango and hearts of palm.

In a small bowl, mix together the oil, honey, lime juice, pecans, and cinnamon. Pour over the surimi mixture and toss.

Turkey Salad
Ensalada de Pavo

4 servings

China likes to use iceberg lettuce for this salad because it has a nice crunch, even after drizzling with a warm dressing. Sliced turkey breast and oranges, together with the fruit and dressing, go very well together. This is a different and tasty salad to have as a starter to your meal.

Ingredients

1 head lettuce, washed and cut into squares
2 large oranges, peeled and cut in slices
4 slices turkey breast, cooked, cut into thin, short slices
2 sprigs mint, finely chopped

2 Tablespoons olive oil
½ teaspoon orange peel, finely shredded
2 Tablespoons fresh orange juice
½ teaspoon ground white pepper
2–3 scallions, finely sliced (white and green parts)
8 prunes without pits, diced

3 small crisp tortillas (known as *horneadas*), broken into bite-sized pieces

In a salad bowl, place the lettuce, slices of orange, sliced turkey, and mint.

Warm the oil in a frying pan; then remove it from the heat. Add the grated orange peel, orange juice, pepper, and scallions. Pour it over the salad while it is still warm. Toss. After tossing the salad, arrange the prune pieces and crisp tortillas on top. Serve.

Pasta in Herb Sauce
Pasta en Salsa de Hierbas

4 servings

Fresh herbs are the key to this pasta sauce. The herb combination is reminiscent of springtime, with the scents of fresh basil, parsley, and green onion. China loves to cook healthy meals for her family, as evidenced by this low-fat sauce. It certainly does not taste low-fat. In fact, the yogurt gives it a bit of tang but no heaviness. The only salt comes from the salted pasta cooking water. So dig in—no guilt found in this sauce recipe.

Ingredients

500 grams (1 pound) pasta (small elbow type)
1 Tablespoon olive oil
1 small onion, diced
1 clove garlic, smashed
2 Tablespoons flour
½ cup vegetable broth
1 cup natural low-fat yogurt
2 Tablespoons parsley, finely chopped
2 Tablespoons fresh basil, finely chopped
2 Tablespoons green onion, finely chopped
ground black pepper to taste

Cook the pasta in well-salted water. Drain and keep it hot.
Heat the oil in a frying pan. Sauté the onion and garlic for 2–3 minutes. Add the flour and broth. Stir continually until it thickens. Add in the yogurt, and heat it without letting it boil or scorch. Turn off the heat and stir in the parsley, basil, green onion, and black pepper.

Serve the pasta in bowls, and bathe it with the sauce.

Mushroom Quiche
Quiche de Champiñones

8 servings

Although it is called a quiche, it is more like a frittata. It can be served at any meal, warm or hot. We used regular white mushrooms and portobellos, but the choice of which mushroom to use is always determined by what is available in our markets. China told me she tested this recipe with many variations of ingredients, including mustards, herbs, and type of onions. She is happy now with this version, and you will be too!

Ingredients

4 eggs, slightly beaten

½ cup low-fat milk
1 Tablespoon Dijon mustard
2 Tablespoons fresh dill, chopped
ground black pepper to taste
1 Tablespoon olive oil
4 green onions, chopped
125 grams (4.5 ounces) fresh white mushrooms, sliced
125 grams (4.5 ounces) fresh mushrooms, sliced (any other type mushroom or more white mushrooms)

Preheat the oven to 175°C/350°F.

Place the eggs, milk, mustard, dill, and pepper in a bowl; beat slightly to mix.

Heat the oil in an oven-safe (29 cm/11 in.) frying pan over medium heat. Add the onions, and sauté for two minutes. Then add the mushrooms (both types that you have chosen), cook, stirring occasionally until they are tender.

Pour the egg mixture over the mushrooms. Cook over low heat for 5 minutes or until it becomes semi-firm around the edges.

Place the frying pan in the oven, and bake until it is golden, about 8 minutes. Cut into wedges and serve.

Tostadas of Fava Beans and Salsa
Tostadas de Habas y Salsa

6 servings

Fava beans make this more of a mid-afternoon meal than a snack. If you are not familiar with dried fava beans, look for them in a bag near the other dried beans. They are yellow and look like large yellow lima beans. The flavor is mild but with a lima-bean type texture. Creamy panela cheese is a perfect complement to their texture. Add as much salsa as you like. China suggests you make other salsas too. She often uses a chipotle salsa made the same way as the salsa below but substituting canned chipotles for the árbol chiles, because she thinks that variety in food is a good thing!

Fava beans cook relatively fast, so 20–30 minutes is all the time you need to cook them.

Ingredients
18 small corn tostadas (7.5–10 cm/3–4 in.) in diameter
(horneadas, baked not fried)
250 grams (8 ounces) dried fava beans
1 Tablespoon oil
1 tomato, diced finely
½ cup onion, diced
1½ teaspoons salt or to taste
50 grams (1¾ ounces) panela or fresh cheese in small cubes

For the salsa
½ cup dried árbol chile
½ cup onion, diced
1 clove garlic

Bring about 6 cups of water to a boil in a medium pan. Meanwhile, sort the fava beans, discarding any clumps of dirt, rocks, and ugly or discolored beans. After the water has come to a boil, add the beans. Do not add salt at this time. Continue to boil them until they are tender.

Heat the oil in a large frying pan over medium-low heat. Add in the diced tomato and onion. Cook until the onion is translucent. Take the cooked beans from their cooking water with a spoon, taking care not to take too much liquid with them. When all the beans have been transferred to the frying pan, start to smoosh the beans and tomato slightly. There should be a combination of smooshed beans with unsmooshed pieces of beans. Sauté them for 5 minutes. Add the salt.

Spread this mixture on the tostadas; then add some of the cheese on top.

For the salsa:
Mix all the salsa ingredients with a mortar and pestle until well smooshed. Spoon over the tostadas and serve.

Pineapple Milkshake
Malteada de Piña

4 servings

Creamy, frothy, fruity are the best ways to describe this drink. This milkshake tastes so good that you will be tempted to have it for breakfast. Great as a midday treat or with lunch. The cinnamon is an interesting touch, because it seems to enhance the flavor of the pineapple. Try to get the canned pineapple in its own juice with no sugar added—you will get more of the real pineapple flavor.

Ingredients
1 can (600 grams/21 ounces) canned pineapple chunks with juice (do *not* drain)
2 cups vanilla ice cream
1 cup low-fat milk
½ teaspoon ground cinnamon

Blend all the ingredients in a blender until smooth. Serve immediately.

Mixed Fruit Mousse
Mousse de Frutas Mixtas

6 servings

This is so light and refreshing, you will want to have some in your freezer at all times—for the family or for when company drops in unexpectedly. It is the easiest frozen dessert you will ever make. No added sugars make this a healthy treat, so dig in!

Ingredients
2 bananas, peeled, cut in pieces and frozen
½ cup low-fat milk
1 cup strawberries, frozen

In a blender, purée the bananas and half of the milk until it is smooth. Add the strawberries and the remainder of the milk. Purée again until it is smooth and starts to look like ice cream.

Place in a glass container, and freeze until it is the consistency you like.

Hazelnut Cake
Pastel de Avellanas

8 servings

The only flour in this recipe is what you use to grease and flour the pan. If your diet is wheat-free, you can use more ground hazelnuts instead. The cake we baked today was baked in a 9-inch cake pan, because China wanted to serve a piece to everyone in attendance. You can bake it in a smaller diameter pan if you want it thicker. You do not need to adjust the baking time. The cake has a spongy texture similar to angel food cake, but because of the nuts, it is a bit more dense. In every bite you get the scent of orange and almonds. Although China does not serve it with whipped cream or ice cream, that thought keeps creeping into my mind.

Ingredients

4 egg whites
3 Tablespoons *fine or superfine* granulated sugar**
3 egg yolks
½ cup ground hazelnuts
4 Tablespoons Maria's cookies, crushed
½ Tablespoon baking powder
1 Tablespoon orange peel, fresh
¼ Tablespoon almond extract

Preheat the oven to 180°C/350°F. Grease and flour a cake pan up to 23 cm/9 inches in diameter.

Beat the egg whites until they are stiff. Slowly add the sugar, a spoonful at a time, beating after each addition until you have achieved a thick meringue.

In a separate bowl, beat the egg yolks until they are light and fluffy. Slowly add the remaining ingredients. Fold the meringue into the yolk mixture to fully incorporate. Pour into the prepared cake pan. Bake for 30–35 minutes. A toothpick inserted into the middle should come out clean. Let it cool slightly in the pan for 5 minutes before removing it from the pan to a cake rack to cool.

** If you do not have fine or superfine sugar, make your own. It is simple to do and may save a trip to the grocery store:
1. Start with a bit more granulated sugar than you will need for the recipe because some of the sugar will turn to dust.
2. Pour the granulated sugar into a blender or food processor fitted with a metal blade.
3. Cover the food processor or blender with a damp towel—this will trap the sugar dust the processing produces. Skipping this step will give your kitchen a lovely sugary coating.
4. Turn on the processor or blender for 30 seconds to 1 minute. Leave the lid on for another 30 seconds for the dust inside to settle. You now have fine to superfine sugar. Store it as you would regular granulated sugar.

Vanilla Pudding
Pudín de Vainilla

4 servings

Pudding with no eggs and no cream—it is wonderful! As you can see, it is low-fat and low-sugar too. And the entire recipe takes less than 5 minutes, start to finish. The pudding is creamy and light—a perfect ending to a heavy dinner.

Ingredients

2 cups low-fat milk
3 Tablespoons cornstarch
3 Tablespoons maple syrup (the kind you use for pancakes)
¼ teaspoon salt
1 Tablespoon vanilla extract

Mix all the ingredients except the vanilla in a pan, stirring well to eliminate the lumps. Heat this mixture over low heat, stirring it constantly until it thickens. Remove from the heat. Stir in the vanilla.

Pour into one large mold or individual sized molds. Serve warm or cold.

Meatballs
Albondigas

4 servings

Who would have thought that a meal like this would come out of Mexico? It is a basic meatball stew with a bit of a twist from the cumin. I love the aroma of cumin, so I try to sneak in a bit more when no one is looking! Serve this stew in bowls so everyone gets some of that wonderful broth.

You will note that there are four recipes for *Albondigas* in this book. They all offer a different flavor. The cooking techniques are the same, and some ingredients are common to all the recipes. Try each one and determine which you like best—that will not be as easy as you might think!

Ingredients

For the sauce:
1 clove garlic
2 tomatoes
½ onion
2 teaspoons ground cumin
6 cups water

For the meatballs:
500 grams (1 pound) ground beef
½ cup rice, cooked
salt and pepper to taste

4 potatoes, peeled and diced
3 carrots, peeled and diced

Prepare the sauce: Add all the sauce ingredients to a blender and purée. Pour into a large pot, and bring to a slow boil.

Prepare the meatballs: Mix the ground beef, rice, salt, and pepper. Knead until thoroughly mixed. Form the meat into small walnut-sized balls.

When the sauce has started to boil, carefully drop in the meatballs, and add the diced potatoes and carrots. Continue to cook over low heat until the vegetables are tender, 15–20 minutes.

Picadillo

8 servings

This is a type of Mexican hash. It is normally plated with a side of rice, but China's is very brothy, much like a stew. Make sure not to overcook the potatoes and squash. They should cook at the same rate and only until they are just tender—you don't want to cook the life out of them. If you cannot find Mexican squash (*calabaza*), then you will need to use a variety similar to zucchini. Make note that zucchini cooks faster and gets mushy if it is overcooked, so put it in the pan when the potatoes are almost cooked.

Ingredients

For the salsa:
½ onion
2 tomatoes
1 clove garlic
1 teaspoon ground cumin
1 liter (4 cups) water

Meat and vegetables:
500 grams (1 pound) ground beef, very lean
3 Tablespoons vegetable oil
4 potatoes, peeled and diced
250 grams (8 ounces) squash, diced
salt and pepper to taste

Purée all the ingredients for the salsa. Set aside.

In a large frying pan, sauté the meat in the oil until it is golden. Add in the potatoes and squash. Season with salt and pepper. Mix in the salsa. Allow to cook over low heat until the vegetables are tender.

Serve with red or white rice and, of course, fresh tortillas.

Karina Ann Betlem

Oriental Chicken Salad
Ensalada Oriental de Pollo

6 servings

This salad is a complete meal in one bowl and is particularly delightful on a warm day. You can even use leftover roasted, sautéed, or poached chicken. The ingredients are fresh-tasting, and the dressing is light. Because this recipe does not call for much chicken, it also makes a great side dish.

Ingredients

For the salad:
2 cups cooked chicken, cold, cut in cubes
1 cup cooked rice, cold
1 cucumber, peeled and diced
1 red bell pepper, diced
2 tomatoes, diced
500 grams (1 pound) corn kernels, cooked (may be canned or frozen)

For the dressing:
1 Tablespoon soy sauce
1 Tablespoon fresh lime juice
1 Tablespoon olive oil

China removes the seeds from the cucumbers and tomatoes before dicing them for the salad. They add no flavor, just unwanted moisture.

Mix all the salad ingredients in a large bowl.

Combine all the dressing ingredients in a different bowl and mix well. Pour over the salad and serve. Garnish with avocado slices.

Mole of Mazatlán
Mole de Mazatlán

2 servings

The wonderful mole in this recipe is actually from China's mother-in-law, Señora Guadalupe Beatriz Ruez Jimenez. Señora Guadalupe was very kind to invite me to her home and into her kitchen one very hot day to make this, so we could include it in China's chapter. Muchas gracias, Señora!

This recipe will probably surprise you in two ways. First, it is extremely simple to make. Many moles have as many as thirty ingredients; this one has only a handful. Second, it uses animal cookies for both flavor and to thicken the sauce. Don't scoff! Many cooks use these small classic cookies in sauces. They are sweet, have a nice vanilla flavor, and dissolve well to thicken a sauce, so the number of ingredients they need to have on hand is diminished. Here is another 30-minutes-or-less recipe—but it sure doesn't taste like it!

Ingredients

These first 4 ingredients will make the broth for thinning out the mole:
2 quarts water
½ medium onion, left whole
1 clove garlic, left whole
½ chicken with skin and bone, cut into 4 or 5 parts

For the Mole:

4 Tablespoons oil, vegetable or canola
2 cinnamon sticks, about 4 inches long
3 whole cloves
5 dried guajillo chiles, stems, seeds, and veins removed
4 dried pasilla chiles, stems, seeds, and veins removed
100 grams animal crackers (cookies)
1 disk Abuelita brand chocolate (90 grams)
1 Tablespoon salt, or to taste
1½ teaspoons sugar, or to taste

Heat the water in a large pan with the onion and garlic. When the water is hot but not boiling, add the chicken pieces and cook, uncovered, skimming the foam off as it cooks. Let it simmer in the hot water for about 10–15 minutes, depending on the size of the chicken pieces.

Meanwhile, heat the oil to medium hot in a frying pan. Add the whole cinnamon sticks, and stir until they are fragrant, about 1 minute. Remove them from the oil and place in a blender jar. Put the cloves in the oil, stir for 2 seconds, and remove them to the blender.

Put the chiles in the hot oil one at a time. Fry on both sides until they look tan colored. Remove to the blender and place another chile in the oil. Repeat this until all the chiles have been fried and placed in the blender.

Toss the animal crackers into the hot oil, and fry on both sides until they are golden. Remove to the blender. Add the chocolate disk to the blender and about 7 to 9 ladles of your hot chicken broth—enough to make it blend smoothly. The mole will have a consistency of pancake batter.

Remove the chicken pieces from the broth and put on a plate. Reserve the broth.

Put the blended mole into a clean large pan and add 4 cups of the broth. Stir to mix well. Add the chicken pieces, and stir to make sure all the little nooks and crannies are filled with mole. Then add the salt (less if you don't want that much salt) and the sugar. It is done!

Serve with white rice, using the mole as a gravy for the rice.

Note: You can easily add eight more pieces of chicken to the cooking broth and then into the mole for a dinner party. This recipe makes a lot of mole, so just use the mole ingredients without changing the quantities.

Señora Guadalupe tells me that if you have any mole left over, you can use it by heating a corn tortilla, placing refried beans down the center, covering the beans with some mole, and topping with fresh cheese (*panela*). Then roll it up and eat it!

Another note: The dried guajillo and pasilla chiles are available on the Mexican food aisle in your grocery store. They are usually packaged in clear cellophane bags. Using both types of chiles gives a dual-flavor layer. Don't skimp on these.

Chicken in Cream with Mushrooms
Pollo en Crema de Champiñones

4 servings

The rich mushroom sauce is tinted with just a hint of green from the flavorful bell pepper. You can save time by cooking the chicken breasts in pieces, rather than whole. The pieces cook faster, and it is almost impossible to overcook them this way. The trick is to stir and watch—don't walk away, or they can overcook. Over medium heat, the chicken pieces will be cooked through in about 4–5 minutes.

Ingredients

½ green bell pepper
250 grams (1 cup) mild sour cream
250 grams (1 cup) media crema (table cream)
1 can mushrooms (184 g/6.5 ounces), drained
1 can cream of mushroom soup
3 Tablespoons vegetable oil
4 chicken breasts, skinless/boneless, cut in pieces
salt and pepper to taste

In a blender, combine the bell pepper, sour cream, media crema, mushrooms, and cream of mushroom soup. Purée until smooth.

Heat the vegetable oil over medium-low heat in a large frying pan. Carefully place the chicken breast pieces in the oil, and sauté until they are almost cooked through. This does not take very long, so don't walk away. (They will continue to cook a bit in the mushroom sauce). Salt and pepper to taste.

Pour the mushroom mixture over the breast pieces. Allow it to come to a slow boil, and serve with white rice and a green salad with tomatoes and cucumbers.

Chicken Sandwiches with Peaches
Sandwiches de Pollo con Durazno

4 servings

China amazes me with her flavor combinations. I would have never considered pairing peaches with onions, but the flavor is a natural! Sweet fresh peaches and onions sautéed in a vinaigrette of dry sherry and vinegar all piled on top of a freshly cooked, hot chicken breast—you can taste it, can't you?

Not the season for fresh peaches in your area? Canned peaches are *not* a substitute. Frozen is okay if they are unsweetened. With this sandwich, China will be your new best friend!

Ingredients

1 Tablespoon vegetable oil
2 cups onion, chopped
¼ cup sugar
2 peaches, peeled, pitted, and chopped
⅓ cup cider vinegar
⅓ cup dry sherry
½ teaspoon ground black pepper

4 medium chicken breasts, boneless and skinless
8 slices multigrain bread

Heat the oil in a frying pan over low heat. Add the onions, and sauté until they are soft but not browned. Sprinkle in the sugar, and heat until it dissolves. Slowly add the peaches, and cook until they are crisp tender. Then stir in the vinegar, sherry, and pepper; heat and set aside.

In a separate pan on medium-high heat, roast the chicken breasts until their juices have dried.

Lightly grill or toast the bread slices. Top each of 4 slices of the toast with a chicken breast; then top that with the peach mixture and cover with the other bread slice. Serve.

Mexican Pork Chops
Chuletas de Cerdo a la Mexicana

4 servings

This meal is so colorful, it just begs to be eaten! No spicy heat here—the poblano only adds a different pepper taste from the bell pepper. You will be able to tell the difference in each tasty bite. When you brown the pork chops, make sure not to overcook them. (No one likes tough, shoe-leather pork chops.) They will finish cooking in the oven.

Ingredients

Oil cooking spray
500 grams (1 pound) pork chops
1 onion, chopped
1 green bell pepper, chopped
1 very small poblano chile, seeded and chopped—*not* charred
400 grams (14 ounces) tomatoes, chopped
2 cups corn kernels
½ cup red salsa, bottled or homemade (Pace works well)
1 ½ Tablespoons Mexican oregano
½ Tablespoon ground cumin

Preheat the oven to 180°C/350°F.

Spray an oven-safe frying pan with the cooking spray. Heat the pan until it is very hot; then brown the pork chops. Remove them from the pan and set aside.

In the same pan, sauté the onion and peppers until they are tender. Add the remainder of the ingredients, stirring frequently until they are heated through.

Put the pork chops back into the pan, nestling them underneath the vegetables. Spoon some of the mixture over top of the chops. Cover the pan tightly with aluminum foil. Place in the preheated oven, and bake 45–50 minutes, until the chops are done but still tender.

Spicy Shrimp
Camarónes Picantes

4 servings

Carrot juice gets very sweet when it is reduced to a thick syrup. Add to this the chipotle chiles and pineapple, and you'll have a plate full of sweet, spicy shrimp. Only a portion of one chipotle chile is used, so it is not spicy hot, just smoky flavored with a wee touch of spice. The pineapple is refreshing and will remind you of a warm summertime shrimp salad. We ate another helping of this later in the day, when it was cold. It lost nothing in flavor, but we found out it was possible to take this on an outing or picnic. For traveling, keep the shrimp cold, and put the ingredients together when you are ready to eat.

Ingredients

3 liters (3 quarts) carrot juice
½ Tablespoon chipotle chile (from canned), minced fine
½ cup vegetable oil
24 medium or large shrimp, peeled and cooked*
6 cups cooked rice
4 cups pineapple chunks, fresh or canned

Pour the carrot juice into a saucepan and bring to a slow boil. Lower the heat to simmer and allow the liquid to reduce for about 40 minutes, until all that remains is a sweet residue.

Mix this sweet residue with the chipotle and oil, stir well, and heat through, about 1 minute.

Serve the shrimp on a bed of rice. Add the pineapple on top and around the plate; then bathe with the carrot sauce.

* Cook the shrimp in either boiling salted water for 2 minutes, or sauté in a pan with butter or oil until they change color.

Batter-Fried Shrimp Tacos
Tacos Capeados

8 servings

Many Latin cultures have their own version of *Tacos Capeados*. In Cuba, for instance, the batter is made with beer, and the fried shrimp are served in a tortilla with purple cabbage. In Mazatlán, the batter is made with mineral water, which makes it light and fluffy, and the shrimp are served with a traditional *Salsa Mexicana* and simple guacamole. You will be able to savor all the layers of flavor in the taco from start to finish! Make them as a main course, or have smaller tortillas for an appetizer or hors d'oeuvre!

Ingredients

1 kilo (2.2 pounds) shrimp
2 cups all purpose flour
1 egg
1 teaspoon baking powder
300 ml (10 ounces) sparkling mineral water
oil to fry the shrimp, about 6 mm / ¼ inch deep in pan
6 tomatoes

1 onion
5 serrano chiles (less if you are watching your heat intake)
2 avocados, peeled with seeds removed
salt
tortillas, corn or flour

Peel and devein the shrimp.

Mix the flour, egg, baking powder, and mineral water gently, until it is a thick batter.

Heat the oil in a medium-sized frying pan over medium heat.

Dip the shrimps into the batter and coat well. Fry the shrimp in the hot oil until they are a deep yellow or golden brown color.

Dice the tomatoes, onion, and chiles into small pieces, and place in a bowl. Stir to combine.

Put the avocados into a blender with salt (to taste) and ¼ cup water. Blend until it is smooth; then empty into a separate bowl.

To serve, place a few shrimps in a tortilla. Allow everyone to garnish their shrimp taco with the tomato salsa and avocado purée.

Karina Ann Betlem

NIEVES

Meet Nieves del Carmen Villegas Garcia

It is difficult to get Nieves to stand still for a photograph. She is constantly on the move. She is a wife and mother of three teenage sons, and she has a full-time job outside the home. A self-proclaimed "lazy cook," she uses many canned or packaged foods in her everyday cooking. Her sister, Sandra, is an accomplished cook, and when it comes to cooking important meals for fiestas or Christmas, Nieves is asked to bring the flowers!

She does, however, enjoy cooking, which she says was awakened in her at the age of seven, when she and Sandra would be shipped off for the holidays and summers to stay with her *abuelita* (grandmother) Juanita in Michoacán, because her mother worked and the girls were not in school.

Her grandmother taught them to make the *nixtamal*, the process of making hominy or pozole corn using slaked lime. Then she taught them how to grind the corn and make corn tortillas and to prepare a delicious mole and ranchero-style casseroles.

The first time that Nieves prepared a complete meal by herself, she had just married. She explained her experience, laughing hysterically. Wanting to impress her new husband with her culinary skills, she prepared a meal of chorizo with eggs. Sounds simple enough. She made the eggs, and then on top of the cooked eggs, she tossed in the raw chorizo to fry. This was backwards. The eggs were so hard, they could have bounced off the floor, while the chorizo was still raw in places

She went to her new mother-in-law with this story and asked for guidance. Her mother-in-law took Nieves under her wing and taught her how to prepare delicious meals, which made her husband a happy man! She was also taught to clean and prepare fish, shrimp, squid, octopus, and crab, the traditional food of the port of Mazatlán.

A quote from Nieves: "*Gracias a estas dos maravillosas y queridas personas es como yo apredi a disfrutar las delicias de cocinar.*" Translation: Thanks to these two wonderful and dear people, it is how I learned to enjoy the delights of cooking.

Sandra and Nieves

Chilaquiles with Cheese in Red Sauce
Chilaquiles al Queso en Salsa Roja

4 servings

Chilaquiles are tortilla chips (either homemade or purchased), covered with a sauce and cheese. In Mexico, this is often a breakfast dish, although it can be eaten at any meal. Some local restaurants serve these with warm shredded chicken on the tortilla chips and then add the sauce. Either way, they are delicious, and you are in control of how spicy you want them. They can be plated on individual plates or on one platter for guests to serve themselves.

Ingredients

1 bag packaged tortilla chips (quantity is your choice)
1 Tablespoon vegetable oil
1 cup red salsa, spicy (purchased bottled or make your own**)
1 can cream of cheese soup
250 grams (8 ounces) shredded cheese
¼ onion, sliced thin

Spread the tortilla chips on a plate.

Heat the oil, and fry the salsa (yes, you are frying a liquid) for 5 minutes. This will not only heat it through but also will dry up some moisture. Add the cream of cheese soup, and stir until it begins to boil. Remove from the heat and immediately pour over the tortilla chips. Sprinkle the shredded cheese on top and garnish with the sliced onion.

** Purchase any type of salsa you wish. If you like Pace, then buy that. No need to blend it; there will be enough liquid in it for the sauce.

Poblano Spaghetti
Espaguetis a la Poblana

2 servings

This spaghetti is about as easy as it gets. Using the canned poblano soup eliminates the steps of charring, peeling, rinsing, and chopping the poblanos. I usually don't eat canned soup, but I love this stuff. The soup should be available on the soup aisle or the Mexican food aisle. Don't be discouraged if you cannot find it. To make your own for this sauce, roast 1 poblano; then peel and remove stem, seeds and veins. Blend with 8 ounces of cream and some salt. It isn't quite the same, but it is still quite good.

Ingredients

250 grams (8 ounces) spaghetti
1 can cream of poblano soup (Campbell's)
¾ cup milk
50 grams (3½ Tablespoons) butter, melted
190 grams (7 ounces) cream cheese
50 grams (3½ Tablespoons) Parmesan cheese, grated

Cook the spaghetti in an abundant amount of salted water until it is *almost* tender. Drain.

In a saucepan, blend the cream of poblano soup, milk, melted butter, and cream cheese. Bring almost to a boil, reduce the heat to low; then add the cooked spaghetti and heat thoroughly for 5 minutes. (This extra 5 minutes will finish cooking the pasta.) Add salt to taste.

Sprinkle Parmesan cheese over the top. Serve with roasted chicken.

Potatoes with Chile Slices
Papas con Rajas

8 servings

These cooks are constantly teaching me new ways to make rajas. I used to think rajas were just chile slices with onions, maybe a little cream, but this one has corn and potatoes. It's a great side dish that goes with just about any type of meat—baked, grilled, or sautéed. Beautiful and appetizing to look at, filled with different colors and textures—you will love rajas.

Ingredients
6 potatoes, peeled, cut in cubes, precooked in salted water, drained
1 cup mild sour cream
1 cup corn kernels, canned or frozen
250 grams (4 ounces) Chihuahua cheese, shredded
4 poblano chiles
3 Tablespoons butter
1 teaspoon salt
freshly ground black pepper to taste

Char the poblano chiles and steam in a covered bowl for 10 minutes. Remove the skin, stems, seeds, and veins. See the "Chile" section of this book for complete instructions. Slice in thin slices.

Melt the butter in a large pan. Add the cooked potatoes and chile slices. When they are coated with the butter and heated thoroughly, add the sour cream, stirring over low heat until the cream is hot but not boiling. Add salt, pepper, and corn. Continue to heat until the corn is hot.

Remove the pan from the heat and sprinkle the cheese over the top. Cover the pan with a lid until the cheese melts. Serve.

Meat with Poblano Chile Sauce
Carne con Salsa de Chile Poblano

6 servings

This definitely is a different take on spaghetti and meatballs! Canned poblano soup is the base for the sauce. It gets jazzed up a bit with the flavors of the meatball ingredients and makes an interesting and tasty alternative to the more common tomato version. A fast meal, it's less than 30 minutes from start to finish. It shows the inventive nature of these cooks. Flavor and appearance are both equally important.

Ingredients
500 grams (1 pound) ground beef

½ cup dry bread crumbs soaked in ¼ cup milk
1 small onion, finely chopped
1 can Campbell's cream of poblano soup
1 egg, beaten
1 Tablespoon oil
¼ Tablespoon oregano
¾ cup milk
salt and pepper to taste

In a large bowl, mix ¼ cup of the cream of poblano soup with the ground meat, soaked bread crumbs, onion, and the egg. Mix well. Form the meat into walnut-sized balls.

In a frying pan with hot oil, fry the meatballs for 10 minutes or until they are golden. Remove the meatballs to a plate. Discard the oil and any bits of meat remaining in the frying pan. No need to wipe it clean—just make sure no bits are in there.

In the same frying pan, stir together the remaining cream of poblano soup, milk, and oregano. Add the meatballs back in and cook them for 10 minutes more or until the meat is well cooked. Add salt and pepper to taste.

Serve over pasta.

Meat in its Own Juice
Carne en Su Jugo

6 servings

This is a classic Mexican dish. In Mazatlán, we even have restaurants named *Carne en Su Jugo*, and that is what they serve. As with all stews, the meat needs to be cooked much longer than you would cook a steak. A pressure cooker for the meat cuts this time dramatically. The flavor of the stew is much like any other beef stew, except it has a zing from the tomatillos, which are a bit tart. A warming meal on a cool day!

Ingredients

1 kilo (2.2 pounds) stew meat, cut in small cubes
salt to taste
2 medium onions
500 grams (1 pound) beans, peruano or pinto
500 grams (1 pound) tomatillos
2 cloves garlic
1 bunch cilantro
1 bunch green onions (fat ones), all but about 2 inches of the green stems removed

Put the meat in a pressure cooker, sprinkle it with salt, and add 1 diced onion. Add about 3 cups of water. Put the lid on, and secure it. Cook over medium-low heat for 45 minutes. When the valve starts to rock, begin the timing. After 45 minutes, remove from the heat, and allow the pressure to release on its own. Do not pour cold water over the pressure cooker; this makes the meat tough.

In a separate pan, cook the beans in water with a little salt to taste.

In a blender, purée the tomatillos, 1 onion, garlic, and cilantro. Place this in a pot, and add the cleaned green onions. When it stars to boil, add the meat with a little of its broth; then the beans with a little of their broth. The amount of broth can vary, depending on how much you want. Continue to boil until the green onions are tender.

Serve with white rice and warm tortillas.

Chicken Crepes
Crepas de Pollo

3 servings (6 crepes)

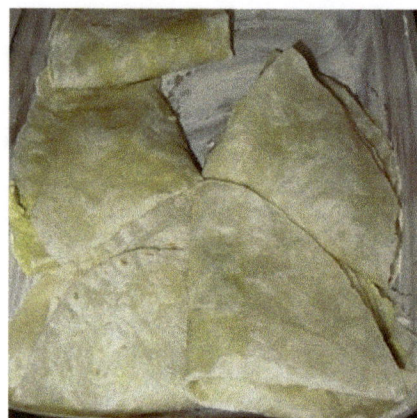

Nieves says she had these crepes at a local restaurant and decided to try to make them at home. She tells me she is a lazy cook, so instead of making homemade crepes, she uses thin flour tortillas. They are wonderful—even though it is the lazy method! They are bathed in a poblano and cream sauce and topped with a few shreds of cheese. Do not completely cover the crepes in cheese, only a pinch for each one.

This easy dish also can be heated in the microwave instead of the oven. Directions are below.

Ingredients
500 grams (1 pound) poblano chiles, charred (stem, seeds, and veins removed)
½ cup milk
1 cup mild sour cream
salt and pepper to taste
½ of a whole cooked chicken breast, shredded
6 crepes or flour tortillas
½ cup Parmesan cheese, grated
butter for greasing the pan

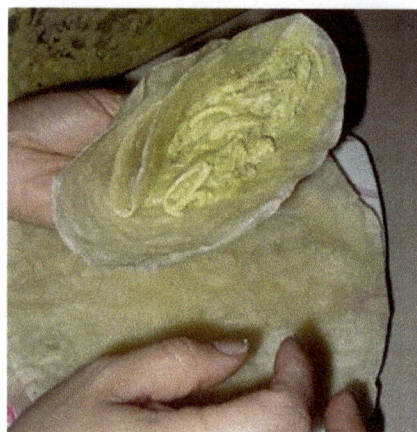

Heat oven to 180°C/350°F.

Char and peel the poblano chiles as directed in the "Chile" section.

Purée the poblano chiles, milk, sour cream, salt, and pepper in a blender until very smooth. Pour into a pan and heat, stirring constantly, until it is slowly boiling. Remove from the heat.

Pour half of this poblano mixture over the shredded chicken, and stir to mix.

Divide the chicken onto the 6 crepes, placing the chicken on only one-quarter of the crepe or tortilla. Fold the crepes into quarters and layer them into a buttered heat-proof dish, overlapping them slightly. (See photo.) Pour the remainder of the sauce over the top of the crepes. Sprinkle with Parmesan cheese, and bake for 10 minutes.

To heat in the microwave: High power for 3–5 minutes until they are hot.

Chicken Breast in Cream
Pechuga ala Crema

4 servings

Nieves is very inventive when some ingredients are in season and therefore at a reduced price in the market. Bell peppers are a good example. You will often find recipes using bell peppers instead of poblanos for an added reason—you don't have to char and peel them. Bell peppers and corn not only look appealing but complement the chicken and cream. This will become a regular in your recipe repertoire.

Ingredients

500 grams (1 pound) chicken breasts, no skin or bone
salt to taste
2 green bell peppers
1 Tablespoon butter
250 grams (8 ounces) onion, finely diced
1 cup mild sour cream
1 chicken bouillon cube
2 cups corn kernels, canned or frozen

Cut the chicken breast in medium cubes, and salt to taste. Cut the bell peppers in small squares. Sauté the onion and peppers in butter. Add the breast to the onion and peppers, and leave on very low heat until the chicken is thoroughly cooked. When the chicken is done, add the sour cream, bouillon cube, and corn. Heat on low for 5 minutes. Serve with white rice.

Savory Chicken Breasts
Pechugas a la Sabrosa

6 servings

Stuffing these chicken breasts with ham and cheese, and then smothering them with a different type of cheese on top makes these little bundles stand out in any crowd. The ham flavor permeates the chicken, while the cheese topper seals in the juices. There are many versions of stuffed chicken breasts, but this one is simple, tasty, and the recipe can be easily increased for a crowd. Slice skinless and boneless chicken breasts in half lengthwise through the center for the "steaks." The result is that the two rolls you see in the photo are actually created from a single chicken breast.

Ingredients

6 chicken breasts
salsa Maggi
12 slices smoked ham
12 slices American cheese
500 grams Chihuahua cheese, shredded
½ teaspoon butter

Preheat oven to 180°C/350°F.

To cut the breasts into steaks, use a sharp knife and slice horizontally through the entire length of the breast. Remove the top layer—you now have two steaks from one breast for a total of 12 steaks.

Spritz a few drops of salsa Maggi on both sides of the breasts; rub it in. Marinate the chicken breasts in the salsa Maggi for 2 hours in the refrigerator.

On top of each breast steak, place one slice of ham and one slice of American cheese. Roll them into logs and place in a buttered heat-proof baking dish. Pour over the remaining Maggi marinade from the chicken. Cover the breast rolls with the shredded Chihuahua cheese.

Bake for 20 minutes.

Chicken with Soy Sauce
Pollo con Salsa de Soya

4 servings

Although this may seem like a lot of soy sauce, it does not taste that way. The soy sauce permeates the vegetables and then the chicken. You still get the fresh vegetable flavor with just a bit of soy saltiness. If you are crunched for time, as Nieves often is, cook the chicken the night before, and refrigerate it until you are ready to mix it with the vegetables and soy sauce. By the time the chicken reheats in the soy sauce, the sauce will have evaporated, and you will have a thick glaze.

Ingredients

1 whole chicken in pieces without skin
ground black pepper to taste
olive oil for sautéing
500 grams (1 pound) carrots, peeled and cut into large squares
500 grams (1 pound) potatoes, peeled and cut into large squares
½ head broccoli, florets separated
½ head cauliflower, florets separated
2 stalks celery, cut into thick slices
2 cups soy sauce

Sprinkle the chicken with the pepper. Heat the oil in a large frying pan, and very slowly cook the chicken until it is done, about 20 minutes.

In a separate pot, steam the carrots, potatoes, broccoli, cauliflower, and celery with 1 cup of the soy sauce and ½ cup water. When the vegetables are tender, drain, and add the vegetables to the chicken pan. Add the other 1 cup of soy sauce, and heat through. Serve over rice with slices of fresh avocado on the side.

Marinated Chicken with Cabbage and Carrot Salad
Pollo Marinado con Ensalada de Repollo y Zanahoria

6 servings

The cabbage and carrot salad is simply flavored but is perfect with the chicken because of its tang from the lime marinade. Together, they make a nice presentation, and the flavors balance each other. Nieves used white cabbage when we cooked together, but says she sometimes uses the purple cabbage because it looks good.

Ingredients

6 pieces chicken without skin
salt and pepper to taste
¼ cup fresh lime juice
½ head cabbage shredded
3 carrots, shredded
½ cup oil
4 Tablespoons mayonnaise

Marinate the chicken in salt, pepper, and lime juice. (Rub enough salt and pepper on the chicken to flavor it but not make a brine.) Let the chicken sit in this marinade in the refrigerator for 2 hours.

Heat the oil in a frying pan over low heat. Remove the chicken from the marinade, and carefully place the pieces in the warm oil. Cover the pan. Cook the chicken slowly until completely cooked, about 20–30 minutes.

Place the shredded cabbage and carrots in a bowl with the mayonnaise. Stir to combine. Let it sit for a few minutes for the flavors to blend. Serve the cooked chicken on top of the salad.

Potatoes with Ham
Papas con Jamón

6 servings

The Mexican version of potatoes au gratin with ham, this is comfort food that is easy to prepare and even easier to eat! By starting with precooked potatoes, the oven time is reduced dramatically, and the cheese does not get over-heated. Another shortcut is the canned cream of cheese soup. I am not sure you would be able to taste that it is canned and not homemade. You can, of course, make your own cream of cheese soup. Do not salt the potatoes when you cook them, because the ham, soup, and cheese all have some salt.

Ingredients

6 large potatoes, peeled, sliced, and cooked (keep hot)
1 cup milk
1 can cream of cheese soup
8 slices ham, diced
150 grams (5¼ ounces) Manchego cheese, shredded

Preheat the oven to 180°C/350°F.

Mix the cream of cheese soup and milk in a bowl. Set aside.

Butter an 8 x 8 oven-proof dish. Put one-third of the potatoes in a layer, then one-third of the ham, and one-third of soup mixture. Repeat two more times. Cover with the Manchego cheese, and bake for 15 minutes or until the cheese melts and browns.

Layered Pork Torte
Pastel Indio

6 servings

Pastel means cake or pie. In this instance, it is more of a layered torte using pork and corn tortillas. Pastel Indio is a common dish throughout the country, not just of a region. There are very few variations, so you will find the same common recipe, no matter where you are in Mexico. The major difference is the use of a prepared canned soup as an ingredient near the big cities, and the use of fresh ingredients in the pueblas or poorer areas. Here, Nieves uses the fresh ingredients, both for cost and flavor.

Ingredients

500 grams (1 pound) poblano chiles, charred (stems, seeds, and veins removed)
½ cup milk
1 cup mild sour cream
4 Tablespoons oil
18 corn tortillas
500 grams (1 pound) boneless pork leg, cooked and shredded
1 cup Chihuahua cheese, shredded

Preheat the oven to 180°C/350°F.

Purée the poblano chiles, milk, and sour cream in a blender until it is smooth. Pour into a pan and heat, stirring constantly, until it is slowly boiling. Remove from the heat.

Heat the oil in a small frying pan, and slightly fry the tortillas. They should be *partially* crisp but not cooked all the way through or browned.

Butter a baking dish (9 x 13) and place a layer of 6 tortillas, overlapping a bit if you need to. Spoon one-quarter of the poblano sauce over the tortillas and then one-third of the pork. Repeat for a total of three layers: **1**. tortillas, sauce, pork **2**. tortillas, sauce, pork **3**. tortillas, sauce, pork, sauce. Please note that layer 3 is different from the other layers. Sprinkle with the shredded cheese. Bake for 15 minutes or until the cheese has melted and browned a little.

Fish Fillet in Squash Flower Sauce
Filete de Pescado en Salsa de Flor de Calabaza

6 servings

With this recipe, you don't have to worry about finding fresh squash flowers. Nieves has created another wonderful sauce using canned soup. Fresh *epazote* is a must-have ingredient, because it gives a hint of that distinctive flavor to the sauce. (If you cannot find fresh, then use dried, but do not omit it.) The fish comes out moist, with a creamy flavorful sauce.

Ingredients

6 fish fillets (red snapper, mahi mahi, or similar fish)
½ cup flour
90 grams (6⅓ Tablespoons) butter
2 Tablespoons oil
1 Tablespoon fresh lime juice
2 serrano chiles, diced, stem and seeds removed
2 Tablespoons fresh epazote, finely chopped
1 can cream of squash soup (also called cream of pumpkin flower soup)
1 cup milk
salt and pepper to taste

Dredge the fillets in the flour, making sure they are well coated. Heat the butter and oil in a frying pan over medium heat. Fry the fillets, turning once until they are golden on both sides, about 7 minutes. Bathe them with the lime juice; set aside.

In the same frying pan, fry the serrano chiles and the epazote for 1 minute. Mix in the squash flower soup and milk. Add the fish back in, and cook for 5 minutes more. Season with salt and pepper to taste.

Serve with white rice. For dessert, a nice lime or lemon sherbet should be served.

Special Shrimp
Camarónes Especiales

6 servings

Shrimp and chipotle chiles are one of those natural flavor combinations, and this recipe does not disappoint! Nieves knows how I love chipotles, so I think she invented this recipe to share with me. (Well, at least, that's my story and I'm sticking to it!) This is a wonderfully fragrant and tasty shrimp dish. Don't be afraid of the spicy heat from the chipotles. You can use fewer and still get the classic smoky flavor.

Ingredients

1 kilo (2.2 pounds) shrimp, cleaned and peeled
3 Tablespoons butter

1½ cup mild sour cream
4 chipotle chiles (from 1 small can)
¼ of a small onion
3 cloves garlic
1 cube shrimp bouillon
1 cup mayonnaise
1 large can sliced mushrooms
salt to taste

Clean the shrimp, remove shell, and devein. Fry the shrimp in the butter until they change color, about 3–4 minutes.

In the blender, liquefy the sour cream, chipotle chiles, onion, garlic, shrimp bouillon, and mayonnaise.

When the shrimp are done, add the liquid from the blender. Heat very slowly, and when it is hot, add the mushrooms, and continue to cook for 5 minutes over low heat. Add salt if necessary.

Serve over white rice or wrapped in a fresh tortilla.

Karina Ann Betlem

RAMÓN

Meet Jesús Ramón Rendón Martínez

Ramón was born and raised in the small village of Mármol de Salcido (Mármol), population 787, not a booming metropolis. It is located in the municipality of Mazatlán and about 30 kilometers north of Mazatlán proper. As you can imagine, coming from such a small village, opportunity for a young boy's education is limited. Ramón was an excellent student and soaked in his education like a human sponge.

Ramón grew up in a very poor family. He is the fourth of five children and as he says, they were a large family living in a small house. His mother was always in the kitchen, cooking. Because he was very close to his mother, he cannot remember a time that he was not hanging out with her in the kitchen, enjoying the smells and chatting with her while she cooked. He would even sit at the kitchen table to do his homework so he could watch her.

As in all big families, everyone has chores to do. Ramón did his the best he could, because his pride would not allow him to do otherwise.

When he was ten years old, Ramón became bored with the standard education he was receiving from school and started to read as many things as he could. He was learning well above his age and grade level and easily surpassed the other kids in his class. As a hobby, he asked his mother to teach him to cook. He was always excited to learn something new and thought that perhaps one day he would take culinary classes at the university. He became proficient at making beef soup and shrimp pozole.

Keeping this bright young boy's mind busy was a challenge for his parents. One day, he discovered soccer on television. He loved to watch the games on TV and would make up strategies for the players as a pretend coach. He tells me about the times when his mother needed to greet someone at the front door, so she had Ramón watch the food to keep it from burning. After all, he had watched his mom many times and had even learned to cook some meals himself. He would get so engrossed in the soccer game, however, that he would not smell the smoke coming from the pot! He laughs now about it, but back then, it wasn't funny, because it meant that the main afternoon meal was ruined, and there would be no food for the family.

When he graduated from high school, Ramón applied for scholarships to attend the university. He was awarded a few for the cost of tuition and books. Without these, he would not have been able to further his education. But this required that he move from Mármol to attend the university, and this meant he needed a job so that he could afford to live in town. That is when I first met Ramón. He was working behind the counter at a local pharmacy.

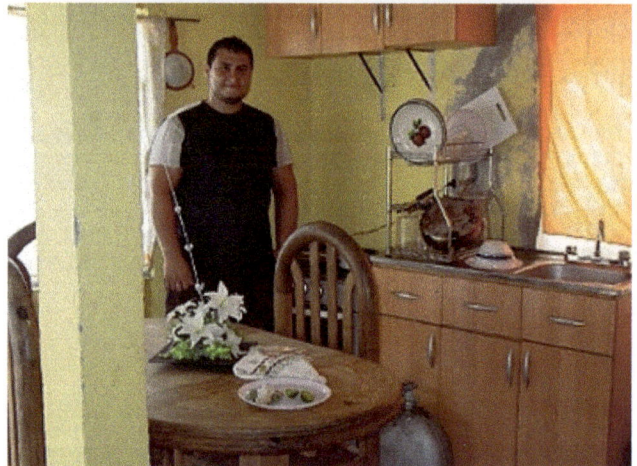

Initially, he moved in with an uncle, but he could not shake the feeling that he was intruding and decided to rent a small place of his own. Cooking became a necessity, and he relied heavily on the knowledge acquired from his mom. Soon, he was refining that knowledge, learning new recipes and inventing some of his own.

At twenty-three years old, he has graduated from the university and is finishing his master's thesis in marine biology. He graduated number one in his class and has received many awards for excellence in education. At present, Ramón is awaiting the approval of more scholarships so that he can continue his education and earn his PhD.

At home with his new wife, Gaby, he is the cook. She told him before they married that she did not know how to cook, and he is quick to point out that "she was not lying!" That is fine with him; he loves to cook, and it is relaxing. He also has plans to attend the Culinary Academy and perhaps have a second career in gastronomy. He says, at the very least, he will learn to be a better cook!

Ramón and Gaby live in a darling little apartment, but it has very few windows that open so not much air circulation. They are working on installing a new operable window, but it is a work in progress. When Ramón and I were cooking together, it was so warm that we both looked like we'd just come from the gym. You will see in the photos that he is quite warm and perspiring. Humidity here gets up in the 90 percent range, so everyone perspires like that at times! He asked that I explain that to my readers.

Fried Pork Rinds in Ranchero Salsa
Chicharrónes Rancheros

4 wervings

Fried pork rinds (*chicharrónes*, pronounced che-char-*roan*-ays) are a very typical snack food, and I love them! Buy some—you can find them on the Mexican food aisle—instead of potato chips. They're very crunchy, and I'll bet you can't eat just one! The "rancheros" part is the salsa you bathe them in. When they are finished cooking, put them in a corn tortilla, and enjoy!

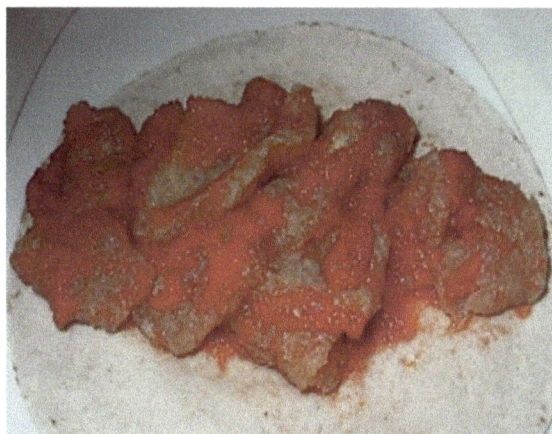

Note: You can make chicharrónes yourself at home, but they are tedious to make, and because of that, no one I know makes their own. They are purchased from a local tortillaria that makes excellent ones—*muy rico!*

Ingredients

1 kilo (2.2 pounds) chicharrónes (pork rinds), already fried
500 grams (1 pound) tomatoes
½ onion
1 or more serrano chile, stem removed
2 cloves garlic
½ teaspoon oregano

salt to taste
1 Tablespoon oil

Cook the tomato, onion, and chile in a small pan of hot water. After 5 minutes, remove them from the water, and place them in a blender. Discard the water. Add the garlic, oregano and salt, liquefy until it is completely smooth.

Heat the oil in a wide pan, add the salsa from the blender, and bring to a boil. While it is boiling, add the chicharrónes, and spoon the sauce over them so that they get well impregnated with the salsa.

Serve with fresh corn tortillas, and let everyone make their own taco.

Mango Ice Cream
Helado de Mango

6 servings

Mango is one of those fruits that I just cannot seem to get enough of. It is always fresh-tasting and has a beautiful orange color. The mango season is short, only about one month, so buy as many as you can get your hands on. To always have some on hand, peel the mango (use a vegetable peeler), take the seed out, and freeze the fruit. This ice cream only takes 1 cup, so you can make it often and not use up your entire store of frozen mango. If you had to eat your way out of a room full of a particular food, what food would you choose? Mine choice would be this mango ice cream! Brain freeze? No problem.

Ingredients

2 eggs
1 can media crema
1 can sweetened condensed milk
1 cup mango pulp, fresh, frozen or canned

Break the eggs into a heat-proof bowl. Whisk well and add in the can of media crema. Place the bowl over a pan of simmering water and continue whisking until the egg/milk mixture is thickened. The eggs will be cooked at this point.

Pour this mixture into a blender and add the other ingredients. Blend until it is totally smooth. Empty this mixture into a wide container, and freeze for 6 hours or until frozen.

Strawberry Cream Pie
Pastel de Fresas con Crema

8 servings

This unique frozen dessert is so simple and has such a wonderful taste that even I imagine I spent more time preparing it! Strawberries and sour cream seem to be a natural combination!

Ingredients

500 grams (1 pound) strawberries
3 cups mild sour cream

2 cups granulated sugar
½ can sweetened condensed milk
100 grams (½ cup) dried unsweetened shredded coconut, pulverized in a blender
1½ Tablespoons butter

Put the strawberries, sour cream, sugar, and milk in a blender. Purée until it is totally smooth.

For the crust: Melt the butter and thoroughly mix into the coconut until it is all moistened. Place in 20–23 cm/8–
–9 inch glass pie pan. Chill in the freezer for 30 minutes. Remove the coconut crust from the freezer, and pour the strawberry cream over the top. Return to the freezer until it has frozen.

Beef Stew
Caldo de Res

6 servings

This is the best stew I have ever eaten! It takes a couple of hours to cook, but it is well worth the time investment and, as an added benefit, your house will smell wonderful. Ramón uses the small beef ribs (larger ones that have been cut up), so that everyone gets some in their bowl. It looks beautiful and enticing, with all the colors and textures in one dish. (In black-and-white, you'll need to use your imagination!) You are going to make this over and over again—I guarantee it!

Ingredients

1 kilo (2.2 pounds) beef ribs or hocks
300 grams (10½ ounces) beef brisket
2 cloves garlic
1 onion
3 stalks of cilantro, chopped including stems
2 corn on the cob, each cut into 3 pieces
⅔ cup garbanzo beans (chickpeas)
salt to taste
¼ head cabbage, chopped
2 large carrots, cut in pieces
1 poblano chile (skin, stem, seeds, and veins removed), chopped
2 large potatoes, peeled and cubed
1 medium squash, peeled and cubed

Rinse the meat and put in a large pot with enough water to totally cover the meat. Add the garlic, onion, cilantro, corn on the cob, and chickpeas. Cook on medium-low to low heat for 1 hour; then add the salt. Continue cooking until the meat is tender, about another 45–60 minutes.

Prepare the poblano by charring and removing the skin. See "Chile" section for complete instructions.

Once the meat is cooked, add the cabbage, carrots, and poblano chile. After another 15 minutes, add the potatoes and squash. Cook for 15–20 minutes longer, until all the vegetables are tender. Adjust the salt if necessary.

Don't forget the tortillas!

Shredded Beef with Vegetables
Machaquita
(Ma-cha-*kee*-ta)

4 servings

The meaning of *machaquita* is "little machaca." Machaca is shredded beef and is one of those foods that is made differently in every household. Let's start with simple shredded beef. You can make some shredded beef by cooking a brisket, seasoned with salt and pepper, until it can be shredded. Cook the brisket any way you prefer, from slow cooking in a crockpot, to boiling it on the stove top, to cooking it in a pressure cooker. Ramón makes his shredded beef in a pressure cooker and keeps some in the freezer for times when he wants a quick meal such as this one.

Ingredients

3 Tablespoons oil
500 grams (1 pound) shredded beef or machaca
1 onion, diced
3 large tomatoes, diced
1 serrano chile, diced
salt and pepper to taste
½ teaspoon ground oregano
1 squash, diced (if you cannot find Mexican squash, a large zucchini will work)
½ cup chicken broth or water

Heat the oil in a large frying pan over medium heat. Drop in the beef and onions, and fry until the onions are almost transparent. Add the tomatoes and serrano chile. Lower the heat and continue to simmer slowly. Gently stir in the salt, pepper, oregano, and the squash. Pour in the chicken broth, cover the pan, and slowly simmer for 15 minutes.

Serve with lots of corn or flour tortillas to wrap around the meat to make either tacos or burritos.

Meatballs
Albondigas

6 servings

These meatballs have diced tomato mixed in with the meat, plus the addition of fresh chopped mint—a delightful flavor combination. This recipe makes enough broth to use as a meatball soup or as a meat main dish with a light gravy, accompanied by rice and beans. Cooking the meatballs directly in the broth without browning first makes them moist and very tender.

Ingredients

For the broth:
4 tomatoes
1 pinch salt
1 pinch ground black pepper
1 cube chicken bouillon
2 liters (2 quarts) water (approximately)

For the meatballs:

500 grams (1.1 pound) ground beef
¼ cup rice (pre-cooked)
1 egg
1 pinch salt
1 pinch ground black pepper
1 tomato, diced, seeds removed
1 slice onion, finely minced
4 mint leaves, chopped

For the broth: Cook the 4 tomatoes in boiling water until the skins split, 5 minutes. Drain and discard the water. Purée the tomatoes in a blender; then place in a pan with the other *broth* ingredients. Heat until it comes to a low boil.

For the meatballs: Knead together all the *meatball* ingredients until they are thoroughly mixed. Form into walnut-sized meatballs. Carefully drop them one at a time into the boiling broth. Cook 30 minutes.

Serve with red rice.

Marinated Meat (Beef or Pork)
Carne Adobada

8 servings

This is about the easiest marinade you will ever make for steaks. Cook the meat immediately after slathering on that beautiful red sauce. Ramón prefers pork steaks, because beef in Mazatlán is much more expensive. Although you can grill your steaks, we used a heavy pan to cook these. The scent of ancho chiles mixing with the aroma of meat cooking fills the air with an earthy sweetness. The most difficult part of this recipe? Waiting for the meat to finish cooking!

Ingredients

8 steaks, beef or pork
2 ancho chiles (stems, seeds, and veins removed)
1 clove garlic
1 pinch oregano
salt and ground black pepper to taste

Salt the steaks on both sides.

Cook the ancho chiles in a small pot of boiling water for 3 minutes. Drain and discard the water. Put them in a blender jar with the garlic, oregano, and black pepper and 2–3 tablespoons of water to allow them to blend. Purée until smooth.

Slather the chile mixture on both sides of each steak. Cook in a hot heavy pan brushed with a little oil or on the grill to your desired doneness. Make sure to breathe in the scents as they cook.

Serve with refried beans and a salad.

Meatloaf
Pastel de Carne

8 servings

The colors in this meatloaf are just as vibrant after it is baked as when you first put it in the oven. Although it may seem like too many peppers in the meat, they are not overpowering. It's simply a nice pepper taste throughout but no spicy heat. When cooked like this, poblanos will remind you of green bell peppers but with a milder taste. By the way, this is good cold, too.

Ingredients

500 grams (1 pound) ground beef
500 grams (1 pound) ground pork
2 poblano chiles (stems, seeds, and veins removed)—do not char
1 can roasted red peppers (185 g/6.5 ounces)
½ cup green olives, pitted
1 cup dry bread crumbs
ground white pepper, to taste
garlic salt, to taste
1 egg
3½ Tablespoons butter

Preheat the oven to 200°C/400°F.

Mix together the beef and pork.

Dice the chiles, red peppers, and olives into small (not tiny) pieces. Add them to the meat along with the bread crumbs, pepper, garlic salt, egg, and butter. Knead together well.

Place in a loaf pan, and bake for 30–45 minutes.

Pulled Pork
Cochinita Pibil

8 servings

Ramón's recipe is definitely *not* the traditional method of preparing *cochinita pibil*. It is, however, just as delicious. Note that it does not use achiote paste but a combination of four different chiles for color and flavor. There is only a mild hint of spiciness, even though he uses ten chiles. The meat falls apart on your fork, which gives you another opportunity to dunk it in the rich-tasting sauce before each bite. Don't waste a drop of the sauce. Any leftovers can be made into breakfast burritos with eggs!

Ingredients

1 kilo (2.2 pounds) pork meat, such as pork leg, butt, or shoulder—no bone
3 tomatoes
½ onion
2 cloves garlic
3 pasilla chiles
3 guajillo chiles
1 cascabel chile

3 árbol chiles
½ Tablespoon oregano
½ teaspoon cumin
2 cups natural orange juice
3 Tablespoons oil (divided usage)

Place the pork in a pot of water, just enough to cover by about 13 mm / ½ inch. Slowly simmer until the meat is tender, about 2 hours. When it is tender, remove it from the broth (reserving the broth), and chop into bite-sized cubes. (This is a bit different than the typical shredding of the pork.)

In another pan of fresh water, place the tomatoes, onion, and garlic. Bring to a boil, and cook for 5 minutes. With a slotted spoon, strain them and place in a blender jar.

Prepare the chiles by removing the stems and seeds. Place them in the hot water you just used for the tomatoes. Let them slowly simmer for 5–7 minutes until they rehydrate. Drain (discard the liquid), and place the chiles in the blender with the tomatoes. Liquefy this with the oregano, cumin, and orange juice. There should be no solid bits, only liquid.

Into the pan you had used to cook the chiles, heat 1 tablespoon oil. Pour in the sauce from the blender. Fry for 2 minutes.

In another larger pan, heat 2 tablespoons oil, and add the cubed meat. Fry for 2 minutes, and then add the sauce to the meat. At this point, add a bit of the meat cooking broth to thin the sauce to your liking. It needs to be a little soupy. Continue to cook over low heat for 10 minutes, adding more broth if needed.

To serve, place the entire pork dish on the table with a large spoon, and allow each person to serve himself or herself. Always have fresh tortillas on hand. You can garnish this dish with sliced red onion, if you like.

Ancho Chiles Stuffed with Tuna
Chiles Anchos Rellenos de Atún

6 servings

Using a dried chile for stuffing may be a new experience for you, but it should be a nice surprise! Good-quality canned tuna is all you put inside these hot little numbers. The coating is egg, and the rellenos are crisp, while the dried chiles are soft. The trick is to have your oil smoking hot—don't burn down the kitchen, but it needs to be extremely hot for the egg coating to get crisp.

Ingredients

6 dried ancho chiles
1 can tuna (140 g/5 ounces)
2 eggs, whites and yolks separated
oil, enough for 6 mm / ¼ inch deep (we used a light olive oil, but use any oil you like)

Wipe the chiles with a damp cloth, and then open the chiles by cutting off the stem end. Remove the seeds and veins. Fill them with the tuna. Toast them lightly on a hot griddle or cast-iron pan. Lightly beat the egg yolks. Beat the egg whites until they are stiff. Carefully fold the whites into the yolks. Dip the stuffed chiles into the eggs, and fry them in smoking-hot oil until they are golden brown, and the tuna is heated through.

Serve with a green salad, tomatoes, and avocados. You also can serve it with a cooked or raw tomato salsa.

Shrimp Empanadas
Empanadas de Camarón

6–8 servings

The rich flavor and brown color of the dough comes from the shrimp heads* and ancho chile. Empanadas take a little practice, but after rolling out just a few of them, you will begin to look like a pro. Use plastic wrap or waxed paper on both sides of the dough to keep it from sticking. You can use a tortilla press, a rolling pin, or the bottom of a plate to flatten the dough. Keep the flattened dough on one piece of plastic wrap or waxed paper to use when folding the dough over the filling.

* If you cannot purchase shrimp with heads, use one shrimp bouillon cube instead. It is not quite the same, but it is an acceptable alternative.

Ingredients

For the empanadas:
1 liter (4¼ cups) water
1 kilo (2.2 pounds) shrimp, preferably with heads, rinsed
1 ancho chile, stem and seeds removed
½ Tablespoon oregano
1 clove garlic
2 teaspoons salt
500 grams (1 pound) corn flour (*not* cornstarch)
oil as needed for frying

For the salsa:
3 árbol chiles
3 poblano chiles
3 medium-sized tomatoes
8 tomatillos
1 clove garlic
2 Tablespoons cilantro leaves
salt to taste

If you are fortunate enough to have whole shrimp with heads available to you, the heads will add good flavor to the broth. Bring the liter of water to a boil, and add all the shrimp, the ancho chile, oregano, garlic, and 2 teaspoons salt. Boil for 3 minutes. With a slotted spoon, remove the shrimp to a bowl; reserve the broth with the chile and its seasonings.

When the shrimp is cool enough to handle, remove the shells and heads. Finely chop the shrimp.

Place the cooked heads and the cooking broth with the chile and its seasonings in a blender. Purée until it is totally smooth. (If you do not have the heads, then blend the same ingredients with 1 or 2 shrimp bouillon cubes.) Pass this mixture through a sieve to remove any unprocessed bits (you don't want to chomp down on a bit of shell or chile seed.) Chill the purée. (Chilling the purée is very important, so do not skip this step.)

When the purée is cold, add it to the corn flour little by little, mixing by hand, to keep a consistent texture. It is not necessary to use all the purée; you need to have a dough that holds together but is not sticky. The dough is ready just before it gets sticky. If it gets sticky, add a wee bit more flour.

Immediately, form the dough into small balls, about the size of a small scoop of ice cream. Place between 2 pieces of plastic wrap or waxed paper, and either press with a tortilla press or roll out with a rolling pin until it is about as thick as a tortilla.

Add a small spoonful of shrimp on one half. Double the tortilla over on itself, so you have a half-moon shape. Use the bottom plastic wrap to assist in folding the empanada in half. Seal the edges by gently pressing with your finger around the opening.

Heat the oil in a frying pan to very hot. Carefully place the empanadas in the oil, and fry on both sides until they are golden brown. Remove to a paper towel to absorb the excess oil.

For the salsa:
Cook all the ingredients (except the cilantro) in a little water, about 7 minutes. Remove everything with a slotted spoon to a blender jar. Add the cilantro. Purée, leaving small chunks in the salsa.

Serve the empanadas with the salsa as a dip. If you desire, you can serve with slices of avocado spritzed with lime.

Shrimp Pozole
Pozole de Camarón

10 servings

The amazing flavor of this soup develops as a result of sautéing the shrimp heads and then using some of the pozole corn cooking broth to deglaze the pan before straining the broth back into the cooked corn. Because you only use one ancho chile, the shrimp flavor is fresh, and the broth tastes light. The only addition to this pozole is a spritz of fresh lime. * If you cannot purchase shrimp with heads, use one shrimp bouillon cube instead. It is not quite the same, but it is an acceptable alternative.

Ingredients

10 cups water
500 grams (1 pound) pozole corn (see *note*)
1 head garlic, cut in half across the head
1 onion, halved
500 grams (1 pound) raw shrimp, with heads*
ground black pepper and salt to taste
5 Tablespoons oil
1 ancho chile, stem and seeds removed
¼ teaspoon oregano

Cook the corn in the water with the garlic bulb for 1 hour. Add the onion and continue cooking until the corn is tender. When the corn is tender, remove and discard the garlic and onion.

Separate the shrimp heads from the bodies, reserving the heads. Peel and devein the shrimp, and rinse them in cold water. Sprinkle with salt and pepper to taste.

Heat the oil in a frying pan over medium heat. When the oil is hot, add the shrimp and cook until they turn red. Transfer them to the pot with the corn. Using the same frying pan and oil, fry the ancho chile for 15 seconds on each side. Remove when crisp, and blend with the oregano until smooth. Pour this into the corn pot.

In the same frying pan, add the raw shrimp heads, and cook until they become red. Ladle out some of the corn water into the pan with the heads. Stir around for 2 minutes. Strain them, putting the liquid back into the corn pot. Discard the shrimp heads. Adjust the salt and pepper, if necessary.

Serve in bowls with a spritz of fresh lime, if desired.

Note: Pozole (also posole) corn is in the refrigerated section of your market. If necessary, you can buy it frozen or canned. Regular sweet corn is *not* a substitute

Shrimp and Nopales Cakes
Tortas de Camarón con Nopales

6 servings

The base for this shrimp cake is dried shrimp. They are purchased in plastic containers or cellophane packages, and they need no refrigeration. It can be a bit tedious to prepare them, but they are such a treat that I know you will want to give this a try! You may be able to purchase the dried shrimp pre-ground in packages. The shrimp have a rather strong flavor, but the nopales and fresh tomato sauce balance it out nicely. You also will see these little babies in many Louisiana dishes, including gumbo.

Ingredients
oil, as needed
250 grams (8 ounces) dry shrimp, peeled, cleaned and ground (see "Ingredients" section)
3 egg whites, beaten until stiff
1 piece squash, shredded (Mexican or zucchini)
750 grams (1½ pounds) tomatoes
1 ancho chile (stem, seeds, and veins removed)
10 sprigs cilantro leaves (no stems), very finely chopped
500 grams (1 pound) nopales, cooked (see "Ingredients" section on how to cook)
1 cube shrimp bouillon
3 fresh limes to spritz over the cooked shrimp cakes

In a large frying pan on medium-high heat, heat enough oil so that it is about 6 mm / ¼ inch deep.

Clean the shrimp according to the instructions in the "Ingredients" section. After cleaning, grind them in a blender or food processor.

Mix together the ground shrimp, eggs, and squash. Form into thick hamburger shapes. Fry them in the hot oil until they are golden brown, 3–4 minutes on each side. Remove from the oil, and drain on paper towels. Discard the oil, and wipe the pan clean with a paper towel. (You will use the pan again.)

Cook the tomatoes in boiling water until the skins split, 3 minutes. Remove them with a slotted spoon, and place in a blender jar. In the same water, place the chile for 3 minutes. Again, with a slotted spoon remove the chile from the water, and place in the blender jar. Purée until smooth, adding a bit of water to assist in the blending. Pour into the frying pan, placed over low to medium heat.

When the tomato mixture is hot, stir in the shrimp bouillon and about ½ cup water to thin out the sauce a bit. When the bouillon has dissolved, add the cilantro, nopales, and the shrimp cakes. Allow them to simmer for 5–10 minutes.

Serve them hot, with a spritz of lime.

ROGELIO

Meet Rogelio Reyes Saavedra
Rogelio is pronounced Row-*hell*-yo

I have known Rogelio for about ten years, and he never ceases to amaze me with his talents. Not only is he an exceptional cook, but he is also a cabinet maker, does remodeling, is a husband, father and *abuelo* (grandpa), *and* he helps out his neighbors when they have a special project that needs taken care of. But his real passion is cooking.

On any Saturday or Sunday, you can travel down Rogelio's street and smell the charcoal heating up on his grill. I like to wait until the chicken is already on the grill before heading over. As I get close, I open the car windows to take in the warm scents wafting in the air. The chicken dripping its juices onto the coals, along with the sweet smell of garlic and chiles, act like an unseen force that gently draws you right up to his grill.

Rogelio is from the state of Michoacán and is one of fourteen siblings. His family was very poor and unable to send him to school. Today, he is self-conscious about that, but makes up for it with his enthusiasm for life!

He recalls that when he was young, his mother concerned herself only with feeding his father, while the children were left to fend for themselves. At the young age of eleven years old, he was abandoned by his parents and sent to sleep on the streets, as there was no room for him in at home. He went looking for work, anything that someone would hire him to do so that he could buy food for himself. In a short time, he walked into a bakery (*panaderia*) and offered to do anything they needed. He was hired to clean the floors. Despite his limited upbringing, Rogelio was a very hard worker and would stay after his work was finished to watch the bakers. The owner of the bakery saw this enthusiasm for knowledge and his excellent work ethic. One day, he told Rogelio that he no longer had to sweep the floors but would be trained as a baker. By now he was thirteen years old. He was trained to make *bolillos*, a bread roll used extensively throughout Mexico. He would also get a raise in salary.

With this raise in salary, Rogelio was able to give his parents money each week to help out the family. When this happened, he was invited back into his parents' home to live. His parents made a small corner available to him with a small cot to sleep on. No one was allowed in his space. He was now a respected contributor to the family.

Kitchen and Garage Combination

When he was thirteen, he met his future wife. She knew nothing about cooking, but Rogelio said not to worry; he would do the cooking in their family. At age fifteen he was married. They have now been married over twenty-five years and have two grown children and one grandson.

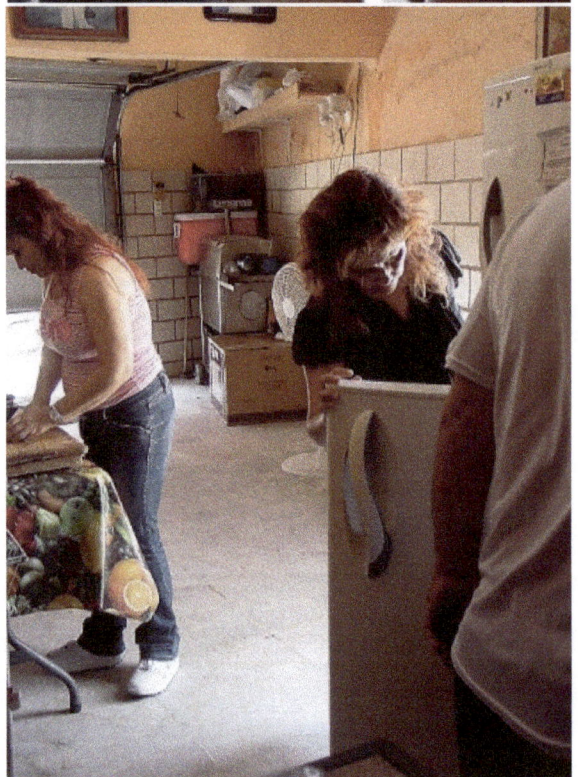

Rogelio continues to cook for his family. He says that when you have good food cooked with love, that love continues to abound, and this makes him a very happy man!

Rogelio's Salsa
Salsa de Rogelio

Makes about 4 cups

I originally had this salsa with Rogelio's *Pollo Asado al Carbon* (barbecued chicken). It was a wonderful complement to the other flavors, but I didn't stop there. I use this particular recipe with several meals each week. This is a versatile salsa that you can use for dipping or as a topping for beef, chicken, fish, or pork. It is wonderful on eggs or in omelets as well. Once you make this, you will find all sorts of reasons to serve it. Make this as spicy or non-spicy as you like. Just adjust the number of jalapeños you use.

Ingredients

1 kilo (2.2 pounds) roma tomatoes, whole—*not* cut up
12 jalapeños, cut off stem (use less if you don't want it spicy hot)
¼ onion, small
¼ cup water
½ teaspoon salt

Place the tomatoes in a dry cast-iron skillet or old pan. Using high heat, char them on all sides. (Charring tomatoes means only getting dark brown/black char marks on them.) They will become very soft. Place them in a blender jar.

Do the same with the jalapeños, turning them so they char on all sides. Add those to the blender. Remember you have 12 chiles, and you do not have to use them all. If you want less heat, start with one. You can always add more, but you cannot take them out! The jalapeños are for flavor, not necessarily heat. Add all the other ingredients to the blender. Blend on medium speed for just a few seconds—you want the salsa to have some small chunks not be puréed.

Pour the salsa into a bowl. Taste it for heat—you should not have much heat if you used one or two. If you want to add more, just whiz a few more jalapeños in the blender, and add by tablespoons to the salsa in your bowl. Stir it around and taste again. Perfect, isn't it?

Red Rice
Sopa de Arroz

Makes 8 servings

Literally, the title means "Soup of Rice," but in reality this is not a soup at all—it's a red rice that has been cooked in a broth. It is a perfect side dish for Rogelio's barbecued chicken, as it has some of the salsa from that recipe in the sauce. It is also great with chicken tacos, burritos—it might be easier to think of a dish this would not be good with! Just make a batch of the salsa, and freeze it in four-tablespoon portions, so you'll be able to make this any time!

Ingredients

1½ cups white rice, uncooked
¼ cup oil (vegetable or canola)
1 slice white onion, finely diced (only 1 slice, not a whole onion)
1 cup tomato purée
4 Tablespoons ancho sauce from Rogelio's *Pollo Asado al Carbon* recipe
1 teaspoon salt
4 cups cold water

Heat the oil in large skillet or saucepan. Add the rice and cook until it is light golden. Add the diced onion slice, tomato purée, sauce, salt, and water. Bring to a low boil; then reduce the heat to low. Cover and let simmer for 20–25 minutes. Serve with the Rogelio's *Pollo Asado al Carbon*.

Doughnuts
Donas

You very rarely see Rogelio without a smile. He is especially happy when he is cooking for a crowd. In this case, he is expecting about 150 kids to converge on his house for a Christmas fiesta. He made a total of 172 donas, and we ran out! Maybe it was because his donas are famous in his colonia. Word travels fast (as does the aroma) when he is cooking for a special event.
Making homemade doughnuts may sound a bit tedious, but this recipe is the easiest I have ever seen. You just mix everything together, let it rise once, roll it out, and cut. Pop them in the hot shortening, and that's it.
The yield is about 4–5 dozen, but they are difficult to count while you are munching on them!

Ingredients

1 kilo (8 cups) flour
1¼ cups granulated sugar
½ Tablespoon salt
4 eggs
1 Tablespoon ground cinnamon
3 Tablespoons yeast, instant
2 bananas *or* 5 strawberries, puréed
2-1/8 cups milk, warmed but not hot (hot milk will kill the yeast)
250 grams (½ pound) vegetable shortening, such as Crisco, for frying *

* The actual amount of shortening depends on the size pan you use. The melted shortening should be deep enough so that the doughnuts do not touch the bottom of the pan.

Heat the shortening in a large pan or deep fryer to 190°C/375°F.

Mix all the ingredients except the vegetable shortening. Knead to totally incorporate all the ingredients. Cover the bowl, and let it rise for 45 minutes. Remove the dough to a floured board.

Roll the dough out to about 13 mm / ½ inch thick. Cut into circles with a floured doughnut cutter or glass. Remember to remove the center portion of each doughnut to create the hole! Rogelio re-rolls the leftover dough from the holes to make more of the larger doughnuts.

Fry them in the hot vegetable shortening until they are golden brown on one side; then flip them over and fry on the other side. Remove them from the oil and allow to drain on paper towels.

While they are still warm, dip them in granulated sugar or melted chocolate.

Orange Chicken
Pollo a la Naranja

4 servings

This chicken cooked with orange juice and raisins really is as sweet and savory as it looks. The chicken poaches in the sweet orange juice, absorbing that wonderful fresh citrus, while the onion and garlic add just a hint of savory flavor. As if that wasn't enough, the raisins plump to a size that makes them look like they are ready to explode! Notice that there is no salt in the entire recipe—with all this flavor, who needs it?

Ingredients
2 Tablespoons oil
1 chicken, cut in pieces, with skin and bones, patted dry
2 small cloves of garlic, very finely minced
1 slice onion (6 mm / ¼ inch thick)
3 oranges
3 Tablespoons butter
100 grams (3½ ounces) raisins
½ cup orange juice

Heat the oil to medium hot in a skillet or large pan with a lid (the lid will be used later in the recipe). Carefully add the chicken, and brown it on all sides. When the chicken has browned, add in the garlic and onion. When the onion and garlic have only begun to change color, squeeze the juice from the 3 oranges onto the chicken. Melt in the butter, and stir to coat the chicken. Add the raisins and the orange juice. Turn the heat to medium low. Cover the pan loosely, and cook until the sauce is dry, and the chicken is sticky with the cooked orange sauce.

Serve with mashed potatoes and crusty bread with butter.

Rogelio's Chicken
Pollo a la Rogelio

4 servings

Rogelio loves to invent recipes, and this is one of his more unusual dishes. The addition of eggs to the chicken is unique, even for Mexico, where recipes are invented by necessity every day. You cook the chicken and eggs separately; then combine them into one pan, and add the tomato sauce to complete the cooking. Nature's combination: chicken and eggs!

Ingredients

1 whole chicken, cut in 8 pieces
2 Tablespoons oil
8 eggs, slightly beaten
canned chipotle chiles, minced (to taste)
10 tomatoes, charred
salt, to taste

Put the chicken in a frying pan with a splash of oil, and cook until it is cooked through.

In another pan, melt the butter, and pour in the beaten eggs. Cook them as you would scrambled eggs, by stirring to break up large pieces of cooked egg. Turn off the heat. Mix in the minced chipotle chiles.

Note: Add chipotles a little at a time, tasting after each addition, because they are very spicy.

Char the tomatoes on all sides in a heavy dry pan until they have dark brown char marks. Put them in a blender, and purée.

Add the eggs and tomato purée to the chicken and stir to combine. Cover the pan and bring the tomato sauce to a boil. Turn off the heat.

Serve the chicken covered with eggs and sauce.

Rogelio's Barbecued Chicken
Rogelio's Pollo Asado al Carbon

Number of servings varies with the size of each chicken

When Rogelio lights up the grill, you can smell it for blocks. I seem to always drive a bit faster going to his house when I know he is grilling! He and Rosie have many family events at their house, and he has been known to grill up to fifty chickens in an afternoon. Can you imagine the aroma throughout the colonia? No matter if it is the first off the grill or the last of the day, you can be sure that it is succulent and the best chicken you have ever eaten. He *is* the king of the grill!

A note about the chickens: Rogelio says the smaller the chicken, the better. It takes much longer to grill larger birds, and the meat tends to get dry and tough.

Ingredients

4 whole chickens, split in half down breastbone and backbone,
1.4 to 1.8 kilos/3 to 4 pounds each, with skin and bones
salt to season chicken

For the Sauce

¼ cup oil (vegetable or canola)
3 dried ancho chiles, open flat, stems and seeds removed
3 heads garlic, outer paper removed, separated into individual cloves

¼ cup white onion, large chunks
1 teaspoon whole black peppercorns
½ teaspoon salt
cold water to thin the sauce a bit

Cut through the wing joint where it attaches to the chicken, being careful not to cut all the way through the meat. It will still be attached to the chicken. Cut deep slits in the skin side of the chicken—one lengthwise through the leg and one more through the breast (see photo). Turn the chicken over, and cut a slit on the other side of the leg. Rub the chicken on both sides liberally with salt. Rogelio does not refrigerate the chicken after this step. Set aside.

For the sauce: *This makes enough sauce for 8 chickens plus some for the rice. The sauce freezes very well.*

Pour the oil into a small frying pan, and heat. When the oil is hot, add one cleaned ancho chile, and fry on both sides (about 5 seconds on each side). Remove from the oil and put into a blender—no need to chop. Repeat with the remaining ancho chiles.

Separate the garlic heads into cloves. It is not necessary to peel the cloves. Place the garlic, onion, peppercorns, and ½ teaspoon salt in the blender. Purée on high, adding ¼ cup of water at a time until it blends smoothly but is still thick enough to spread with your hands. Reserve at least 4 large tablespoons of the sauce for the rice.

Rub the sauce liberally onto the chicken and into the slits on both sides. Set aside to marinate while you get your coals ready. Again, do not refrigerate—the chicken needs to be at room temperature.

Light your charcoal and let it heat until coals are mostly white; then spread them out in an even layer. The other option is to heat your gas grill to medium temperature. Place the grill about 4 inches above the coals for medium to medium-low heat.

Place the chicken, skin side up, and grill for 7 minutes. Turn the chicken over, and grill the skin side for 7 minutes. Take each chicken half off the grill, and using a meat cleaver or sharp heavy knife, cut the halves into 4 or 5 pieces.

Place the pieces back on the grill and continue cooking for 15 more minutes, turning often. Remove to a platter.

This chicken is great hot or cold and transports well to a picnic or potluck..

** Note: In Mexico, cooks would never use briquettes or gas grills. They use only natural charcoal, which imparts a wonderful smoky wood flavor. Use gas if you must, but *do not* use briquettes—they will taint the flavor of your chicken! Natural charcoal should be widely available in your area.

To light that charcoal *without* lighter fluid, just soak some newspaper in inexpensive cooking oil; then place the charcoal on top and light the paper. This same system works if you have a charcoal chimney to light your charcoal.

Serve with Steamed Onions on the Grill, Sopa de Arroz (red rice cooked in a broth), and Rogelio's Salsa. (All recipes are included in this chapter.)

Steamed Onions on the Grill

Serving size is ½ onion

Cut medium-sized white onions in half through the bulb end. Place ½ teaspoon butter in the middle of a square of foil, and place a half onion, cut side down, on the butter. Wrap tightly, and place around the edges of the grill with the chicken. When the onions are soft to the touch, they are done.

Pozole (Posole) from Michoacán
Pozole de Michoacán

Servings: Makes enough for the whole neighborhood

When another of the cooks suggested that she make pozole for me, Rosie (Rogelio's wife) called me aside and very quietly told me that it would not be the "real" pozole but that she and Rogelio would make the "real" pozole from Michoacán for me!

Rogelio and I had decided on a day to cook this wonderful soup. We were working very smoothly together in his garage/kitchen. Rosie, who does not cook *at all*, came in after Rogelio had all the ingredients in the pot and announced that it did not have enough ancho chiles. Rogelio rolled his eyes, looked at me, and we both started laughing. He did the only thing a husband could do to keep peace in the house—he added more chiles!

This recipe was a bit unusual, but the end result was very tasty. When I make it at home, however, I do vary the meat selection a bit.

Ingredients
1 pork head, cleaned (your butcher should have already done this for you)
4 pork feet with legs, also cleaned
2 kilos (4½ pounds) pork back bones with meat
3 kilos (6½ pounds) pozole corn (see note)
4 large heads of garlic, divided usage
2 large onions, divided usage
water to cover the pork
8 ancho chiles, stem, seeds, and veins removed
(he started with 4, but Rosie said 8)
¼ cup oil
3 teaspoons salt
½ cup Mexican oregano, whole leaf

Chile Árbol Salsa
250 grams (8 ounces) árbol chiles
2 large garlic cloves
1 teaspoon salt

In a huge soup pot, place the head, feet, back bones, corn, 1 head of garlic (cut in half across—no need to peel), and 1 onion (cut in half). Add enough water to cover all the ingredients. *Do not* add salt at this time. Cover the pot, and boil this mixture for 3 hours.

After 3 hours, turn down the heat, and continue to simmer.

Heat the oil in a small skillet. When it is hot, quickly fry each ancho chile until it is crisp, about 5 seconds each side. Place in a blender. Then, to the blender add 1 onion, 3 rounded teaspoons salt, and 3 large heads of garlic. Remove the outer paper and stems, but it is not necessary to peel them. Pour in enough water to almost fill the blender jar. Blend on high until it is totally smooth and no bits of any kind can be seen. If you need more water to make it free flowing, then add as much as you need. Pour this into the soup pot. Simmer for another 5 minutes. Turn off the heat. Rub the oregano between your hands, over and into the soup pot so that the leaves get crushed. Stir.

Remove the meat pieces from the pot, and place on a large platter. Ladle the soup into bowls, and serve the meat on a side plate.

Pozole is usually served with side dishes of salt, fresh lime halves, tortilla chips, very finely shredded raw cabbage, and fine slices of white onion. The *chile árbol salsa* (recipe below) is part of the Michoacán tradition as well. Other accompaniments can include sliced avocado and shredded cheese (but Rosie would not agree!).

Note: Pozole corn is in the refrigerated section of your market. If necessary, you can buy it frozen or canned. You can use hominy corn—they are very similar. Regular sweet corn is *not* a substitute.

Chile Árbol Salsa

Put the chiles in a pot of water. Simmer until they are soft—timing does not matter; you can keep them warm as long as you like. Drain and put them in a clean blender with the garlic and salt. Add just enough water to allow it to blend. Pour into a bowl, and allow everyone to add as much as they like to their pozole.

Árbol chiles are very hot, but some of the heat is removed by the hot soaking water. Discard the water after soaking the chiles.

Fish in the Oven
(Microwave oven, actually)
Pescado al Horno

1 serving

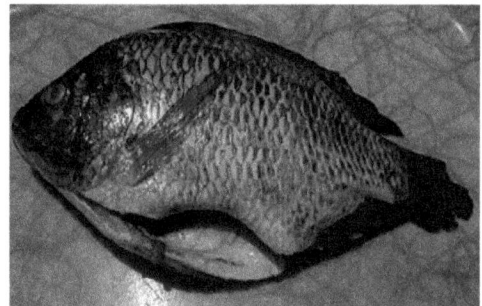
Mojarra talapia

We have given instructions for one fish. You will probably want to increase the portions of this delicious fish for your friends and family. The bacon imparts its flavor throughout the fish and keeps it moist while it cooks in the microwave. Rogelio is a versatile cook and experiments constantly. You never know what he will try next, but I am willing to test whatever he is cooking!

Ingredients

400 grams mojarra talapia, cleaned**
20 grams (.7 ounces) ham
20 grams (.7 ounces) bacon
20 grams (.7 ounces) Chihuahua cheese
1 teaspoon butter

Cut all the ingredients, except the fish, in little pieces. Slather the already-clean fish, inside and out, with the butter. Then fill the fish with all the ingredients, spread out evenly inside the fish. Put into the microwave. Cook on 80 percent for 15 minutes. Check that the fish is cooking evenly and if necessary, put it in again for 5-minute increments until it is cooked through.

Note: The microwave we used is 1,000 watts. The time will vary depending on the size and wattage of your microwave.

Serve with limes, guacamole, salsa Mexicana, or with avocados placed around the plate.

** You can buy a larger fish to feed two or three people. Increase the stuffing ingredients just a bit, and cook for the same time. You may need to cook it a bit longer, depending on the size and variety of the fish you choose. Remember when microwaving, less time is better.

Sierra Ceviche
Ceviche de Sierra

5 servings

Sierra is a fish known as the Mexican mackerel. There is another ceviche recipe in this book using sierra, but it is similar only in name and the use of the sierra fish. If you cannot find sierra, get any other mild-tasting fleshy fish, and grind it yourself in the food processor or meat grinder. I have tested red snapper and talapia as substitutes, and both of those worked very well. Either of these two substitutes should be readily available in your area.

This ceviche is remarkably fresh tasting. Of course, the limes give it a fresh taste, as do the fresh tomatoes, crunchy onion, and chiles. A word of warning: use caution adding all the serranos if you are heat-sensitive. Add a little at a time, and *taste* as you go. Offer a side dish of diced serranos to your guests, so that they can add their own. Rogelio often does that very thing, because even some Mexicans don't like the heat.

Ingredients
1 kilo (2.2 pounds) ground sierra fish (raw)
2 teaspoons salt
500 grams (1.1 pound) limes, juiced
1 kilo (2.2 pounds) tomatoes, small dice
4 stems cilantro, finely chopped
3 medium onions, finely diced
250 grams (8 ounces) serrano chiles, very finely diced—seeds removed, if necessary
½ teaspoon ground black pepper
1 bag corn chips

Put the fish into a bowl with the salt and pour the lime juice over it. Let sit in the refrigerator for 20–30 minutes. Drain off the lime juice, squeezing out as much of the juice as possible. Place the fish into a serving dish. It has now been cooked chemically and is no longer raw.

Add the tomatoes, cilantro, onions, chiles, and black pepper. Stir to combine. Serve with corn chips as dippers.

Breaded Shrimp
Camarónes Empanizados

5 servings

If you love breaded shrimp, this is probably the easiest recipe you ever will make. They are crunchy on the outside and tender on the inside, without being greasy. Rogelio does not serve these with a dipping sauce, but he does have a bowl of lime slices on the table to squeeze over the shrimp. He uses either medium or jumbo shrimp, depending on the price at the market that day.

Ingredients

1 kilo (2.2 pounds) medium or jumbo shrimp
3 eggs, beaten
1½ cup dried bread crumbs, seasoned with salt and pepper to taste
2 cups oil for frying

Peel and clean the shrimp by removing the shells and cutting down the backs to remove the veins.

Heat the oil in a medium frying pan on medium heat. Depending on the size pan you have, you may need more oil—the level should reach halfway up the uncooked shrimp.

Dip the shrimp one at a time in the beaten egg, then into a dish of dried bread crumbs, then again into the egg, and again in the bread crumbs, so that you have 2 layers of egg and crumbs. Put a few breaded shrimp into the hot oil, and fry on both sides until golden but not overcooked. This only takes a few minutes, so keep a watchful eye on those shrimp. Remove to paper towels.

Serve with vegetables and/or rice.

Karina Ann Betlem

Q

R

S

www.ingramcontent.com/pod-product-compliance
Lightning Source LLC
Chambersburg PA
CBHW040259100426
42811CB00011B/1319